Demystifying Cryptography with OpenSSL 3.0

Discover the best techniques to enhance your network security with OpenSSL 3.0

Alexei Khlebnikov

BIRMINGHAM—MUMBAI

Demystifying Cryptography with OpenSSL 3.0

Associate Group Product Manager: Mohd Riyan Khan

Publishing Product Manager: Shrilekha Malpani

Senior Content Development Editor: Adrija Mitra

Technical Editor: Nithik Cheruvakodan

Copy Editor: Safis Editing

Book Project Manager: Kirti Pisat

Proofreader: Safis Editing

Indexer: Sejal Dsilva

Production Designer: Alishon Mendonca

Marketing Coordinator: Ankita Bhonsle

First published: October 2022

Production reference: 1071022

Published by Packt Publishing Ltd.
Livery Place
35 Livery Street
Birmingham
B3 2PB, UK.

978-1-80056-034-5

www.packt.com

To my beloved mother, Tatyana Khlebnikova, who, through a lot of effort, care, love, and support, brought me up to the point where I could continue my own development further.

– Alexei Khlebnikov

Foreword

Having been a coder for more than three decades, I've come across fellow techies who could write a book, or even 10, about common but intricate technologies many times. However, very rarely have I come across someone who can explore topics as deeply as Alexei Khlebnikov.

I've had the pleasure of working with him and being his friend for several years now and I am looking forward to really diving into this book. I would certainly say it's a subject that deserves our greatest attention.

In this book, we will be taken on a journey through the basics of OpenSSL, general cryptography, cryptography modes, the "joys" of certificates, and the making of TLS connections. All in great detail if I understand Alexei correctly, which I am very certain I do.

This is an important book, looking closely at technologies we take for granted and that are used basically everywhere to secure our online presence.

There are practical examples and step-by-step explanations of essential concepts to help you along. By the end of the book, you'll be able to use the most popular features of OpenSSL in your products, whether web or desktop.

The book is certainly interesting for the doers, but also for managers and others who think security is important but lack knowledge about it. Don't worry – an in-depth understanding of mathematics is not needed to read this book and learn from it.

In my view as a lifelong techie, learning new things or maybe diving deeper into topics you have some starting knowledge on is rewarding and helpful and it keeps us all on our toes!

Take it away, Alexei!

– *Jarle Adolfsen*

Serial entrepreneur, CTO at bspoke, former CTO at Link Mobility, and a pioneer in computer graphics in the late 1980s and early 1990s

Contributors

About the author

Alexei Khlebnikov has more than 20 years of professional experience in IT where he has worked in a host of different roles – software developer, system administrator, DevOps engineer, technical leader, architect, and project manager. During these years, Alexei has worked with many technologies – security, artificial intelligence, web development, embedded, mobile, and robotics. Among other companies, Alexei worked for Opera Software on the famous Opera internet browser. Alexei has always been interested in security. He was one of the maintainers of the security-related Opera browser modules, responsible for cryptography, SSL/TLS, and integration with OpenSSL. He was also a member of the security architect group, responsible for the security of the Opera browser. Now, Alexei lives in Oslo, Norway, and works as a senior consultant for bspoke AS. He is also the leader of the architect group at his current employer.

First and foremost, I want to thank my beloved wife, Larisa, and son, Dmitry, for their continued love and support, and for supporting me while I was writing this book and spending less time with them. I also want to thank all the editors, managers, and other people at Packt Publishing who worked on this book, as well as the technical reviewer, Kris. Their help and valuable advice helped me improve the book to the benefit of its readers.

About the reviewer

Krzysztof Kwiatkowski is a cryptography engineer who focuses on problems at the intersection of cryptographic research and implementation. He holds an MSc degree in mathematics with a specialization in computational methods. With a career spanning over 15 years, Kris has worked on a variety of topics related to cryptography, communication, and software security from compact embedded to large distributed systems. Currently, he is concentrating on the implementation of modern, quantum-safe cryptographic schemes, and helping organizations to migrate towards them.

I'd like to thank my wonderful and loving family, who understand my busy schedule and always stand by my side.

Table of Contents

3

Message Digests   55

4

MAC and HMAC

71

5

Derivation of an Encryption Key from a Password

83

Part 3: Asymmetric Cryptography and Certificates

6

Asymmetric Encryption and Decryption

95

7

Digital Signatures and Their Verification   119

8

X.509 Certificates and PKI   137

Part 4: TLS Connections and Secure Communication

9

Establishing TLS Connections and Sending Data over Them   163

10

Using X.509 Certificates in TLS   193

11

Part 5: Running a Mini-CA

12

Preface

Security and networking are essential features of software today. The modern internet is full of worms, Trojan horses, men-in-the-middle, and other threats. This is why maintaining security is more important than ever.

OpenSSL is one of the most widely used and essential open-source projects on the internet for this purpose. If you are a software developer, system administrator, network security engineer, or DevOps specialist, you've probably stumbled upon this toolset in the past – but how do you make the most out of it? With the help of this book, you will learn the most important features of OpenSSL, and gain insight into its full potential.

This book contains step-by-step explanations of essential cryptography and network security concepts, as well as practical examples illustrating usage of those concepts. You'll start by learning the basics such as how to perform symmetric encryption and calculate message digests. Next, you will discover more about cryptography: MAC and HMAC, public and private keys, and digital signatures. As you progress, you will explore best practices for using X.509 certificates, public key infrastructure, and TLS connections.

By the end of this book, you'll be able to use the most popular features of OpenSSL, allowing you to implement cryptography and TLS in your applications and network infrastructure.

Who this book is for

This book is for software developers, system administrators, DevOps specialists, network security engineers, and analysts, or anyone who wants to keep their applications and infrastructure secure. Software developers will learn how to use the OpenSSL library to empower their software with cryptography and TLS. DevOps professionals and sysadmins will learn how to work with cryptographic keys and certificates on the command line, and how to set up a mini-CA for their organization. A basic understanding of security and networking is required.

What this book covers

Chapter 1, OpenSSL and Other SSL/TLS Libraries, will outline what OpenSSL is and what its strengths are and take a look into OpenSSL's history and at what's new in OpenSSL 3.0. We will also compare OpenSSL to other SSL/TLS libraries.

Chapter 2, Symmetric Encryption and Decryption, will cover the important concepts in symmetric encryption – ciphers, encryption modes, and padding. We will overview modern ciphers, encryption modes, and padding types and recommend which technology to use in which situation. Usage of these technologies will be illustrated by command-line and C code examples.

Chapter 3, Message Digests, will explore why message digests, also known as cryptographic hashes, are needed and where they are used. We will get an overview of modern cryptographic hash functions that calculate message digests and recommend which hash function to use in which situation. The calculation of message digests will be illustrated by command-line and C code examples.

Chapter 4, MAC and HMAC, will explain why **Message Authentication Codes (MACs)** are needed and where they are used. Since it's a popular MAC type, **Hash-based MAC (HMAC)** will be discussed. We will also learn about how to combine HMAC with encryption and about the Cryptographic Doom Principle. The calculation of HMAC will be illustrated by a code example.

Chapter 5, Derivation of an Encryption Key from a Password, will show why a password itself cannot be used for encryption and why key derivation is needed. We will overview modern key derivation functions and recommend which one to use when. Then, encryption key derivation will be illustrated by command-line and C code examples.

Chapter 6, Asymmetric Encryption and Decryption, will unpack why asymmetric encryption is needed, how it works, and how private and public keys are used to achieve encryption and decryption. Encryption and decryption using RSA will be illustrated by command-line and C code examples.

Chapter 7, Digital Signatures and Their Verification, will clarify why digital signatures are needed and where they are used. We will overview modern digital signature algorithms, such as RSA, ECDSA, and EdDSA, and recommend which digital signature scheme to use in which situation. Digital signing and signature verification will be illustrated by command-line and C code examples.

Chapter 8, X.509 Certificates and PKI, will detail what X.509 certificates are, why they are needed, and where they are used. We will also explain how certificates sign other certificates and how certificate signing chains are formed, as well as what **Public Key Infrastructure (PKI)** is and how certificate verification is used to verify identities – for example, the identities of websites. The usage of the techniques mentioned will be illustrated by command-line and C code examples.

Chapter 9, Establishing TLS Connections and Sending Data over Them, will break down what the TLS protocol is, why it is needed, and why it is used so widely. We will also learn what the difference between SSL and TLS is. Then, we will learn how to establish and shut down a TLS connection, as well as how to send and receive data over TLS. Working with TLS will be illustrated by command-line and C code examples.

Chapter 10, Using X.509 Certificates in TLS, will elaborate on how to work with X.509 certificates in TLS and why certificates are important for TLS. We will also learn how to verify a remote certificate. Then, we will learn how to further check the certificate validity using a CRL and OCSP. Finally, we will learn how to use a client certificate. Working with certificates will be illustrated by command-line and C code examples.

Chapter 11, Special Usages of TLS, will look into special usages of TLS: TLS pinning, using non-blocking networking mode, and TLS connections over non-standard sockets or special networking layers using OpenSSL **Basic Input-Output Objects** (**BIOs**). The usage of the techniques mentioned will be illustrated by C code examples.

Chapter 12, Running a Mini-CA, will instruct you on how to run your own mini-CA in order to control certificates and build PKI into an organization. Running a mini-CA will be illustrated by example configuration files and commands.

To get the most out of this book

You will have to install OpenSSL on your computer in order to run the command-line and C code examples. If you haven't installed it yet, *Chapter 2, Symmetric Encryption and Decryption*, will help you to do so. To build the C code examples, you will need a C11-compatible C compiler and a linker. You will have to install these development tools following their respective documentation. All the examples have been tested on Kubuntu Linux 22.04 using GNU C Compiler, GNU Linker (LD), and GNU Make from the Linux distribution mentioned. Other development tools, such as LLVM Clang or Microsoft Visual C++, should also be compatible with the code examples in this book.

Software/hardware covered in the book	System requirements
OpenSSL 3.0	<ul><li>Linux, FreeBSD, macOS, Windows, or any other OS supported by OpenSSL</li><li>A C compiler – for example, GNU C Compiler</li><li>A linker – for example, GNU Linker (LD)</li><li>Your favorite C/C++ IDE or code editor</li><li>A build tool – for example, GNU Make (optional)</li></ul>

If you are using the digital version of this book, we advise you to type the code yourself or access the code from the book's GitHub repository (a link is available in the next section). Doing so will help you avoid any potential errors related to copying and pasting code.

While explanations of OpenSSL features and code examples are sometimes very detailed, the book is meant to provide guidance, not to replace the OpenSSL documentation. If you are wondering about details of OpenSSL functionality that are not covered by the book, feel free to consult the OpenSSL documentation, the OpenSSL source code, or just experiment with your own code using OpenSSL!

Download the example code files

You can download the example code files for this book from GitHub at `https://github.com/PacktPublishing/Demystifying-Cryptography-with-OpenSSL-3`. If there's an update to the code, it will be updated in the GitHub repository.

We also have other code bundles from our rich catalog of books and videos available at `https://github.com/PacktPublishing/`. Check them out!

Download the color images

We also provide a PDF file that has color images of the screenshots and diagrams used in this book. You can download it here: `https://packt.link/c0WEO`.

Conventions used

There are a number of text conventions used throughout this book.

`Code in text`: Indicates code words in text, database table names, folder names, filenames, file extensions, pathnames, dummy URLs, user input, and Twitter handles. Here is an example: "SSH user public keys are pinned on the server in the `authorized_keys` file."

A block of code is set as follows:

```
if (pinned_server_cert)
    X509_free(pinned_server_cert);
if (pinned_server_cert_file)
    fclose(pinned_server_cert_file);
```

Any command-line input or output is written as follows:

```
$ ./tls-server 4433 server_keypair.pem server_cert.pem
*** Listening on port 4433
```

Bold: Indicates a new term, an important word, or words that you see onscreen. For instance, words in menus or dialog boxes appear in **bold**. Here is an example: "Reduced maintenance because you don't need to make a **Certificate Signing Request (CSR)** and communicate with a CA. You can even use a self-signed certificate."

> **Tips or Important Notes**
> Appear like this.

Get in touch

Feedback from our readers is always welcome.

General feedback: If you have questions about any aspect of this book, email us at `customercare@packtpub.com` and mention the book title in the subject of your message.

Errata: Although we have taken every care to ensure the accuracy of our content, mistakes do happen. If you have found a mistake in this book, we would be grateful if you would report this to us. Please visit `www.packtpub.com/support/errata` and fill in the form.

Piracy: If you come across any illegal copies of our works in any form on the internet, we would be grateful if you would provide us with the location address or website name. Please contact us at `copyright@packt.com` with a link to the material.

If you are interested in becoming an author: If there is a topic that you have expertise in and you are interested in either writing or contributing to a book, please visit `authors.packtpub.com`.

Share Your Thoughts

Once you've read *Demystifying Cryptography with OpenSSL 3.0*, we'd love to hear your thoughts! Scan the QR code below to go straight to the Amazon review page for this book and share your feedback.

`https://packt.link/r/1800560346`

Your review is important to us and the tech community and will help us make sure we're delivering excellent quality content.

Part 1: Introduction

Each journey starts with a first step. Our first step will be to learn about what OpenSSL is, take a look at its history, and learn about what's new in OpenSSL 3. We will also review other SSL/TLS libraries that are competitors of OpenSSL.

This part contains the following chapter:

- *Chapter 1, OpenSSL and Other SSL/TLS Libraries*

1
OpenSSL and Other SSL/TLS Libraries

Currently, there are several libraries available to developers who want to add support for cryptography or SSL/TLS features to their applications. This chapter will help you compare different libraries and learn about the strengths of OpenSSL. You will also learn a bit about OpenSSL's history and what's new in OpenSSL 3.0.

In this chapter, we are going to cover the following topics:

- What is OpenSSL?
- The history of OpenSSL
- What's new in OpenSSL 3.0?
- Comparing OpenSSL with GnuTLS
- Comparing OpenSSL with NSS
- Comparing OpenSSL with Botan
- Comparing OpenSSL with lightweight TLS libraries
- Comparing OpenSSL with LibreSSL
- Comparing OpenSSL with BoringSSL

What is OpenSSL?

OpenSSL is an open source software toolkit that includes a **cryptography** and **SSL/TLS** library, as well as command-line utilities that use the library to provide some useful functionality on the command line, such as generating encryption keys and **X.509 certificates**. The main part of OpenSSL is its library, which means that OpenSSL is mainly useful for software developers. However, system administrators and DevOps specialists will also find OpenSSL's command-line utilities very useful.

SSL stands for **Secure Sockets Layer**. It is a protocol designed to provide secure communications over insecure computer networks. An insecure computer network means a network where the transmitted data can be read or even changed by a malicious intermediate network node. An example of such an insecure network is the internet. Secure communication is where transmitted data cannot be read or changed. SSL achieves communication security by using **symmetric** and **asymmetric** cryptography. The SSL protocol was invented in 1995 by the *Netscape Communications Corporation* and was deprecated in 2015 in favor of its successor, the TLS protocol. **TLS** stands for **Transport Layer Security**.

The OpenSSL toolkit was created before the SSL protocol became deprecated, so it contains "SSL" instead of "TLS" in its name.

OpenSSL was historically licensed under the *BSD-style license*, but since version 3.0, it is licensed under *Apache 2.0 license*, which is also BSD-style. This license allows OpenSSL to be used in both open source and closed source applications.

OpenSSL supports a lot of **cryptographic algorithms**, among which are algorithms for **symmetric** and **asymmetric encryption**, **digital signatures**, **message digests**, and **key exchange**. OpenSSL supports **X.509 certificates**, **SSL**, **TLS**, and **DTLS** protocols, as well as other cryptography-related technologies that are less popular.

OpenSSL has been around for a while and during its development, it gained support for a lot of operating systems. OpenSSL was originally developed for Unix-like operating systems. Up until now, OpenSSL supports different variations of Unix, including *GNU/Linux*, *BSDs*, and old and new commercial Unixes, such as *IBM AIX* and *macOS*. OpenSSL also supports popular non-Unix operating systems such as *Microsoft Windows*, mobile OSes such as *Android* and *iOS*, and even old and exotic OSes such as MS-DOS and VMS.

Through many years of OpenSSL development, the library has received numerous optimizations, including *assembly optimizations* for the most popular CPU architectures, such as **x86**, **x86_64**, and **ARM**. OpenSSL is currently one of the fastest existing crypto and TLS libraries.

Because of its universality, support for a lot of algorithms and operating systems, and because of its speed, OpenSSL has become the de facto industry standard. OpenSSL is so popular that other TLS libraries make so-called OpenSSL **compatibility layers** so that those libraries can be used via OpenSSL **application programming interfaces** (**APIs**).

OpenSSL is quite a popular library but what did its path to the widespread adoption look like? Let's find out by walking through the OpenSSL history.

The history of OpenSSL

The OpenSSL library is based on the **SSLeay library** by Eric Andrew Young. The *eay* in SSLeay stands for *Eric Andrew Young*. SSLeay's development started in 1995 as an open source implementation of the SSL library. Back then, the *NSS* library was not available. Later, Tim Hudson joined the development team. But in 1998, both Eric and Tim were hired by the *RSA Corporation* and did not have time to develop SSLeay further.

SSLeay was forked as OpenSSL in 1998, which means that OpenSSL has become SSLeay's successor. The initial founding members were Mark Cox, Ralf Engelschall, Stephen Henson, Ben Laurie, and Paul Sutton. The very first version of OpenSSL, numbered 0.9.1, was released on December 23, 1998, merely a week after Eric and Tim joined the RSA Corporation and effectively stopped working on SSLeay.

Over many years, a lot of people and companies contributed a lot of code and other work to OpenSSL. The list of contributing companies is impressive: Oracle, Siemens, Akamai, Red Hat, IBM, VMware, Intel, and Arm, among others.

Currently, OpenSSL development is managed by the OpenSSL Management Committee, which consists of seven members. The core development team, which has commit rights, consists of approximately 20 people. Only two people work full-time on OpenSSL. The other contributors either do so in their spare time or as a part of their work in the contributing companies.

The history of OpenSSL is interesting, but what does the future hold for it? Let's find out about the latest changes in the toolkit.

What's new in OpenSSL 3.0?

One major change in **OpenSSL 3.0** is its license. A software project does not change its license very often during its lifetime. The OpenSSL project used its *BSD-style* open source license until version 3.0. Since version 3.0, it uses *Apache License 2.0*.

OpenSSL 3.0 is a release with big changes in the internal architecture of the library. The architectural changes are not finished and will be continued in OpenSSL 4.0. The concept of **OpenSSL operation implementation providers** was introduced. A **provider** is a unit of code that provides the implementation of cryptographic algorithms. The existing OpenSSL cryptography code will mostly be available via *Default* and *Legacy* providers. **Engines** are still supported in OpenSSL 3.0 but have been deprecated in favor of providers. Support for **ENGINE API** may be removed in OpenSSL 4.0. There is also support for third-party providers that allow independent developers to plug their cryptographic algorithms into OpenSSL.

Another interesting feature of OpenSSL 3.0 is **Kernel TLS (KTLS)**. When using KTLS, an application can create a special **TLS socket**, similar to a TCP socket. OpenSSL then performs a **TLS handshake** and hands the negotiated encryption key and other data to the **operating system kernel** in the form of **TLS socket options**. Then, the actual data transmission in the TLS protocol is handled by the KTLS code. Such TLS offloading to the kernel can speed up data transmission on high-load systems where performance is important, especially when the kernel can use hardware acceleration for **Advanced Encryption Standard** (**AES**) and thus offload the main CPU. Of course, KTLS support is needed both in the TLS library and in the operating system kernel. At the time of writing, only the Linux and FreeBSD kernels support KTLS.

Some other notable changes in OpenSSL 3.0 include the following:

- Support for the **Certificate Management Protocol**.
- A simple HTTP/HTTPS client.
- **Advanced Encryption Standard Galois/Counter Mode with Synthetic Initialization Vector (AES-GCM-SIV)** encryption.
- New **Message Authentication Code (MAC)** algorithms, such as **GMAC** and **KMAC**.
- New **Key Derivation Function (KDF)** algorithms, such as **SSKDF** and **SSHKDF**.
- New high-level APIs, such as **EVP_MAC**, **EVP_KDF**, and **EVP_RAND**.
- Low-level APIs deprecated in favor of newer higher-level APIs.
- Code cleanup.
- Error handling reworked.
- Old insecure algorithms are no longer available at the default security level.
- Interactive mode has been removed from the openssl command-line tool.

OpenSSL is a solid mature software toolkit, so the most important features are already implemented in it. As a result, the latest changes don't contain that much new functionality for a lot of users. The latest release focuses on architectural improvements to the library.

While OpenSSL is the most popular crypto/TLS library, it's not the only one. We'll compare OpenSSL to its competitors in the following sections.

Comparing OpenSSL with GnuTLS

GnuTLS is a free software TLS library that was created for the needs of the **GNU Project**. When GnuTLS was created, most applications of the GNU Project were distributed under the *GPL 2.0 license*, which is incompatible with the old OpenSSL license. The authors of the GPL 2.0 licensed software had to include a licensing exception if they wished to link with OpenSSL. GnuTLS was originally licensed under *LGPL 2.0*, so it did not require such licensing exceptions.

Currently, GnuTLS is licensed under *LGPL 2.1*. This license allows users to use the library in **free and open source software** (**FOSS**) projects. It is also allowed to use the library in closed source projects, but with certain conditions, such as only **dynamic linking**.

GnuTLS does not include cryptography, big-number arithmetic functionality, and some other functionality that OpenSSL includes. Instead, GnuTLS *uses other libraries* from the **GNU ecosystem** that provide the needed functionality: **Nettle** for cryptography, **GMP** for big-number arithmetic, **Libtasn1** for **ASN.1** (short for **Abstract Syntax Notation One**), and so on.

An interesting feature of GnuTLS is that it supports not only X.509 certificates but also OpenPGP certificates. Unlike an X.509 certificate, which is signed by its issuer at the time of being issued, an OpenPGP certificate supports the so-called *web of trust*, can have multiple signatures, and signatures can be added once the certificate has been issued. Unfortunately, OpenPGP certificates have not gained popularity for usage in **TLS connections**.

Apart from OpenPGP certificate support, GnuTLS and its crypto library, Nettle, support fewer crypto algorithms than OpenSSL, and performance-wise, they are a bit slower than OpenSSL. GnuTLS and Nettle, however, support all popular algorithms.

Should you choose OpenSSL or GnuTLS? I recommend that you choose GnuTLS if you are developing GPL-licensed software; otherwise, choose OpenSSL.

Another competitor to OpenSSL is the NSS library, which we will discover in the next section.

Comparing OpenSSL with NSS

Network Security Services (**NSS**) is the first SSL/TLS library. It originated as security code inside the *Netscape Navigator 1.0* browser, released in 1994 by Netscape Communications Corporation. Netscape also invented the SSL protocol, the predecessor of the TLS protocol. Netscape Navigator was succeeded by Netscape Communicator, which was succeeded by the Mozilla browser, which was finally succeeded by Firefox. Soon after the release of Netscape Communicator 4.0 in 1997, the Netscape security code was released as a separate library, named **Hard Core Library** (**HCL**). HCL was later renamed NSS.

The NSS library is licensed under *Mozilla Public License 2.0*, which allows application developers to use the library in both open source and closed source applications.

Notable applications that use the NSS library are applications of Mozilla Foundation, such as Firefox and Thunderbird, some applications from Oracle and Red Hat, and some open source office applications such as LibreOffice and Evolution. While this is a list of solid and respected companies and applications, despite NSS having a long history, it did not become as popular as OpenSSL. I am unsure why. Some people say that OpenSSL is easier to use and has better documentation.

Should you choose NSS or OpenSSL? I recommend OpenSSL because it has better documentation and a larger community of developers and users.

Both NSS and GnuTLS provide their main API in **C**. However, the **Botan** library is different, as we'll find out in the next section.

Comparing OpenSSL with Botan

Most TLS libraries are written in **C** and provide their main API in C. Botan is a TLS library written in **C++11** that adopted **C++17** in version 3.0. Botan provides its main API in **C++** but also provides **API bindings** for **C** and **Python**. Third-party projects provide API bindings for Ruby, Rust, and Haskell. There are also experimental API bindings for Java and Ocaml.

It's also worth mentioning that the Botan library has good documentation. Botan is distributed under a simple **two-clause BSD license**, which allows users to use the library in both open source and closed source applications.

I recommend Botan for developers who want to use the C++ API and are willing to accept a less popular library with a smaller developer community. If you want to use the C API or want a more performant library with a larger developer community, then stick with OpenSSL.

The Botan library has a larger footprint on your storage than OpenSSL, unlike lightweight TLS libraries, which we will discuss next.

Comparing OpenSSL with lightweight TLS libraries

Some **lightweight TLS libraries** are available. They are targeted at embedded markets such as **Internet of Things (IoT)** devices or other small devices that many people use but they aren't considered computers. This includes payment terminals at your local grocery store, smartwatches, smart light bulbs, and industrial sensors of different kinds. Such devices usually have *weak CPUs*, *low memory*, and *small storage space*.

Lightweight TLS libraries usually become lightweight through *modularity*, the possibility to compile only the needed modules, support fewer cryptographic algorithms and protocols, and have less advanced APIs; that is, they expose fewer features and settings to application developers using the library.

The most well-known lightweight TLS libraries are **wolfSSL** (formerly yaSSL, also known as Yet Another SSL), **Mbed TLS** (formerly PolarSSL), and **MatrixSSL**.

The most advanced of the three libraries seems to be wolfSSL. It supports a lot of cryptographic algorithms, including new algorithms such as **ChaCha20** and **Poly1305**.

The latest versions of wolfSSL have *assembly optimizations* and are very performant. According to the *benchmarks* on the wolfSSL website, woflSSL's raw encryption performance is often on par and will in some cases even noticeably faster than OpenSSL – about 50% faster. Other information on the internet suggests that older versions of wolfSSL are noticeably slower than OpenSSL. If you are interested in performance, then I suggest that you run benchmarking on the target hardware and with the newest versions of the libraries. This is because both libraries are in constant development and newer versions may contain more optimizations.

Mbed TLS and MatrixSSL support noticeably fewer cryptographic algorithms.

WolfSSL and MatrixSSL are dual-licensed under *GPL 2.0* and a commercial license. The GPL 2.0 license only allows users to use the library in GPL-compatible FOSS applications. The commercial license allows users to use the library in *closed source* applications.

Mbed TLS is licensed under *Apache License 2.0*, which allows users to use the library both in open source and closed source applications.

While the lightweight TLS libraries claim to be significantly smaller, approximately 20 times smaller than OpenSSL, they are not so small in their default configurations. Here are the sizes of the libraries, compiled for an *Ubuntu 22.04 x86_64* machine:

- wolfSSL (version 5.2.0, libwolfssl.so): 1,768 KiB

- Mbed TLS (version 2.28.0, libmbedtls.so + libmbedcrypto.so): 664 KiB

- MatrixSSL (version 4.5.1, libssl_s.a + libcrypt_s.a + libcore_s.a): 1,772 KiB

- OpenSSL (version 3.0.2, libssl.so + libcrypto.so): 5,000 KiB

To cut down on the library's size, the user of the library has to compile it themselves and disable all the modules that they do not need.

OpenSSL also has a *modular design* and allows you to exclude unneeded modules from the compilation. However, this is more difficult than with lightweight libraries. Some OpenSSL modules are hard to exclude because other modules have dependencies on them, even if they shouldn't. And some OpenSSL modules are just very big, particularly the x509 module, since it contains the code for working with X.509 certificates. Thus, while it is possible to cut down the size of compiled OpenSSL, it is not possible to cut down as much as with the lightweight TLS libraries.

Use a lightweight TLS library if OpenSSL does not fit into your device. Otherwise, use a *full-size* TLS library, such as OpenSSL.

The last two TLS libraries that we will review originated from OpenSSL itself. Let's find out why the pristine OpenSSL was not good enough for some.

Comparing OpenSSL with LibreSSL

LibreSSL is a fork (derived code) of OpenSSL that was created in 2014 by the OpenBSD Project as a response to the infamous Heartbleed vulnerability that was found in OpenSSL. LibreSSL was founded to increase the *security* and *maintainability* of the library by removing old, unpopular, and no longer secure cryptographic algorithms and other features.

OpenBSD is a Unix operating system, one of the **BSD** systems family aimed at security. OpenBSD developers do not only develop the operating system kernel and utilities. Another famous software project is **OpenSSH**. Other software projects started as applications for OpenBSD, such as OpenNTPD, OpenSMTPD, and others. This now includes LibreSSL.

After forking, the LibreSSL developers removed a lot of the original OpenSSL code that they considered old or insecure. They claimed that they removed approximately half of the OpenSSL code within the first week. They also added a few new cryptographic algorithms such as **Advanced Encryption Standard in Galois/Counter Mode** (**AES-GCM**) and **ChaCha-Poly1305**. In addition to adding and removing code, some existing code was reworked and hardened in some places.

Despite LibreSSL's aim to increase security, there were some vulnerabilities in LibreSSL that did not affect OpenSSL, such as CVE-2017-8301.

In the last few years, OpenSSL also did some work on improving the security and maintainability of the library and deprecated/removed some code – though not as much code was removed as in LibreSSL. However, more code and new features were added.

OpenSSL has much more development resources than LibreSSL, which means it advances much faster. For example, from the end of 2018 until the beginning of 2021, LibreSSL has merged approximately *1,500 patches from 36 developers*. During the same time, OpenSSL has merged more than *5,000 patches from 276 developers*. Apart from the core OpenSSL development team, OpenSSL receives code contributions from big companies such as Oracle, Red Hat, IBM, and others.

While the focus of LibreSSL is providing a TLS library for the OpenBSD project, it also aims to support other platforms and remain API-compatible with OpenSSL. At the time of writing, the LibreSSL API is compatible with OpenSSL 1.0.1, but does not include all the newest APIs from OpenSSL 1.0.2 and later.

Since its fork from OpenSSL, LibreSSL became the default TLS library on OpenBSD, but on most other operating systems, the adoption has been low. Most Linux distributions continued using OpenSSL, and some decided to try LibreSSL as a system-wide option but decided to drop such support later. Most commercial application vendors that used OpenSSL also decided to stick with it.

In the competition between OpenSSL and LibreSSL, OpenSSL is winning. I recommend that you choose OpenSSL unless you are developing software specifically for the OpenBSD community, in which case you should consider LibreSSL.

Another fork of OpenSSL has been created by the mighty Google corporation, as we'll explore in the next section.

Comparing OpenSSL with BoringSSL

BoringSSL is another fork of OpenSSL that was made public in 2014. BoringSSL was made for the needs of the Google corporation. For years, Google maintained its own patches for OpenSSL for use in various Google products, such as *Chrome*, *Android*, and the server's infrastructure. Finally, they decided to *fork* OpenSSL and maintain their fork as a separate library.

Like LibreSSL, in BoringSSL, Google removed a lot of the original OpenSSL code, which was responsible for supporting old and unpopular algorithms and features. Google also added some functionality that does not exist in OpenSSL. For example, the **CRYPTO_BUFFER** functionality allows you to deduplicate X.509 certificates in memory, thus reducing memory usage. It also allows you to remove OpenSSL's X.509 and ASN.1 code from the application if OpenSSL is linked statically to the application. The X.509 code is a sizeable part of OpenSSL.

Unlike LibreSSL, BoringSSL does not aim for **API compatibility** with OpenSSL, or even with former versions of BoringSSL. Google wants to change the library API at will. It makes sense because Google controls both BoringSSL and the major software projects that use the library, which makes it possible to synchronize the API changes in BoringSSL and those projects. If the API is not kept stable, it is possible to free up development resources that would otherwise be spent on maintaining the old APIs.

But this also means that if someone outside Google wants to use BoringSSL, they should be ready for *breaking changes* in the library API, at the least suitable times. This is very inconvenient for developers who use the library. Google understands this and states that although BoringSSL is an open source project, it is not for general use.

My opinion is that BoringSSL was made open source mostly for third-party contributors to Google projects, such as Chrome and Android.

I do not recommend using BoringSSL in your applications due to its **API instability**. Furthermore, OpenSSL has more features, better documentation, and a much larger community.

With that, we have reviewed several competitors of OpenSSL. You should now understand the main differences between the popular TLS libraries and which library should be used in which case.

Let's proceed to the summary.

Summary

In this chapter, we have learned what OpenSSL is and why it's needed. We also walked through the history of OpenSSL and had a glimpse into its future. We reviewed other TLS libraries and competitors to OpenSSL and highlighted their strengths and weaknesses.

You should now have a better understanding of which TLS library you should choose in any given situation. And if the situation is not special, I recommend that you choose OpenSSL since many other people have chosen the same, which implies that OpenSSL is the most popular TLS library and the de facto industry standard.

Now that you know why you should choose OpenSSL, you need to learn how to use it. The next few chapters will be practical ones in that we will learn how to use OpenSSL's powerful features – from symmetric encryption to creating TLS connections with X.509 certificates.

Part 2:
Symmetric Cryptography

In this part, we will learn about symmetric cryptography and its accompanying technologies, such as cryptographically strong message digests, message authentication codes, and generating symmetric cryptographic keys from passwords. This section contains a review of the symmetric ciphers, such as AES and ChaCha, and message digest algorithms, such as SHA-256, supported by OpenSSL. The usage of all the technologies mentioned will be illustrated using command-line and C code examples. We will learn how to initialize and un-initialize OpenSSL and will write our first programs that use the OpenSSL library.

This part contains the following chapters:

- *Chapter 2, Symmetric Encryption and Decryption*
- *Chapter 3, Message Digests*
- *Chapter 4, MAC and HMAC*
- *Chapter 5, Derivation of an Encryption Key from a Password*

2
Symmetric Encryption and Decryption

In this chapter, we will learn about the important concepts of symmetric encryption – cipher, encryption mode, and padding. There will be an overview of modern ciphers, encryption modes, and padding types and recommendations on which technology to use in which situation. The usage of those technologies will be illustrated by code examples. This is the first chapter that will contain code examples; thus, we will also need to learn how to initialize older versions of the OpenSSL library if we ever want to run our code with an older version of OpenSSL.

We are going to cover the following topics in this chapter:

- Understanding symmetric encryption
- An overview of the symmetric ciphers supported by OpenSSL
- Block cipher modes of operation
- Padding for block ciphers
- How to generate symmetric encryption keys
- Downloading and installing OpenSSL
- How to encrypt and decrypt with AES on the command line
- Initializing and uninitializing OpenSSL library
- How to compile and link with OpenSSL
- How to encrypt with AES programmatically
- How to decrypt with AES programmatically

Technical requirements

This chapter will contain commands that you can run on a command line and C source code that you can build and run. For the command-line commands, you will need the `openssl` command-line tool with OpenSSL dynamic libraries. For building the C code, you will need OpenSSL dynamic or static libraries, library headers, a C compiler and, a linker. If you don't have OpenSSL components installed, this chapter will teach you how to install them.

We will implement some example programs in this chapter in order to practice what we are learning. The full source code of those programs can be found here: `https://github.com/PacktPublishing/Demystifying-Cryptography-with-OpenSSL-3/tree/main/Chapter02`.

Understanding symmetric encryption

Symmetric encryption is used for encrypting data with an **encryption key**. Note that an encryption key is not the same as a **password**, but an encryption key can be derived from a password. How to do so will be explained in a *Chapter 5, Derivation of an Encryption Key from a Password*.

Symmetric encryption is called symmetric because the same key is used both for encryption and decryption operations. There is also **asymmetric encryption**, where different keys (public and private) are used for encryption and decryption. Asymmetric encryption will be covered in *Chapter 6, Asymmetric Encryption and Decryption*.

In order to symmetrically encrypt something, you have to use a **symmetric encryption algorithm**. This kind of algorithm is also called a **cipher**. It is worth noting the term *cipher* has a broad meaning and can refer to any encryption or encryption-related algorithm, including algorithms for symmetric and asymmetric encryption, message digests, and even a set of algorithms used during a TLS connection – for example, `ECDHE-ECDSA-AES256-GCM-SHA384`. In the course of this book, we will use the term *cipher* to mean different things depending on the current context. For example, right now, the context is symmetric encryption – thus, we are using *cipher* to denote a symmetric encryption algorithm.

Useful data that is being encrypted is called **plaintext**, even if it is not text. Images, music, videos, archives, or databases, anything you want to encrypt is plaintext in encryption terms.

The result of encryption process, encrypted data, is called **ciphertext**. Ciphertext almost never looks like text, but this terminology is still used in the industry.

Using the given terminology, we can say that encryption transforms plaintext into ciphertext and decryption transforms ciphertext back into plaintext.

In order to encrypt some plaintext, you have to do the following:

1. Choose an encryption algorithm (cipher).
2. Generate an encryption key.
3. Generate an **initialization vector (IV)**.

4. Choose the **cipher operation mode.**

5. Choose the **padding type.**

6. Encrypt the plaintext with the cipher, key, and padding using the chosen cipher operation mode.

Depending on the cipher and its operation mode, some of these steps may not be required. For instance, stream ciphers and some block cipher operation modes do not require padding.

Someone with little experience in cryptography may ask, "why do I have to choose so many parameters? When I used encrypted archives, my archiver only asked me for a password, not for a cipher, a key, an IV, a mode, or a padding type!" The answer is that an archiver or another user-friendly tool handles all those things behind the scenes, makes most of these choices on behalf of the user, and generates an encryption key from the user-supplied password.

Nevertheless, we are going to learn a bit about the basic encryption concepts mentioned in order to make conscious choices and understand how those concepts work together. We will start by learning about encryption algorithms (or ciphers).

An overview of the symmetric ciphers supported by OpenSSL

In this section, we will review the symmetric encryption algorithms supported by OpenSSL, but, first, we need to introduce some concepts that will help us to understand the differences between ciphers, their properties, and their advantages and disadvantages. Symmetric ciphers are divided into two categories: block ciphers and stream ciphers.

Comparing block ciphers and stream ciphers

Block ciphers operate on blocks of data. For example, a popular **Advanced Encryption Standard** (**AES**) cipher has a **block size** of 128 bits, meaning that the cipher encrypts or decrypts data in 128-bit blocks. If the amount of data is larger than the block size, the data is split into blocks of the needed size needed for processing. If the **plaintext** length is not multiple of the block size, the last block is usually padded up to the block size according to the chosen **padding type**. Thus, in most **block cipher operation modes**, the **ciphertext** length is always a multiple of the block size.

What happens during encryption by the block cipher, explained simply? Input to the encryption is a block of plaintext (for example, 16 bytes), the encryption key, and possibly some cipher operation mode-specific data (for example the previous ciphertext block or the IV). Individual bytes of the plaintext are put into a list or a matrix. Then, different logical and arithmetical operations are performed on the plaintext bytes, the encryption key bytes, and the additional operation mode-specific data bytes: **bit rotations**, **eXclusive OR** (**XOR**), addition or subtraction, or the exchange of full or partial bytes in the list or matrix. The output of those operations is a ciphertext block of the same size as the input plaintext block. For decryption, the input is a ciphertext block, the encryption key, and the operation mode-specific data. The operations from the encryption phase are performed in the opposite order and, as a result, the ciphertext block is transformed back into the plaintext block:

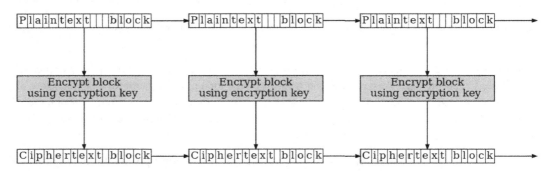

Figure 2.1 – How block ciphers work

Stream ciphers do not operate on blocks but operate on single bytes or even bits of data. This means that stream ciphers do not need padding. They also do not have operating modes, although some researchers are trying to introduce operation modes for stream ciphers too. These characteristics of stream ciphers make them easier to use, especially for streamed data, easier to implement, and faster to perform than block ciphers. However, cryptographers believe that the existing stream ciphers are generally less secure than block ciphers and it is easier to further weaken the security of a stream cipher through an implementation mistake than it is with a block cipher.

How do stream ciphers work, explained simply? During both encryption and decryption, a stream cipher generates a so-called **pseudorandom cipher digit stream** or **keystream**, based on the encryption key and the **IV** or **nonce** (**number used once**). The cipher takes bytes of the encryption key and the IV and performs logical and mathematical operations on them in order to generate an infinite stream of seemingly random bytes. This is the keystream we refer to. We can say that a stream cipher, when generating the keystream, works like a **pseudorandom number generator** (**PRNG**), which is **seeded** by the encryption key and the IV. On encryption, the ciphertext stream is produced by combining the keystream with the plaintext stream. Usually, the keystream bytes and the plaintext bytes are just XOR-ed. On decryption, the same keystream is generated and combined with the ciphertext stream. If the *ciphertext stream* was produced by XOR-ing the *keystream* with the *plaintext stream*, then the *plaintext stream* is recovered by using the same XOR operation, but this time, on the *keystream* and the *ciphertext stream*. In order to produce the same keystream for decryption, the same encryption key and IV must be used:

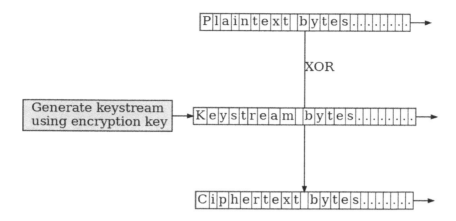

Figure 2.2 – How stream ciphers work

Understanding symmetric cipher security

When cryptographers are talking about security of a cipher, they usually measure **cipher security** or **cipher strength** in **security bits**. For example, if an attacker needs to perform 2^{256} computational operations to break a cipher, then the cipher security is 256 bits.

The maximum amount of security bits a cipher can have is the length of the used encryption key. For example, if a cipher uses a 256-bit encryption key, its strength is no more than 256 bits. It's rather easy to prove. Let's imagine an attacker has some ciphertext, does not have the encryption key and the corresponding plaintext, but can distinguish the valid plaintext from random data. The attacker's goal is to recover the encryption key or the plaintext. If the **key length** is 256 bits, then there are 2^{256} possible encryption keys that can be used with the current cipher. The attacker can use **brute force**, also known as the **exhaustive search** approach – that is, trying every possible key for decrypting the ciphertext. Then, they must try no more than 2^{256} times – that is, perform 2^{256} computational operations at most.

Here, a computational operation does not mean a very basic operation, such as a **Central Processing Unit** (**CPU**) instruction, but a complete attempt at decrypting a small amount of ciphertext, such as one ciphertext block. The important thing here is that the amount of the computational operations depends on the key length. Decryption of one ciphertext block is very fast and cheap on modern CPUs, but doing such an operation 2^{256} times would take billions of years. Encryption security is based on the attacker's necessity to perform an infeasible number of operations to decrypt the ciphertext or recover the key.

It's important to understand that the computational complexity grows exponentially depending on the key length – meaning, breaking a 256-bit key is not two times more computationally expensive than breaking a 128-bit key. It is 2^{128} times more computationally expensive. Longer keys require more computational power during normal operation than shorter keys but in the case of symmetric encryption, this difference is not significant. Therefore, it makes sense to use longer keys.

Most ciphers aim to be as strong as their key allows. In practice, security researchers often find smarter ways to attack encryption than just brute force. This way, security of a cipher may weaken – for example, from 256 to 224 security bits. A cipher is considered secure if, after applying the smartest possible attack, it still retains enough security bits.

How many bits of security is enough?

As of 2021, the consensus among security researchers and the recommendation of the US' **National Institute of Standards and Technology** (**NIST**) is the following:

- 112 bits of security should be enough until 2030.
- 128 bits of security should be enough until the next revolutionary breakthrough in technology or mathematics.

One such technological breakthrough is expected in the coming years. This is **quantum computing**. Quantum computers already exist, but they are quite expensive and still not powerful enough to be used for cryptography breaking. Quantum computing is expected to *halve* the number of security bits for **symmetric cryptographic algorithms**. It means that ciphers that were previously 256-bit strong will become only 128-bit strong and those that previously were 128-bit strong will reduce their cryptographic strength to only 64 bits.

As we previously noted, security researchers are constantly looking for smarter ways to break cryptography. Thus, the effective security of any cipher is usually a bit lower than its key length.

Popular symmetric ciphers support key lengths of up to 256 bits.

Given the preceding considerations, I recommend using 256-bit symmetric encryption keys with a strong symmetric cipher whenever possible. This amount of security bits should be enough for the foreseeable future, even considering ongoing security research and the ongoing development of quantum computing.

Reviewing the AES cipher

AES is the most popular modern symmetric cipher. If you are unsure which symmetric cipher to use, use this cipher. This cipher is both fast and secure. AES is a block cipher with a block size of 128 bits. There are three variants of the AES cipher, using keys of different lengths: 128, 192, and 256 bits. Those three variants are called AES-128, AES-192, and AES-256, respectively.

There was a lot of research about AES security to find smarter ways than brute force to break the cipher. AES stands quite strong against these attempts. The current best attacks reduce AES security strength by only 2 bits: to 126, 190, and 254 bits of security for AES-128, AES-192, and AES-256, respectively.

It is worth mentioning though that modern x86 and x86_64 CPUs have hardware acceleration for AES, called **Advanced Encryption Standard New Instructions (AES-NI)**, making the already-fast AES cipher even faster. Some ARMv8 CPUs support an optional **ARMv8 Cryptographic Extension** that also accelerates AES.

AES uses an encryption algorithm called **Rijndael**. Rijndael supports more block sizes and key lengths than when standardized as AES. Thus, we can say that AES is a subset of Rijndael. Many people use the terms *AES* and *Rijndael* interchangeably, as synonyms. The Rijndael algorithm was developed by two Belgian cryptographers, *Vincent Rijmen* and *Joan Daemen*. The name *Rijndael* is based on parts of the authors' surnames, *Rij* and *Dae*.

Why does AES have *Standard* in its name? Because AES was standardized in 2001 by NIST as the standard encryption algorithm for sensitive commercial and (US) government information. It is worth mentioning that AES is not the only cipher used for the US government's sensitive information, but AES is the most popular symmetric cipher in the world that the general public has access to.

Reviewing DES and 3DES ciphers

Data Encryption Standard (**DES**) was the previous encryption standard, the predecessor of AES. It is a block cipher with a block size of 64 bits and a key length of 56 bits. Both the block size and key length are too short for the cipher to be secure. Cryptography researchers further reduced the DES security to 39 to 41 security bits. In practice, a DES key can be recovered on a modern consumer-grade PC in a matter of days or even hours.

3DES or **Triple DES** is a cipher based on the usual DES. Basically, 3DES is DES applied three times with two or three different keys. 3DES security is considered to be 112 bits for the three-key variant and only 80 bits for the two-key variant.

It is not recommended to use DES or 3DES ciphers for new encryptions. However, DES was in use for many years and some organizations may still have old data encrypted by DES. Some legacy systems may have also implemented 3DES but not AES for network security and so 3DES may be needed for interoperability. If the usage of old insecure ciphers is needed for legacy systems, it is strongly recommended to limit this usage to internal networks and migrate to more modern ciphers as soon as possible.

3DES is three times slower than usual DES. DES itself is a rather slow cipher compared to AES and other competitors. On modern workstations, the slowness of DES or 3DES should not be significant, but if a server serves a lot of clients using a slow cipher, this slowness may be significant. It is one more reason to migrate to a faster and more secure cipher.

Reviewing the RC4 cipher

RC4 is an old stream cipher that can use keys with a length of 40 to 2,048 bits. The cipher was very popular in the past because of its speed and the simplicity of its implementation, but over the years, many flows were discovered in the algorithm and it is now considered insecure. For example, one of the attacks reduces the security of RC4 with 128-bit keys to just 26 bits.

An interesting fact about RC4 is that, for a period of time in 2013, RC4 was used as the main SSL/TLS cipher, because all the block ciphers used in SSL 3.0 and TLS 1.0 were targeted by the infamous **Browser Exploit Against SSL/TLS (BEAST)** attack, but RC4, being a stream cipher, was not affected by it.

The problem with RC4 is the same as with DES. RC4 was popular for a long time in the past and some organizations may still have old data encrypted by RC4. Some organizations may also have legacy systems in use that do not support modern encryption algorithms. The recommendation to such organizations is the same as with DES: migrate to modern systems and ciphers and in the meantime, limit the usage of RC4-affected data or network streams to the organization's internal networks.

At the time of writing, popular modern web browsers still support 3DES for interoperability with old servers, but do not support single DES or RC4 anymore.

Reviewing the ChaCha20 cipher

ChaCha20 is a modern stream cipher. It is secure and fast. ChaCha20 can be used with a 128-bit or 256-bit key. The main variant of the cipher uses a 256-bit key and OpenSSL only supports the main variant. At the time of writing, there are no known attacks that can reduce the security of the full 20-round ChaCha20 cipher – thus, its security remains the same as the key length, 256 bits.

The ChaCha20 cipher is developed by *Daniel J. Bernstein (DJB)*, a famous cryptography and security researcher. DJB is also known for his other projects, such as **qmail**, **djbdns**, **Poly1305**, and **Curve25519**. ChaCha20 is a performance-optimized modification of the **Salsa20** cipher from the same author. ChaCha20 became popular when Google started to use it in their Chrome browser, together with the Poly1305 **message authentication code (MAC)** algorithm from the same author. Then, support for ChaCha20 and Poly1305 was also added to OpenSSH. Becoming a popular stream cipher, ChaCha20 has effectively become the successor of RC4.

As mentioned earlier, ChaCha20 is a fast cipher. ChaCha20 is faster than AES in software implementations. Hardware AES acceleration on x86 or x86_64 and ARMv8 makes AES faster than ChaCha20, but this acceleration is not included in all CPUs. For instance, low-end ARM CPUs, used in mobile and other devices, do not have such optimization, nor do they have as much processing power as x86_64 CPUs in desktop computers. Therefore, ChaCha20 may be preferred on low-end devices over AES, especially for encrypting network data streams.

One minor disadvantage of ChaCha20 is that it uses a **block counter**, which is only 32-bit. Because of that, the cipher is only considered secure on contiguous plaintexts that do not exceed 256 GiB of data. It should be enough for network data streams but might not be enough for the encryption of large files. A workaround is to split very long plaintexts into shorter chunks, at most 256 GiB, and reset the block counter and **nonce** before encrypting each chunk.

Reviewing other symmetric ciphers supported by OpenSSL

OpenSSL supports some other symmetric ciphers that are less popular than the four ciphers mentioned above.

Some of them, such as **Blowfish, CAST5, GOST89, IDEA, RC2**, and **RC5**, are block ciphers with a block size of 64 bits or with variable block sizes, whose OpenSSL implementation uses a block size of 64 bits. Those ciphers are not recommended to use for very long ciphertexts (longer than 32 GiB) because of **collision attacks** and the **birthday paradox**. The solution for this issue is to split long plaintexts into chunks smaller than 32 GiB and use a different encryption key and IV for each chunk. The algorithms using 64-bit blocks are quite old. Many of them were developed in the 1990s and some even in the 1970s.

Other algorithms, such as **ARIA, Camellia, SEED**, and **SM4**, are block ciphers with 128-bit block sizes. With 128-bit block sizes, you can encrypt very long plaintexts without worrying about collision attacks, up to 256 exabytes.

Some of the less popular algorithms are good, but some have technical disadvantages compared to AES. Many of the old algorithms are significantly slower than AES, up to 10 times slower, but most of the less common ciphers supported by OpenSSL are still secure. We are not going to review every less common cipher in detail, but the following are worth mentioning.

The less popular ciphers can be grouped into the following categories.

National ciphers

National ciphers are developed and standardized in a particular country. There is usually a lot of pride around the national cipher in the crypto community of the country where the cipher was developed. Often such ciphers are good, but not very popular outside of the country of origin.

CAST5, also known as **CAST-128**, is a cipher developed by Canadian researchers *Carlisle Adams* and *Stafford Tavares* in 1996. The name *CAST* represents the initials of the cipher authors, but also has a connotation of randomness, which makes sense, because a good cipher produces ciphertext that looks like random data. The CAST5 cipher uses 128-bit keys. No known attack has been developed yet on the full 16-round CAST5. Therefore, its security level remains at 128 bits. An interesting fact about CAST5 is that for a long time, it was the default symmetric cipher in the **GNU Privacy Guard (GnuPG)** software, until the default was changed to AES. For some time, CAST5 was also the default cipher in the original **Pretty Good Privacy (PGP)** software. CAST5 is one of the standard ciphers used by the Canadian government. You may be required to use this cipher if your software interacts with the computer systems of Canadian state organizations.

GOST89, also known as **Magma**, is an old government standard cipher from the USSR and Russia. It was developed in 1970s by the KGB and first published as a classified standard in 1989. GOST89 has a successor cipher, **GOST2015**, also known as **Kuznyechik**, but GOST89 is not declared obsolete. **GOST** stands for **GOvernment STandard**. GOST89 uses 256-bit keys. Extensive cryptoanalysis has been done on GOST89 and the best theoretical attack reduces the security of GOST89 to 178 bits, at the cost of impractical memory and storage requirements. Some cryptanalysts point out that insecure **S-boxes** exist for GOST89, but OpenSSL includes only secure GOST89 S-boxes. As GOST89 is one of the government standards of the Russian Federation, you may be required to use this cipher if your software interacts with the computer systems of Russian state organizations.

SEED and ARIA are ciphers from South Korea. Both are in use in South Korea, but seldom elsewhere in the world. SEED was developed in 1998 and ARIA was developed in 2003. Both are block ciphers with a block size of 128 bits. ARIA is based on AES and supports the same key lengths as AES – 128, 192, and 256 bits. SEED uses 128-bit keys. No practical attack on SEED or ARIA has been developed at the time of writing – hence, the security of the ciphers is believed to be the same as the key length. ARIA is optimized for hardware implementations, also in low-end hardware. In software implementation it is one-and-a-half to two times slower than AES. SEED and ARIA are the national standards of South Korea. You may be required to use this cipher if your software interacts with the computer systems of South Korean state organizations.

Camellia is a 128-bit block cipher developed in 2000 in Japan by NTT and Mitsubishi Electric. The cipher is named after the *Camellia japonica* flower. The Camellia cipher is similar in design to AES and has security and performance comparable to AES. AES-NI instructions in x86_64 CPUs can be used for the hardware acceleration of Camellia. Much of AES-related cryptanalysis also applies to Camellia. As AES, Camellia supports keys of 128, 192, and 256 bits. Camellia is a patented cipher but is available under a royalty-free license. Camellia is one of the standardized ciphers in Japan. You may be required to use Camellia if your software interacts with the computer systems of Japanese state organizations.

SM4 is another cipher from the East – this time, from China. The year of its development is not publicly known, as the cipher was secret for some time and was declassified in 2006. The cipher uses 128-bit blocks and 128-bit keys. As with the Camellia cipher, AES-NI instructions in x86_64 CPUs can be used for the hardware acceleration of SM4. Several cryptanalytical attempts were made, but no attack has been developed on the full 32-round SM4 cipher yet – thus, its security remains at 128 bits. SM4 is a Chinese national standard for encryption and is used for wireless **Local Area Networks (LANs)** in China. You may be required to use SM4 if your software interacts with the computer systems of Chinese state organizations.

The RC cipher family

The RC family is a collection of ciphers developed by a famous cryptographer *Ron Rivest*. RC stands for Ron's Code or Rivest Cipher. RC2, the predecessor of RC4, is and old cipher developed in 1987. RC2 is vulnerable to related-key attacks. Not very much research has been done on this cipher by independent cryptanalysts, but the cryptography community is skeptical about the security of RC2. Another drawback of RC2 is that being a variable key length cipher, RC2 supports short insecure keys.

RC5 was developed in 1994. The cipher is notable for the simplicity of its implementation. It is a cipher with a variable key length (0 to 2,040 bits) and variable block size (32, 64, or 128 bits). OpenSSL only supports 64-bit blocks for RC5 and keys up to 2,040 bits. The default key length in OpenSSL is 128 bits – it is also the length recommended by the author of the cipher. No practical attack on RC5 has been developed yet, but, like RC2, RC5 supports short insecure keys, which is a drawback.

Other ciphers

International Data Encryption Algorithm (IDEA) was developed in 1991 as an intended replacement for DES. IDEA is known as the default cipher in PGP version 2, which was the time when PGP became widespread. IDEA was covered by patents at the time of its creation, but the last patent expired in 2012. Because of the patents, GnuPG could not use IDEA in its core code. For the same reason, the author of PGP decided to change the default cipher to CAST5 in PGP version 3. The cipher uses 128-bit keys. The best-known attack reduces its security to 126 bits. The Blowfish cipher was developed by probably the most famous cryptography researcher in the world, *Bruce Schneier*. Schneier developed Blowfish as a free-to-use, symmetric cipher in 1993 when most other ciphers were proprietary and patent-encumbered. Blowfish is a variable-length cipher, supporting key lengths of 32 to 448 bits. So far, no practical attack has been developed against full 16-round Blowfish. But Blowfish, being a variable-key-length cipher, supports short insecure keys. Thus, it is not possible to say upfront whether Blowfish-encrypted data is encrypted securely. The decrypting software has to examine the key length, make a decision about the security level of the encrypted data, and inform the user whether the decryption process is interactive, but not all software does it. That's a second weakness of Blowfish, in addition to its small 64-bit block size. The author of Blowfish has developed a successor to Blowfish, Twofish, which uses a 128-bit block size and key lengths of minimum 128, 192, or 256 bits. He recommends the users of Blowfish to migrate to Twofish.

Block cipher modes of operation

Block ciphers can operate in different **encryption modes**, also known as **modes of operation**. As we already know, block ciphers encrypt plaintext data block by block. Encryption modes specify how blocks of ciphertext are chained together. We are now going to review most popular operation modes.

Reviewing the Electronic Code Book mode

The simplest operation mode is **Electronic Code Book (ECB)**. In this mode, each plaintext block is encrypted into a ciphertext block using only the encryption key, without using an **IV** or previous plaintext or ciphertext blocks. Then, the ciphertext blocks produced are concatenated.

The ECB mode can be illustrated by the following image:

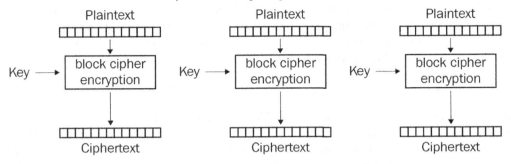

Electronic Codebook (ECB) mode encryption

Figure 2.3 – How ECB mode works

Image Source: Wikipedia, licensing: Public Domain

In the ECB mode, the same plaintext always produces the same ciphertext. It is a security issue because patterns in the plaintext are preserved in the ciphertext and are visible to an observer.

Let's consider the following image and its encrypted representation:

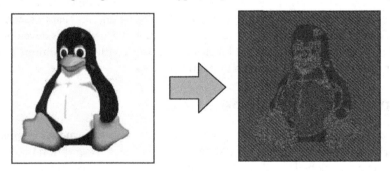

Figure 2.4 – An example of an image and its encrypted representation

The source of the both penguin images: `https://isc.tamu.edu/~lewing/linux/`, *author: Larry Erwing, licensing: "Permission to use and/or modify this image is granted provided you acknowledge me lewing@isc.tamu.edu and The GIMP if someone asks"*

As illustrated, even though the second image is encrypted, we can see what was been drawn and that the ECB mode does not provide efficient encryption protection. Therefore, we should use a smarter operation mode – for example, **Cipher Block Chaining (CBC)** mode.

Reviewing CBC mode

In CBC mode, the ciphertext of the current block depends on the ciphertext of the previous block. How does that work? Unlike ECB mode, where every plaintext block is encrypted as is, in CBC mode, the current plaintext block is XOR-ed with the previous ciphertext block and then the result of the XOR operation is encrypted, producing the current ciphertext.

What happens with the very first plaintext block, for which no previous ciphertext exists? The first plaintext block is XOR-ed with an IV. An IV is a block of data used for initializing the cipher. In many modes, including CBC, the IV is usually generated randomly and is the same size as the cipher block size. The IV is *usually* not kept secret and is stored together with the ciphertext because it is needed for decryption. However, *sometimes*, when possible and it makes sense, for example, in TLS protocol version 1.1 and above, the IV is transmitted in the encrypted form.

The CBC operation mode can be illustrated by the following diagram:

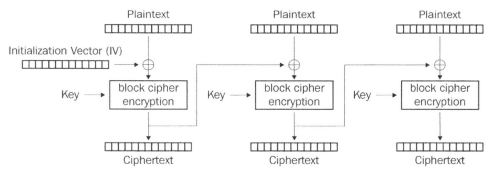

Cipher Block Chaining (CBC) mode encryption

Figure 2.5 – How CBC mode works

Image source: Wikipedia, licensing: Public Domain

Here is an encryption of the same penguin image in CBC mode:

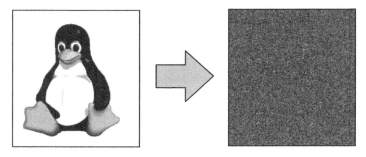

Figure 2.6 – An example of image encryption in CBC mode

The source of both the penguin image and the pseudo-randomness image: `https://isc.tamu.edu/~lewing/linux/`, *author: Larry Erwing, licensing: "Permission to use and/or modify this image is granted provided you acknowledge me lewing@isc.tamu.edu and The GIMP if someone asks"*

As illustrated, the patterns in the original image were not preserved during the encryption. It is impossible to say, observing the encrypted image, what was drawn in the original image. As we can see, CBC mode provides good encryption protection. It hides both the exact original data from an observer and the relationships between parts of the original data. Other non-ECB modes of operation produce similar seemingly random images.

The IV used in the CBC mode must be unpredictable for a given message, in order to resist the **chosen-plaintext attack**. An easy way to satisfy that requirement is to generate the IV randomly.

In almost any encryption mode, including CBC, an IV must only be used for one message encrypted with the given encryption key and must not be reused for another message. Therefore, we can say that an IV is usually a **nonce**. For some operation modes, it is said that the IV is derived from a nonce.

CBC mode was invented in 1976 and for many years, it was the most popular mode of operation, both for file and network traffic encryption. Nowadays, GCM (described a bit later) is becoming more popular, especially for networking. CBC mode remains quite good for file encryption. GCM is based on the **Counter (CTR)** mode, which we will review next.

Reviewing CTR mode

In CTR mode, plaintext itself is not processed by the encryption algorithm, as with AES. Instead, a sequence of counter blocks is encrypted by the block cipher. For example, each counter block may consist of a concatenated 64-bit random nonce and an actual 64-bit integer counter, incrementing for each next block. The important things are that the first counter block is not reused for the encryption of another plaintext with the same encryption key and all the counter blocks are different.

The simplest and most popular way to increment a counter is to just add 1 to it, but this way is not mandatory. Other operations, such as adding or subtracting more than 1, or something more complex, such as XOR and bit shifting, are also acceptable. The important thing is that the counter sequence will not start to repeat itself.

OK, in CTR mode, we are encrypting some counter sequence instead of the plaintext, but how does this help us? How do we protect the plaintext? We take the encrypted *counter* blocks and XOR them with the *plaintext* blocks. The result of that XOR operation is our ciphertext.

CTR operation mode can be illustrated by the following diagram:

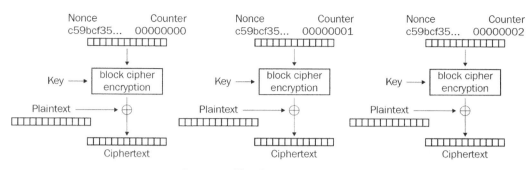

Counter (CTR) mode encryption

Figure 2.7 – How CTR mode works

Image source: Wikipedia, licensing: Public Domain

We can say that CTR mode converts a block cipher into a stream cipher. Indeed, the sequence of *encrypted* counter blocks is our keystream! We XOR that keystream with the plaintext, just as we do when using a stream cipher!

We can think about the first counter block in a similar way as that of the IV. Similar to the IV in CBC mode, the first counter block (or at least its random part) is usually saved together with the ciphertext because it is needed for the decryption. The counter block incrementation method is also usually not a secret. In the case of OpenSSL, it can even be looked up in the OpenSSL code. Therefore, all counter blocks are known to a possible observer or attacker, But *encrypted* counter blocks are not known to the observer if they do not possess the encryption key. If the observer could obtain the encrypted counter blocks (the keystream), they would be able to recover the plaintext just by XORing the keystream with the ciphertext.

The IV used in CTR mode must never be reused with the same encryption key for another message. If you reuse it, the same keystream will be generated for encrypting multiple messages. Two ciphertexts encrypted with the same keystream can be XORed and the result will be the same as XORing the corresponding plaintexts. Plaintexts often have much less randomness than the keystream and thus, a plaintext recovery attack becomes much easier than an attack on the ciphertext. Furthermore, if the chosen plaintext attack is possible, then the keystream can be recovered just by XORing the plaintext and the ciphertext, and then the recovered keystream can be used to decrypt any message encrypted by the same keystream or produced by the same key and IV. While IV uniqueness is a very important requirement in CTR mode, IV unpredictability is not a requirement in this mode, unlike in CBC mode. This is because CTR's resistance against the chosen plaintext attack is based on the unpredictability of the next keystream block, not on the unpredictability of the IV. Some cryptographers criticize CTR mode because the block cipher is fed with non-secret data in order to produce the keystream. However, nowadays, CTR mode is widely accepted and respected by cryptographers, such as *Niels Ferguson* and *Bruce Schneier*, who believe that it is secure. It is also worth mentioning that the CTR mode was invented by two other respected cryptographers, *Whitfield Diffie* and *Martin Hellman*, who are famous for inventing the **Diffie-Hellman (DH) key exchange** method used in TLS.

As CTR mode converts a block cipher to a stream cipher, it has the same advantages as stream ciphers. In CTR mode, plaintext padding is not needed and thus, padding oracle attacks are avoided. The keystream can also be precalculated in advance, not necessarily at the time of encryption. Finally, encryption and decryption operations just XOR the keystream with the plaintext – hence, different plaintext blocks can be encrypted or decrypted in parallel using the precalculated keystream.

CTR mode serves as the basis for the more advanced **Galois/Counter mode (GCM)**.

Reviewing GCM

In GCM, the ciphertext is produced in the same way as in CTR mode. The counter blocks are encrypted with a block cipher, producing the keystream. Then, the keystream is XORed with the plaintext, producing the ciphertext.

The difference from CTR mode is that GCM not only *encrypts the plaintext* but also *authenticates the ciphertext*. This means that the knowledge of the encryption key allows us to verify the **integrity** of the ciphertext or, in other words, detect unauthorized changes to the ciphertext if the verification has failed. This detection is useful because many attacks work by changing the ciphertext, feeding the changed ciphertext to an **oracle**, and analyzing the oracle feedback.

An **oracle** in cryptography is a program, device, or network node that possesses an encryption key and is able encrypt or decrypt data. An oracle gives some feedback, sometimes in the form of (correctly or incorrectly) encrypted or decrypted data, sometimes in the form of an error message, or sometimes, an oracle exposes other information – for example, the time taken to decrypt. This can differ between successful and unsuccessful decryption. The oracle feedback allows an attacker or a cryptanalyst to get data that may help to break the encryption.

Authenticated encryption (AE) modes, such as GCM, make it possible to detect unauthorized changes to the encrypted data and refuse to use the corrupted data.

Some authenticated encryption modes allow us to combine encrypted and unencrypted data for authentication. This is needed for storing or transmitting data that is not confidential but is related to encrypted confidential data and needs protection from unauthorized changes. These encryption modes are called **authenticated encryption with associated data (AEAD)**. GCM is an AEAD mode – extra data added will only be authenticated but not encrypted.

How does GCM authenticate the ciphertext? Each ciphertext block is converted into a number and is used in the finite field arithmetic over the *Galois* field, together with an initial block, which depends on the encryption key. Hence, the mode of operation is called the *Galois*/Counter mode. The authentication operation produces an authentication tag that can be used by the decrypting party to verify the integrity of the ciphertext.

The output of the encryption in GCM then contains the IV, ciphertext, and authentication tag.

GCM operation can be illustrated by the following diagram:

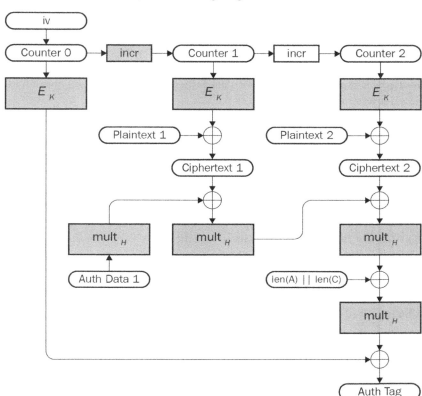

Figure 2.8 – How GCM works

Image authors: D. McGrew and J. Viega at NIST, licensing: Public Domain

GCM is a bit special. It only works on 128-bit block sizes and requires a 96-bit IV. Thus, it is impossible to use it with old 64-bit block ciphers. OpenSSL can only use GCM with the AES cipher.

GCM and other AE modes authenticate the data. If the decrypting party wants to verify the ciphertext integrity, it must process the whole ciphertext in order to validate the authentication tag. Usually, decryption and validation are done simultaneously. Hence, if the validation fails, the decrypted data should be discarded.

The requirement for the IV in AES-GCM is the same as in CTR mode: the IV must be unique, meaning that the same IV must not be reused with the same encryption key for another message. If the IV is reused, the same attacks that apply in CTR mode can also apply in AES-GCM. In addition, an attacker can recover the key used for authenticating the messages (not the encryption key). With the authenticating key, the attacker can produce fake authentication tags and inject unwanted, seemingly authenticated data into the ciphertext stream.

GCM is currently the most popular block encryption mode used in the TLS protocol. GCM has been supported since TLS 1.2. Older versions of the TLS protocol used CBC mode.

The TLS protocol always verifies encrypted data integrity, even if a non-AE encryption mode is used. The TLS protocol uses MACs for verification. On the internet, a lot of bad things can happen to the passing traffic. Someone can try **Man in the Middle (MITM)** attack on your data. Someone else can try to use your server as an oracle. Therefore, data authentication is more important on the network than on a local filesystem.

As we have mentioned, GCM is vulnerable to various attacks if the key-IV pair is reused for another message. As a response to that weakness, **Advanced Encryption Standard in Galois/Counter Mode with a Synthetic Initialization Vector (AES-GCM-SIV)** mode has been invented.

Reviewing AES-GCM-SIV

AES-GCM-SIV is a variant of the AES cipher in GCM. The distinctive feature and advantage of AES-GCM-SIV is that this algorithm provides resistance to IV or nonce misuse, meaning that the algorithm ensures that the same IV will not be reused for different messages.

AES-GCM-SIV does not take the IV as a part of the input data, as most encryption modes do. Instead, this algorithm takes the second secret key for authentication. AES-GCM-SIV generates the authentication tag based on the plaintext, additional authenticated data, and the authentication key. The generated authentication tag is also used as the IV for the plaintext encryption. This generated IV is called the **Synthetic Initialization Vector (SIV)**. As the IV depends on the plaintext, it will be different for different plaintexts.

A disadvantage of AES-GCM-SIV is that the algorithm needs two passes over the plaintext: one for generating the auth tag and IV and another one for encryption.

Other block cipher operation modes

There are many other operation modes for block ciphers, such as **propagating CBC (PCBC)**, **cipher feedback (CFB)** mode, **output feedback (OFB)** mode, **Counter with CBC-MAC (CCM)** mode, **Carter-Wegman + CTR (CWC)** the **Sophie Germain Counter Mode (SGCM)**, and so on. Those modes are not very popular; therefore, they will not be reviewed here.

Choosing the block cipher operation mode

The best block cipher operation mode supported by OpenSSL is believed to be GCM. GCM supports authentication in addition to encryption, does not require padding, and thus is immune to padding oracle attacks. GCM also allows to precalculate the keystream and parallelize encryption and decryption. If you use GCM, be sure to use a different IV for every plaintext that you encrypt with the same encryption key. It is very important – otherwise, your encryption will not be secure.

The former de facto standard block cipher operation mode is CBC. You will probably find a lot of CBC usage in existing software and a lot of existing data encrypted using CBC. CBC mode needs padding applied to plaintext. If you develop or support software that uses CBC mode, you will have to understand what padding is.

Padding for block ciphers

In CBC mode, block ciphers encrypt plaintext data block by block – but what happens to the last plaintext block, which in most cases, is smaller than the block size? It cannot be encrypted as is, because a block cipher requires a complete data block as input. Thus, the last plaintext block is padded up to the block size.

OpenSSL can add padding automatically when finalizing encryption and remove it when finalizing decryption. This feature can be disabled – in such a case, the developer must pad and unpad the plaintext data himself.

Cryptographers invented different types of padding. For symmetric encryption, OpenSSL only supports **Public Key Cryptography Standard number 7 padding (PKCS #7 padding)**, also known as **PKCS7 padding**, simply **PKCS padding**, or **standard block padding**. PKCS #7 padding consists of N bytes, each having the value N. For example, if the cipher block size is 16 bytes (128 bits) and the last block of plaintext is only 10 bytes of data, then the padding length will be 6 bytes and each padding byte will have a value of 0x06. The padding will look as follows: 0x06 0x06 0x06 0x06 0x06 0x06.

As we see, PKCS #7 padding has the advantage that it encodes the length of padding, thus indirectly encoding the length of the useful plaintext data in the last block. Hence, the exact length of the whole plaintext data does not need to be transmitted along with the data. For what it's worth, the length of the last data block is concealed from an observer of the ciphertext because the padding bytes are encrypted together with the last useful data bytes.

What happens if the plaintext length is a multiple of the block size and the last plaintext block fully fills the to-be-encrypted block? In such a case, PKCS #7 padding is added anyway. A block of padding-only bytes is appended to the plaintext as the last block for encryption. For modern ciphers with 128-bit block sizes, 16 bytes of padding are appended, each with a value of 0x10. If seemingly unneeded padding was not added, it would be impossible to know after the decryption of the last block whether the last byte was a padding byte or a plaintext data byte.

What does it mean that OpenSSL *supports* PKCS #7 padding? It means that OpenSSL will automatically add padding on encryption, remove padding on decryption, and check whether the existing PKCS #7 padding is correct. The existing padding would not be correct if the decrypted plaintext did not finish with N bytes to the value of N. In this case, OpenSSL will return an error when trying to finalize the decryption.

Note that PKCS #7 padding is sometimes called PKCS #5 padding. PKCS #5 padding uses the same padding principle (N bytes to the value of N) but is only defined for blocks up to 64 bits.

The disadvantage of PKCS #7 padding is that the resulting ciphertext is susceptible to padding oracle attacks. However, padding oracle attacks are only possible if an attacker can force the encryption of a lot of attacker-controlled plaintext with the same encryption key – for example, by sending data using JavaScript on TLS connections. If we control all the encrypted plaintext (for example, we just encrypt a file), then it is impossible, or very hard, at least, to accomplish the padding oracle attack.

If you control the encryption method and want to avoid padding oracle attacks, you can pad and unpad manually with random data. In this case, you will have to store or send the length of the plaintext, or at least of the last plaintext block, with the ciphertext.

How to generate a symmetric encryption key

Generating an encryption key for symmetric encryption is surprisingly easy. You just request the needed amount of random bytes from your **cryptographically secure random generator**!

Which random generator is considered *cryptographically secure*? It is a random generator that generates bytes that are extremely hard to predict. The unpredictability of generated random bytes is accomplished by using the entropy caused by unpredictable events from the outside world. Often, cryptographically secure random generators use the entropy caused by the unpredictable timing of the input from a keyboard and mouse. If the keyboard and mouse are unavailable, for example, when an application is running in a container, then another source of entropy can be used, such as microfluctuations in the CPU speed. Another common entropy source is a ring oscillator that can be included in the CPU or another chip.

What is the correct amount of random bytes? It is the same as the key length of your chosen cipher. For example, if you have chosen AES-256, you will need 256 random bits or 32 random bytes.

Some ciphers, such as DES or IDEA, have classes of weak keys, which render the encryption by those keys insecure, but for all popular ciphers, the probability of randomly generating a weak key is very low.

Where do you get a *cryptographically secure* random generator? It depends on your **operation system (OS)**. For example, on Linux, you can get secure random bytes from a /dev/random device, running the following command on the command line:

```
$ xxd -plain -len 32 -cols 32 /dev/random
```

Here and in the rest of the book, command-line examples follow these conventions:

- Lines beginning with $ represent commands entered at the command prompt.
- The $ prefix itself is the command-line prompt.
- The rest of the line after the $ prefix is the entered command.
- Lines not beginning with $ represent the output of the commands.

If you want to generate secure random bytes in your C code, OpenSSL provides the RAND_bytes() function, which uses an OS-dependent **cryptographically secure pseudorandom generator (CSPRNG)** and will provide you with the requested amount of secure random bytes. You can also use that function on the command line using the openssl rand command:

```
$ openssl rand -hex 32
```

The obtained encryption key can be used for symmetric encryption. It must also be saved in a safe place or securely transmitted to the decrypting party in order to decrypt the ciphertext later.

In many cases, you don't need a random encryption key, but need a key generated deterministically – for example, from a password or a passphrase. In such cases, you need to use a **Password-Based Key Derivation Function (PBKDF)**. More information about PBKDFs will be given in *Chapter 5, Derivation of an Encryption Key from a Password*.

Downloading and installing OpenSSL

We have now learned enough about the building blocks of symmetric encryption. It is time to use our knowledge to encrypt some data using OpenSSL, but first, we need to get the required components of OpenSSL.

The OpenSSL toolkit is distributed from its official website (https://www.openssl.org/) in the form of source code. If you are a software developer, you can compile OpenSSL using the documentation supplied with the source code. Compiling OpenSSL from the source is the preferred way if you want a particular version of OpenSSL or want to compile it with specific options.

You can also get OpenSSL in a compiled form. Almost all Linux distributions contain OpenSSL in the form of one or several installable packages. For example, in order to install OpenSSL on Debian or Ubuntu Linux, you only need to issue one command:

```
$ sudo apt install openssl libssl3 libssl-dev libssl-doc
```

Another Linux distribution may use a different command, but for any Linux distribution, the installation will be similar. Users of FreeBSD, NetBSD, or OpenBSD can install OpenSSL from BSD ports. Users of macOS can also install OpenSSL using a package manager, such as Homebrew or MacPorts.

It is also possible to install OpenSSL on Windows using a package manager for Windows, such as Scoop, Chocolatey, or winget. But, unlike on other operating systems, on Windows, users often do not use package managers and use standalone installation packages. These standalone installers are also made for OpenSSL by third-party developers. The incomplete list of those installers can be found at https://wiki.openssl.org/index.php/Binaries.

What do you get on your system after installing OpenSSL? The OpenSSL toolkit consists of the following components:

- Dynamic libraries
- Static libraries
- C header files
- The `openssl` command-line tool
- Documentation

What is the purpose of each component?

The dynamic libraries (`.so` or `.dll` files) are needed for linking applications that use the OpenSSL library dynamically and the subsequent execution of those applications. The OpenSSL toolkit includes two libraries, `libcrypto` and `libssl`. `libcrypto` contains an implementation of cryptography algorithms and `libssl` contains an implementation of SSL and TLS protocols. `libssl` depends on `libcrypto` and cannot be used without it. `libcrypto`, on the other hand, can be used without `libssl`, if only crypto functionality is needed, without SSL/TLS. On systems with package managers, such as Linux and BSDs, a package with OpenSSL dynamic libraries is usually called `libssl`, optionally with the version suffix – for instance, `libssl3`. The `libssl` package must be installed if any other installed package needs the OpenSSL library. There are many applications that use the OpenSSL library – hence, the `libssl` package will be installed on most systems.

Static libraries (`.a` or `.lib` files) are needed for linking OpenSSL statically into applications. When a static library is linked to an application, that static library is included in the application executable file and is not needed to be available at runtime, unlike dynamic libraries. Therefore, static libraries are only needed during development. On systems with package managers, a package with OpenSSL static libraries is usually called `libssl-dev`, `libssl-devel`, `openssl-devel`, or something similar. Note the `dev` or `devel` suffix – it gives a hint that the package is needed for development.

C header files are needed for the compilation of C/C++ applications that need OpenSSL. They are only needed for development – thus, on systems with package managers, they are included in the same package as static libraries – that is, `libssl-dev`, `libssl-devel`, or `openssl-devel`.

The `openssl` command-line tool is needed for using OpenSSL functionality on the command line without having to write your own applications. The tool is very useful for system administrators and DevOps engineers. On systems with package managers, the `openssl` tool is usually contained in a package with the same name, `openssl`. The `openssl` package may contain **man** (**manual**) pages for the `openssl` tool, or those man pages may reside in a separate package with documentation.

As every library, OpenSSL needs documentation. Originally being a library for Unix, OpenSSL supplies documentation for its **Application Programming Interface (API)** in the form of man pages. On systems with package managers, a package with the documentation may be called `libssl-doc`, `openssl-man`, or similarly. The package may also include code examples. Note that OpenSSL also has its man pages in HTML format available on its official website: `https://www.openssl.org/docs/manpages.html`.

Now, when we have the OpenSSL components installed, let's get our feet wet with some encryption.

How to encrypt and decrypt with AES on the command line

We are going to encrypt a file using the `openssl` command-line tool.

Let's generate a sample file:

```
$ seq 1000 >somefile.txt
```

Using our knowledge of the symmetric encryption concepts, we are choosing the following parameters for our encryption:

- Cipher: AES-256

- Operation mode: CBC (we should have chosen GCM, but that mode is not supported by the command-line tool)

- Padding type: standard block padding

How can we find out how to encrypt the command line from the documentation? We can begin with the `openssl` tool man page:

```
$ man openssl
```

On that man page, we can see different *subcommands* that the `openssl` tool supports. From the man page, we can figure out that we need the `enc` subcommand. We can then refer to the `openssl-enc` man page for documentation on the `enc` subcommand:

```
$ man openssl-enc
```

From the `openssl-enc` man page, we can figure out which parameters the subcommand needs. We see that the `enc` subcommand needs an encryption key and IV, among other parameters. We can just generate those values randomly with the `rand` subcommand. Its documentation can be read in the usual way:

```
$ man openssl-rand
```

OK, we have read enough documentation – let's generate a 256-bit encryption key using our recently acquired knowledge:

```
$ openssl rand -hex 32
74c8a19fee9e0710683afe526462ce8a960ca1356e113b-
f3a08736a68a48eca0
```

We also need to generate a 128-bit IV, the same length as the block size:

```
$ openssl rand -hex 16
4007fbd36f08cb04869683b1f8a15c99
```

Finally, let's encrypt some files:

```
$ openssl enc \
  -aes-256-cbc \
  -K \
74c8a19fee9e0710683afe526462ce8a960ca1356e113b-
f3a08736a68a48eca0 \
  -iv 4007fbd36f08cb04869683b1f8a15c99 \
  -e \
  -in somefile.txt \
  -out somefile.txt.encrypted
```

`openssl` is not printing anything to the terminal. By old Unix tradition, that means a successful execution. In unsuccessful cases, errors would be printed.

Let's check that the encrypted file has been created:

```
$ ls -o somefile.txt*
-rw-rw-r-- 1 alexei 3893 Jul 27 20:17 somefile.txt
-rw-rw-r-- 1 alexei 3904 Jul 27 20:26 somefile.txt.encrypted
```

Note that the encrypted file is 11 bytes longer (3904 versus 3893 bytes) and 3,904 is a multiple of 16. As you may have guessed, the extra 11 bytes are padding for the 16-byte blocks.

If you examine the contents of the encrypted file, you will see seemingly random binary data, as expected.

Let's try to decrypt the file:

```
$ openssl enc \
  -aes-256-cbc \
  -K 74c8a19fee9e0710683afe526462ce8a960ca1356e113b-
```

```
f3a08736a68a48eca0 \
  -iv 4007fbd36f08cb04869683b1f8a15c99 \
  -d \
  -in somefile.txt.encrypted \
  -out somefile.txt.decrypted
```

Again, there's no output, meaning the execution was successful.

Let's check that the decrypted file has exactly the same contents as the original one. We can do it by looking at the file's contents in an editor, but it is more reliable to compare their checksums:

```
$ cksum somefile.txt*
1830648734 3893 somefile.txt
1830648734 3893 somefile.txt.decrypted
4000774547 3904 somefile.txt.encrypted
```

As we can see, both size (3893) and checksum (1830648734) match for somefile.txt and somefile.txt.decrypted, meaning that the files are identical. The size and checksum of somefile.txt.encrypted are different, as expected.

If you are on Windows and do not have the cksum command, you can use OpenSSL's **message digest** calculation functionality to calculate cryptographically strong checksums (message digests):

```
$ openssl dgst somefile.txt*
SHA256(somefile.txt)= 67d4ff71d43921d5739f387da09746f405e425b-
07d727e4c69d029461d1f051f
SHA256(somefile.txt.decrypted)= 67d4ff71d43921d5739f-
387da09746f405e425b07d727e4c69d029461d1f051f
SHA256(somefile.txt.encrypted)= 5a6a88e37131407c9dc9b8601b-
3195c8a33c75a20421a1733233a963ba42aef3
```

Message digests are much more reliable than checksums produced by the cksum command, but the calculation of cryptographically strong message digests is much slower. In our case, we don't expect somefile.txt.decrypted to be specially crafted for achieving a special checksum. Thus, we don't need the advantages of cryptographically strong checksums – cksum checksums will do just fine. Also, it's a bit more difficult to compare digests in the openssl dgst output, because the digests are not lined up. Message digests will be covered in detail in *Chapter 3, Message Digests*.

What will happen if we try to decrypt the file using the wrong encryption key or IV? Let's find out. Note that the first byte of the key has been changed from 0x74 to 0x00:

```
$ openssl enc \
  -aes-256-cbc \
```

```
  -K 00c8a19fee9e0710683afe526462ce8a960ca1356e113b-
f3a08736a68a48eca0 \
  -iv 4007fbd36f08cb04869683b1f8a15c99 \
  -d \
  -in somefile.txt.encrypted \
  -out somefile.txt.decrypted
bad decrypt
140283139302720:error:06065064:digital envelope routines:EVP_
DecryptFinal_ex:bad decrypt:../crypto/evp/evp_enc.c:610:
```

The decryption has failed, but how did openssl detect the failure? Decryption is just a sequence of arithmetical and logical operations on a block of 16 bytes. We did not use authenticated encryption to check the data integrity. We also did not provide openssl with any checksum for checking the result of the decryption. It is the standard padding that helped! The decryption of the last block resulted in a block of garbage data, which did not have the right padding at the end, and openssl detected that.

Let's take a look at the checksum listing:

```
$ cksum somefile.txt*
1830648734 3893 somefile.txt
1498277506 3888 somefile.txt.decrypted
4000774547 3904 somefile.txt.encrypted
```

Note that the decrypted file is 16 bytes shorter that the encrypted file (3888 versus 3904 bytes). This is because until the last encrypted block, it was impossible to detect failure, and openssl wrote all the blocks to the output file except the last one. The checksums of somefile.txt and somefile. txt.decrypted are different, as expected. The contents of somefile.txt.decrypted look like garbage because we tried to decrypt with the wrong key.

What if we used a cipher operation mode that did not require padding – for example, CTR? Let's try to decrypt our file in CTR mode:

```
$ openssl enc \
  -aes-256-ctr \
  -K 00c8a19fee9e0710683afe526462ce8a960ca1356e113b-
f3a08736a68a48eca0 \
  -iv 4007fbd36f08cb04869683b1f8a15c99 \
  -d \
  -in somefile.txt.encrypted \
  -out somefile.txt.decrypted
```

No output, meaning that `openssl` did not detect any errors. Remember we have tried to decrypt with the wrong key and in the wrong mode! The decryption result cannot be right. Let's examine the file sizes and the checksums:

```
$ cksum somefile.txt*
1830648734 3893 somefile.txt
1916084428 3904 somefile.txt.decrypted
4000774547 3904 somefile.txt.encrypted
```

The checksums of `somefile.txt` and `somefile.txt.decrypted` are different, as expected. The contents of `somefile.txt.decrypted` look like garbage, as expected. Note the size of `somefile.txt.decrypted`: `3904`, the same size as `somefile.txt.encrypted`. We were decrypting in CTR mode – thus, all the (wrongly) decrypted data was considered plaintext without padding. The padding was neither checked nor removed. That's why the decrypted file size is the same as the encrypted file size and that's why `openssl` could not detect decryption failure.

As we can see, it is quite useful to have some checksum or message digest in order to check the decryption result.

We have played enough with the command line so far. Let's write our first program that uses OpenSSL as a library.

Initializing and uninitializing OpenSSL library

As of version 1.1.0, the OpenSSL library does not require explicit initialization and uninitialization. The library will automatically initialize and uninitialize.

However, it is still possible to initialize OpenSSL explicitly if some non-standard initialization is needed. It is also possible to uninitialize explicitly, but it is discouraged, especially in multithreaded programs or if OpenSSL may be used by both the program and another library in the same process. Note that after uninitialization, it is not possible to initialize OpenSSL again.

Explicit initialization is done by calling the `OPENSSL_init_ssl()` function. Explicit uninitialization is done by calling the `OPENSSL_cleanup()` function.

Older versions of OpenSSL, below 1.1.0, will not initialize automatically. If you need to use an old OpenSSL version, you have to initialize it explicitly, using now-deprecated functions called `SSL_library_init()` and `EVP_cleanup()`.

You can read the API documentation for these functions on their man pages:

```
$ man OPENSSL_init_ssl
$ man OPENSSL_cleanup
$ man SSL_library_init
$ man EVP_cleanup
```

Most OpenSSL functions have a man page that has the same name as the function name. It is a good source of documentation. As was mentioned before, the man pages are also available on the OpenSSL website in HTML format.

Let's write a simple program that will only initialize and uninitialize OpenSSL, just to demonstrate how to make calls to the library and compile and link a program that uses OpenSSL. Here is its complete source code:

```c
// File: init.c
#include <openssl/ssl.h>
#include <stdio.h>
int main() {
    printf("Initializing OpenSSL...\n");
    OPENSSL_init_ssl(0, NULL);
    printf("Unintitializing OpenSSL...\n");
    OPENSSL_cleanup();
    printf("Done.\n");
    return 0;
}
```

The source code of the init program is also available on GitHub: https://github.com/PacktPublishing/Demystifying-Cryptography-with-OpenSSL-3/blob/main/Chapter02/init.c.

The program looks very simple. Let's find out how to compile and link it with OpenSSL.

How to compile and link with OpenSSL

How to compile and link your program with OpenSSL depends on how you installed OpenSSL. If you are on Unix, you could install OpenSSL C headers and library files into the include and lib system directories, such as /usr/include and /usr/lib/x86_64-linux-gnu. In such a case, compilation and linking can be accomplished using one simple command:

```
$ cc init.c -lssl -lcrypto
```

The headers and library files will be looked up in the include and lib system directories. Therefore, it's not necessary to explicitly specify directories for header and library searches. The output executable will be called a.out.

If are on Unix and the preceding command did not work for you, check that you installed the OpenSSL development package, such as libssl-dev or openssl-devel.

If you have not installed OpenSSL system-wide or do not want to use system-wide installation, you will have to specify paths to the OpenSSL C headers and library files explicitly:

```
cc \
  -I/path/to/openssl/c/headers \
  -L/path/to/openssl/library/files \
  -o init \
  init.c \
  -lssl -lcrypto
```

Note that we also used the `-o init` switch to specify the output executable name, because `a.out` is not the most descriptive name. Note that `-lssl -lcrypto` switches also reside on the command line after the source file name. This is important. Libraries must be specified after the files that want to use them. If one library uses another, the library that uses another library is specified before the used library.

The specified library path may include dynamic or static OpenSSL libraries. Either type is supported. If both dynamic and static libraries are available, the linker will choose the dynamic libraries.

This method of calling the compiler directly with only a few switches is OK for small programs. For larger programs, you will want to use a build tool, such as GNU Make, BSD Make, or CMake, or an IDE, where you will specify the needed paths and switches and avoid repeating them on the command line.

If you are using Microsoft Windows, you will likely use an IDE, such as Microsoft Visual Studio. You will need to specify paths to the OpenSSL C headers and library files because on Windows, there is no concept of system include and library paths. However, don't underestimate the power of command-line build tools because they are quite useful for build automation and **Continuous Integration**.

Here is a sample `Makefile` file that can be used by the `make` tool to build our `init` program:

```
# File: Makefile
CFLAGS  += -I/usr/include
LDFLAGS += -L/usr/lib/x86_64-linux-gnu
LDLIBS  += -lssl -lcrypto
init:
```

In this sample `Makefile` file, we used implicit `make` compilation rules, providing compiler options via implicit variables. If the OpenSSL headers and libraries are in the system paths, we can omit the switches with paths to the implicit `CFLAGS` and `LDFLAGS` variables. `make` and the compiler cannot figure out by themselves which libraries are needed for linking; thus, we cannot omit the `-lssl -lcrypto` switches to the `LDLIBS` variable.

In order to build with `make`, just run the following:

```
$ make
```

Do so from the same directory where the `Makefile` and `init.c` files reside.

Let's check that our compiled executable is linked with `libssl` and `libcrypto`:

```
$ ldd init
        ...
        libssl.so.3 => /lib/x86_64-linux-gnu/libssl.so.3
(0x00007fd72096a000)
        libcrypto.so.3 => /lib/x86_64-linux-gnu/libcrypto.so.3
(0x00007fd72068d000)
        ...
```

Finally, let's run the executable!

```
$ ./init
Intitializing OpenSSL...
Unintitializing OpenSSL...
Done.
```

The output is as expected.

We have got our feet wet – written and built a very easy application that calls OpenSSL but does not really do anything useful. It was helpful for learning how to build programs that use OpenSSL. Let's build on our success by developing a more useful program – one that encrypts a file, similar to `openssl enc`.

How to encrypt with AES programmatically

When using `OpenSSL` as a library, we do not have to limit ourselves to the functionality that the `openssl` tool provides. `openssl` is a good tool, but it does not expose the whole functionality of OpenSSL. For instance, `openssl enc` does not support encryption or decryption in GCM, but OpenSSL as a library allows us to do that.

In this section, we are going to develop a program that can encrypt a file using an AES-256 cipher in GCM. We will call our program `encrypt`.

In order to avoid passing too many values on the command line, we will store the IV and authentication tag in the encrypted file. Unlike the encryption key, the IV and auth tag are public information and do not have to be kept secret. The format of the encrypted file will be the following:

Position, bytes	Length, bytes	Content
0	12	IV
12	?	Ciphertext
?	16	Authentication tag

Table 2.1 – The encrypted file format

Our encryption program will need three command-line arguments:

1. Input file name
2. Output file name
3. Encryption key, hex-encoded

Here is our high-level plan for the implementation:

1. Generate a random IV and write it into the output file
2. Initialize encryption
3. Encrypt chunk by chunk, reading plaintext chunks from the input file and writing the resulting ciphertext chunks into the output file
4. Finalize encryption
5. Get the authentication tag and write it into the output file

Let's figure out how to perform all those stages.

Implementing the encryption program

Here is how we implement the encryption:

1. First, let's allocate the input and output buffers:

    ```
    const size_t BUF_SIZE = 64 * 1024;
    const size_t BLOCK_SIZE = 16;
    unsigned char* in_buf  = malloc(BUF_SIZE);
    unsigned char* out_buf = malloc(BUF_SIZE + BLOCK_SIZE);
    ```

    Those are buffers that will be used for reading input data and storing output data before writing. Note that the output buffer is a bit longer than the input buffer. This is because in some cases, according to OpenSSL documentation, encryption may produce ciphertext longer than plaintext, up to BLOCK_SIZE - 1 bytes longer. In our case, it should not happen, but let's follow the OpenSSL documentation anyway.

2. The generation of the IV is easy – we just have to use the `RAND_bytes()` function that we already mentioned:

    ```
    RAND_bytes(iv, IV_LENGTH);
    ```

3. Then, we have to initialize encryption. The first thing we have to do for initializing encryption is to create a cipher context:

    ```
    EVP_CIPHER_CTX* ctx = EVP_CIPHER_CTX_new();
    ```

Let's talk a bit about the `EVP_` prefix and the `_CTX` suffix. When developing programs using OpenSSL, you will see and use those acronyms very often.

EVP stands for **Envelope** and denotes the usage of the **Envelope API**. The Envelope API is a high-level API allowing us to accomplish high-level operations – for example, encrypting a long plaintext in the needed operation mode. The Envelope API will provide the developer with a collection of data structures and functions for the task, such as the initialization of encryption, setting a key and IV, adding plaintext chunks for encryption, finalizing encryption, and getting post-encryption data, such as an authentication tag. In contrast to the Envelope API, OpenSSL also has the old encryption API and functions such as `AES_encrypt()`, `AES_cbc_encrypt()`, and `AES_ofb128_encrypt()`. That old API has a number of disadvantages:

- Inconsistency in naming. For example, the `AES_ofb128_encrypt()` function has a block size (`128`) in the name, but `AES_cbc_encrypt()` does not.

- Higher-level functions, such as `AES_cbc_encrypt()` and lower-level functions, such as `AES_encrypt()`, which encrypts only one block, are mixed in the same `AES_` namespace. This is confusing.

- The choice of the cipher – for example, *AES*, *SEED*, or *Camellia* – is communicated via the function name prefix – that is, `AES_`, `SEED_`, or `Camellia_`. The cipher operation mode is also communicated via function name: substrings such as `cbc` or `ofb128`. This leads to the need for many similar functions to exist, one for each combination of ciphers and operation modes. Instead, cipher and operation modes should have been passed as function parameters.

- The collection of functions is incomplete. For example, the `AES_ctr128_encrypt()` function for encrypting in CTR mode may or may not be listed in OpenSSL header files. It depends on the OpenSSL version. Functions for some ciphers – for example, ARIA and SM4, are not available in the old API at all.

- The authors probably recognized the issue with a lot of similar functions, did not want to have a separate decryption function for each encryption function, and thus decided to communicate an encryption or decryption action via a function parameter. As a result, in order to decrypt in CBC mode, the library user has to call a function called `AES_cbc_encrypt()`, but pass an `enc=0` parameter to indicate decryption. Meanwhile, to only decrypt one block, the developer has to call the `AES_decrypt()` function. Quite inconsistent.

- It is impossible to add extra parameters for encryption or decryption when calling higher-level functions – for example, enabling or disabling padding. The developer then has to use the block-level `AES_encrypt()` function and program the desired operation mode himself.

- Functions supporting operation modes can only take full plaintext or ciphertext. It is impossible to supply data chunk by chunk – for example, if data does not fit into the memory buffer or we are performing streaming encryption. This is a very serious drawback.

Fortunately, the mentioned issues are solved in the EVP API. The old encryption API is officially deprecated since OpenSSL 3.0.

Now – about the CTX abbreviation. **CTX** stands for **Context**. When developing with OpenSSL, you will see and use a lot of contexts – for encryption, the calculation of message digests and message authentication codes, key derivation, TLS connections, TLS sessions, and TLS settings. What is a context? It is a C structure that stores data relevant to the current operation. Some contexts are more high-level and they store settings that can be applied to several operations of the same kind – for example, to several TLS connections.

In our case, `EVP_CIPHER_CTX` stores the cipher type, the encryption key, the IV, flags, and the current internal state of the encryption operation. It is possible to set data, such as key and IV, into `EVP_CIPHER_CTX` and get data out of it, such as an authentication tag. The `EVP_CIPHER_CTX` object is supplied to all functions that we need to call during encryption in our chosen operation mode:

1. OK, we have created our `EVP_CIPHER_CTX` object. The next thing we have to do is to initialize the context and the encryption process with the chosen operation mode, key, and IV:

    ```
    EVP_EncryptInit(ctx, EVP_aes_256_gcm(), key, iv);
    ```

2. Initialization is done. Now, we can encrypt chunk by chunk, using the `EVP_EncryptUpdate()` function:

    ```
    while (!feof(in_file)) {
        size_t in_nbytes = fread(in_buf, 1, BUF_SIZE, in_
    file);
        int out_nbytes = 0;
        EVP_EncryptUpdate(
            ctx, out_buf, &out_nbytes, in_buf, in_nbytes);
        fwrite(out_buf, 1, out_nbytes, out_file);
    }
    ```

3. Encryption is almost done. Now, we have to finalize it using the `EVP_EncryptFinal()` function:

    ```
    int out_nbytes = 0;
    EVP_EncryptFinal(ctx, out_buf, &out_nbytes);
    fwrite(out_buf, 1, out_nbytes, out_file);
    ```

Encryption finalization is an operation that depends on the used cipher and mode. For example, in the CBC mode, the finalization operation adds padding to the last data block and encrypts it, producing the last ciphertext block. It means that the finalization operation may produce data – thus, it takes the output buffer as one of the parameters.

4. In GCM, the finalization operation calculates the authentication tag, which reminds us that we have to get it from the context object and write into the output file:

```
EVP_CIPHER_CTX_ctrl(
    ctx, EVP_CTRL_GCM_GET_TAG, AUTH_TAG_LENGTH, auth_
tag);
fwrite(auth_tag, 1, AUTH_TAG_LENGTH, out_file);
```

5. The last operation that we need to do is to free the EVP_CIPHER_CTX object that is no longer required in order to avoid memory leaks:

```
EVP_CIPHER_CTX_free(ctx);
```

Those were all the OpenSSL operations that we needed!

The full source code of the encryption program can be found on GitHub as an encrypt.c file: https://github.com/PacktPublishing/Demystifying-Cryptography-with-OpenSSL-3/blob/main/Chapter02/encrypt.c.

At the given URL, you can find the complete implementation but almost without error handling, so that the error handling doesn't clutter the code and the code flow is more visible.

Here is another implementation, encrypt-with-extended-error-checking.c, with extended error handling: https://github.com/PacktPublishing/Demystifying-Cryptography-with-OpenSSL-3/blob/main/Chapter02/encrypt-with-extended-error-checking.c.

The code is not as readable as in the first implementation, but the second implementation may be useful for debugging and troubleshooting.

A small remark about the usage of the goto statement in the code – we all know the statement "*Go To Statement Considered Harmful*" and we should not overuse it. Some developers think that goto should not be used at all, but sometimes, goto is useful – for example, for deduplicating the cleanup code, as in the preceding examples. In C++, we would be able to use destructors for automatic cleanup, but in C, we don't have that possibility.

Running the encrypt program

Let's try to run our `encrypt` program:

1. Generate a sample file for further encryption:

   ```
   $ seq 20000 >somefile.txt
   ```

2. Encrypt the file:

   ```
   $ ./encrypt somefile.txt somefile.txt.encrypted \
   74c8a19fee9e0710683afe526462ce8a960ca1356e113b-
   f3a08736a68a48eca0
   Encryption succeeded
   ```

3. Check the files sizes and checksums:

   ```
   $ cksum somefile.txt*
   3231941463 108894 somefile.txt
   3036900166 108922 somefile.txt.encrypted
   ```

The original and the encrypted files are different, as expected. The encrypted file is 28 bytes longer because it contains the IV and auth tag in addition to the ciphertext.

Looks good so far – but can we decrypt what we encrypted?

How to decrypt with AES programmatically

In this section, we are going to develop the `decrypt` program that can encrypt a file encrypted by the `encrypt` program.

Our decryption program will be similar to the encryption program and will also take three command-line arguments:

1. Input file name
2. Output file name
3. Encryption key, hex-encoded

This time, the input file is the encrypted file created by the preceding `encrypt` program.

Let's make a high-level plan, similar to how we did before:

1. Read the IV from the input file.
2. Initialize decryption.

3. Decrypt chunk by chunk, reading plaintext chunks from the input file and writing the resulting plaintext chunks into the output file.

4. Read the authentication tag from the input file and set it into the cipher context.

5. Finalize decryption.

As we can see, the decryption plan is very similar to the encryption plan – initalize, process, and finalize. Let's see how it is implemented in the concrete code.

Implementing the decrypt program

Here is how we implement the decryption:

1. We read the IV:

   ```
   size_t in_nbytes = fread(iv, 1, IV_LENGTH, in_file);
   size_t current_pos = in_nbytes;
   ```

   Note the `current_pos` variable. This time, we cannot rely on reading up to the end of the input file and need to track our position in the input file.

2. We initalize the decryption. Note that this time, we initialize using the `EVP_DecryptInit()` function instead of `EVP_EncryptInit()`:

   ```
   ctx = EVP_CIPHER_CTX_new();
   EVP_DecryptInit(ctx, EVP_aes_256_gcm(), key, iv);
   ```

3. The main part is decrypting chunk by chunk. For decryption, we use the `EVP_DecryptUpdate()` function instead of `EVP_EncryptUpdate()`:

   ```
   while (current_pos < auth_tag_pos) {
       size_t in_nbytes_left = auth_tag_pos - current_pos;
       size_t in_nbytes_wanted =
           in_nbytes_left < BUF_SIZE ?
           in_nbytes_left : BUF_SIZE;
       in_nbytes = fread(in_buf, 1, in_nbytes_wanted, in_
   file);
       current_pos += in_nbytes;
       int out_nbytes = 0;
       EVP_DecryptUpdate(
           ctx, out_buf, &out_nbytes, in_buf, in_nbytes);
       fwrite(out_buf, 1, out_nbytes, out_file);
   }
   ```

Note this part of the decryption loop:

```
size_t in_nbytes_wanted =
    in_nbytes_left < BUF_SIZE ?
    in_nbytes_left : BUF_SIZE;
```

Here, we are avoiding reading too much from the input file in order to avoid reading the authentication tag into the ciphertext buffer.

4. When we have read and decrypted the ciphertext, it's time read the authentication tag and set it into the cipher context:

```
fread(auth_tag, 1, AUTH_TAG_LENGTH, in_file);
EVP_CIPHER_CTX_ctrl(
    ctx, EVP_CTRL_GCM_SET_TAG, AUTH_TAG_LENGTH, auth_
tag);
```

We have to set the authentication tag before finalizing the decryption – otherwise, the finalization operation will fail.

5. Finally, for finalizing the decryption, we have to use the EVP_DecryptFinal() function instead of EVP_EncryptFinal():

```
int out_nbytes = 0;
EVP_DecryptFinal(ctx, out_buf, &out_nbytes);
fwrite(out_buf, 1, out_nbytes, out_file);
```

The authentication tag will be validated during the finalization operation. Therefore, finalization will fail in any of the following cases:

*   The authentication tag has not been set to the cipher context.

*   The ciphertext has been corrupted.

*   A wrong key, IV, or auth tag has been used for the decryption.

The full source code of the decrypt program can be found on GitHub as a decrypt.c file: https://github.com/PacktPublishing/Demystifying-Cryptography-with-OpenSSL-3/blob/main/Chapter02/decrypt.c.

There is also an alternative implementation, decrypt-with-extended-error-checking.c, with extended error checking, useful for debugging and troubleshooting: https://github.com/PacktPublishing/Demystifying-Cryptography-with-OpenSSL-3/blob/main/Chapter02/decrypt-with-extended-error-checking.c.

We have implemented our decryption program. Let's run it.

Running the decrypt program

Time to run our `decrypt` program and examine the checksums of the produced files:

1. Decrypt the file using the `decrypt` program:

```
$ ./decrypt somefile.txt.encrypted somefile.txt.decrypted
\ 74c8a19fee9e0710683afe526462ce8a960ca1356e113b-
f3a08736a68a48eca0
Decryption succeeded
```

2. Looks good! Let's check the file checksums:

```
$ cksum somefile.txt*
3231941463 108894 somefile.txt
3231941463 108894 somefile.txt.decrypted
3036900166 108922 somefile.txt.encrypted
```

The original and the decrypted files have the same size and checksum. Our decryption has indeed succeeded!

3. What will happen if we supply the wrong key to our decryption program? Let's check! We are expecting an error message and garbage in the erroneously decrypted file. Let's use the version of the program with the extended error checking this time:

```
$ ./decrypt-with-extended-error-checking \ somefile.txt.
encrypted somefile.txt.decrypted \
74c8a19fee9e0710683afe526462ce8a960ca1356e113b-
f3a08736a68a48ec0a
Could not finalize decryption
Decryption failed
```

As expected, decryption failed at the finalization operation. The authentication tag validation failed because of the wrong encryption key.

4. Let's look at the files:

```
$ cksum somefile.txt*
3231941463 108894 somefile.txt
502982927  108894 somefile.txt.decrypted
3036900166 108922 somefile.txt.encrypted
```

The original and the decrypted files have the same size, but different checksums. If we examine the contents of the decrypted file, we will only see garbage. That's how changing only one byte in the key affects the decryption.

What advice can I give to developers working with encryption? Be very careful with the implementation and use the correct encryption key!

We have learned how to encrypt, decrypt, and check that the decryption was correct. Let's proceed to the summary.

Summary

In this chapter, we have learned what symmetric encryption is and how it differs from asymmetric encryption. We also learned what a cipher is, what block ciphers and stream ciphers are, how cipher security is measured, and how much security is enough. Then, we learned which ciphers are supported by OpenSSL, which you should use in which situation, and which ciphers you should avoid. We also learned which cipher operation modes exist, how they differ, and which you should use.

We discussed padding, why it exists, and in which cases you should use it. We also covered oracle and how to download and install OpenSSL. We explored and saw what is included in the OpenSSL toolkit, how to initialize the OpenSSL library, and how to compile and link your program with the OpenSSL library. Finally, we learned how to generate an encryption key and an IV, how to encrypt and decrypt a file using the OpenSSL command-line tool, and how to encrypt and decrypt a file programmatically using the OpenSSL library.

In this chapter, we used checksums in order to check whether files were identical. It was very useful. We also mentioned message digests, which are cryptographically strong checksums. In the next chapter, we will learn more about message digests, specifically which message digest algorithms are supported by OpenSSL and how to calculate message digests using OpenSSL.

3

Message Digests

In this chapter, we will learn about **message digests**, also known as **cryptographic hashes**. Message digests, which are produced by cryptographic hash functions, have many important applications, such as data integrity checking, password verification, digital signatures, secure network protocols such as TLS, and even blockchains. We will provide an overview of the cryptographic hash functions supported by **OpenSSL** and recommendations on which hash functions to use and which to avoid. Then, in the practical part of this chapter, we will learn how to calculate a message digest using the command line and C code. After reading this chapter and trying the practical part, you will know why message digests are needed and how to calculate them.

We are going to cover the following topics in this chapter:

- What are message digests and cryptographic hash functions?
- Why are message digests needed?
- Assessing the security of cryptographic hash functions
- Overview of the cryptographic hash functions supported by OpenSSL
- How to calculate a message digest on the command line
- How to calculate a message digest programmatically

Technical requirements

This chapter will contain commands that you can run on a command line and C code that you can compile and run. For the command-line commands, you will need the `openssl` command-line tool, along with the relevant OpenSSL dynamic libraries. To build the C code, you will need OpenSSL dynamic or static libraries, library headers, a C compiler, and a linker.

We will implement an example program in this chapter, in order to practice what we are learning. The full source code of that program can be found here: `https://github.com/PacktPublishing/Demystifying-Cryptography-with-OpenSSL-3/tree/main/Chapter03`.

What are message digests and cryptographic hash functions?

A **message** in cryptography is any piece of data, big or small, that is processed by a **cryptographic algorithm**.

A **cryptographic hash function** is an algorithm that maps a message of arbitrary size to a relatively short (for example, 256 bits) fixed-size array of bits. This fixed-size bit array is called a **message digest** or a **cryptographic hash**.

In other words, a message digest is the output of a cryptographic hash function. As we mentioned in the previous chapter, we can say that a message digest is a cryptographically strong checksum.

A good cryptographic hash function has the following properties:

- It is *deterministic*, meaning that processing the same message must always yield the same message digest.

- It is *irreversible*, meaning that it must be impossible or extremely difficult to recover the original message by its digest. The only way to reverse the hash should be *brute force* and it must be too computationally expensive to do.

- It must be computationally infeasible to find two distinct messages with the same digest. If two or more different messages with the same digest are found, then this is known as a **hash collision** or simply a **collision**.

- Any change to the message, big or small, must result in an extensive change to the digest – so extensive that it would be impossible to relate the two digests to each other. Such an extensive reaction, even to a small change, is called the **avalanche effect**.

It's not difficult to understand what message digests are, but *why are they needed*, and *why are they important?*

Why are message digests needed?

Message digests have many applications. The most obvious one is **data integrity verification**.

Data integrity verification

When you're downloading software from the internet, you will often find the message digest of the distribution package close to the download link. As an example, look at the OpenSSL download page at https://www.openssl.org/source/:

KBytes	Date	File
14627	2021-Sep-07 12:00:26	openssl-3.0.0.tar.gz (SHA256) (PGP sign) (SHA1)
9603	2021-Aug-24 13:46:31	openssl-1.1.1l.tar.gz (SHA256) (PGP sign) (SHA1)
1457	2017-May-24 18:01:01	openssl-fips-2.0.16.tar.gz (SHA256) (PGP sign) (SHA1)
1437	2017-May-24 18:01:01	openssl-fips-ecp-2.0.16.tar.gz (SHA256) (PGP sign) (SHA1)

Figure 3.1 – The OpenSSL download page fragment

Next to the download link, you will see links called SHA256 and SHA1. These contain the message digests for the corresponding .tar.gz files. When the required .tar.gz file is downloaded, the digest of the downloaded file can be calculated and compared to the expected digest. If the digests match, then the file may not have been corrupted or otherwise changed while being transmitted and saved. If the file was changed, the calculated digest would look very different from the expected digest, because of the *avalanche effect*. In our case, the OpenSSL distribution package is a rather small download, and the official OpenSSL website is a trusted source, so the chance of the download being corrupted is very small. But imagine if you were downloading something big, such as a Linux installation image, or you received a distribution from an unofficial source and wanted to check that it's not been tampered with. Here, you can obtain the correct digest from the official website and check if the digest of the untrusted download matches.

Message digests are also applicable to stored data. If some data is stored for a long time, it may be corrupted because of storage media errors or other unexpected changes. Verification via message digest is a reliable way to check that the data has not been corrupted.

Basis for HMAC

Message digests form the basis for **Hash-based Message Authentication Codes (HMACs)**. HMAC is a **Message Authentication Code (MAC)** that combines a secret key and a cryptographic hash function for data authentication. HMAC will be covered in more detail in *Chapter 4, MAC and HMAC*.

Digital signatures

When a message is digitally signed, the digest of that message is signed. It is worth mentioning that digital signatures are used not only for documents. They are often used for signing drivers, applications, and even cryptography objects, such as the **X.509 certificates** that are used in the TLS protocol. Digital signatures will be covered in more detail in *Chapter 7, Digital Signatures and Their Verification*.

Network protocols

Security-enabled network protocols, such as TLS and SSH, use the HMACs and digital signatures of transmitted data at different protocol stages. As we mentioned previously, cryptographic hash functions are needed for HMAC and digital signatures, so they are also needed for secure network protocols.

Password verification

Most modern operating systems and websites do not store passwords in plaintext. Often, a salted password hash is stored instead. Salted means that some salt is added to the password before hashing. Salt is a small amount of random data, which can be as small as 2 bytes, that is prepended or appended to the password so that the same passwords will have different hashes and be more difficult to break with the help of a known hash. The salt itself is not a secret and is usually stored together with the hash. When a password is verified, it is concatenated with the stored salt and hashed. Verification is successful if the computed digest is the same as the one that was stored.

Content identifier

As one of the features of a good cryptographic hash function is an extremely low probability of a hash collision, message digests can be used for identifying objects. Let's look at some examples of how cryptographic hashes are used for identification.

When verifying an X.509 certificate, the issuer certificate is looked up by its name and the cryptographic hash of its public key.

Modern **Source Code Management** (**SCM**) systems, such as Git and Mercurial, use cryptographic hashes to uniquely identify stored objects, such as files, commits, branches, and tags. Such an identification scheme also ensures the integrity of the code repository.

Some peer-to-peer filesharing networks, such as eDonkey, use message digests to identify shared files.

Blockchain and cryptocurrencies

Blockchain blocks are linked together using cryptographic hashes. Newer blocks refer to the old blocks by their hashes. Such referencing ensures the integrity of the chain and the impossibility to change older blocks since any block change will also change its hash. Hence, its identity will also change, and the changed block will stop being part of the blockchain.

The most well-known application of blockchain technology is **cryptocurrencies**. But it's not the only one. The aforementioned **Git** and **Mercurial** SCMs use the same kind of link between their stored objects, so they are also based on blockchain technology. There are also many other uses of blockchain: in trading, medicine, and other areas. The blockchain would be impossible without cryptographic hash functions and message digests.

Proof-of-work

A **proof-of-work** system gives its client a cryptographic challenge that can only be overcome if the client performs a certain amount of computational work. One such challenge is **partial hash inversion**, meaning that the client has to find some piece of data whose partial message digest is the same as requested in the challenge. If a good cryptographic hash function is used, the client has to perform some brute force work. The data that's found will be proof that the client performed the work.

Proof-of-work systems can be used for cryptocurrency mining, processing a cryptocurrency transaction, and preventing **denial-of-service** attacks or **spam**.

Let's explain this concept using the spam prevention example. Imagine that a mail client connects to a mail server and wants to send an email to one or several addresses. The server gives the client proof-of-work challenges – one for every target address. If the client wants to send the message to one or only a few addresses, it will need to spend only a small volume of computational resources, which will not be a big burden. However, if a spammer wants to send the same mail to a million addresses, the volume of computational work will be unbearable.

The important property of a proof-of-work system is that it is much easier to check the performed work than to perform it.

Why does only a partial hash have to be found in a proof-of-work challenge? Because reverting the full hash of a good cryptographic hash function is too expensive and can take billions of years. The purpose of a proof-of-work challenge is to prevent service abuse, not to block the service completely.

As we can see, cryptographic hash functions and message digests are very important and have a lot of good appliances. But cryptographic hash functions are only useful if they are secure. Let's learn about the popular attacks that are performed on message digest functions, how can we measure their security, and how much security is enough for a hash function.

Assessing the security of cryptographic hash functions

The two most important types of attacks that can be performed on cryptographic hash functions are collision attacks and preimage attacks. A collision attack tries to find two messages that produce the same message digest, while a preimage attack aims to find a message that produces the predefined message digest. Performing a collision attack is easier than performing a preimage attack on the same hash function because the message search is not limited to a single target message digest.

The security level of a cryptographic hash function is the computational complexity of the collision attack. The security level is measured in security bits, similar to the security level of symmetric encryption algorithms. For example, if the complexity of the collision attack is $2,128$ hash evaluations, then the security level is 128 bits.

The security level of a cryptographic hash function depends on the size of its output message digest. If the message digest's size is n bits, the maximum attack complexity is 2n/2 for the collision attack and 2n for the preimage attack. It is impossible to have a higher complexity than 2n/2 for the collision attack because the birthday attack, which is based on the birthday paradox, can always find collisions in 2n/2 time.

For example, the **SHA-256** function has a 256-bit hash size, a 2^{128} collision attack complexity, a 2^{256} preimage attack complexity, and a security level of 128 bits. It is also said that the function's collision resistance level is 128 bits and that its preimage resistance level is 256 bits.

How many security bits is enough? The same as for symmetric encryption algorithms:

- 112 bits of security should be enough until 2030.

- 128 bits of security should be enough until the next revolutionary breakthrough in technology or mathematics.

So far, we know how hash function security is measured and how much security is enough. Next, we will learn about which cryptographic hash functions are supported by OpenSSL and how secure they are.

Overview of the cryptographic hash functions supported by OpenSSL

In this section, we will review the cryptographic hash functions supported by OpenSSL and their properties, such as security, speed, and message digest size. We will also learn a bit about the history of those hash functions.

Reviewing the SHA-2 family of hash functions

The **SHA-2** family contains the most popular modern cryptographic hash function, SHA-256. SHA-256 outputs a 256-bit digest and has a collision resistance level of 128 bits.

SHA-256 is widely used. It is currently the default hash function that's used in the TLS protocol, as well as the default signing function for X.509 certificates and SSH keys. Several cryptocurrencies, including Bitcoin, use SHA-256 to verify transactions and proof of work. The popular Git SCM is migrating to SHA-256 hashes for its blockchain implementation and object identification processes. SHA-256 is used in many security protocols and software, such as SSH, IPsec, DNSSEC, PGP, and more. SHA-256 is also a popular choice for password hashing in Unix systems.

In addition to SHA-256, the SHA-2 family also includes the following hash functions:

- SHA-224, which is a modification of SHA-256 with a changed *initialization vector* and *truncated output* (224 bits). Its collision resistance is 112 bits.

- SHA-512, which has an algorithm similar to SHA-256 but operates on 64-bit words instead of 32-bit words. It outputs a 512-bis message digest and has a collision resistance of 256 bits.

- SHA-384, SHA-512/256, and SHA-512/224, which are modifications of SHA-512 with changed initialization vectors and truncated output. The functions output message digests of 384, 256, and 224 bits and have collision resistances of 192, 128, and 112 bits, respectively.

SHA-2 functions were developed by the United States **National Security Agency** (**NSA**) and first published by the **National Institute of Standards and Technology** (**NIST**) in 2001 as a federal standard. SHA-2 algorithms are patented, but the patent is available under a royalty-free license.

SHA stands for **Secure Hash Algorithm**. SHA-2 functions are currently considered secure, but cryptanalysts are slowly and steadily advancing their attacks on SHA-2. While the attacks are advancing, there are currently no successful attacks on full versions of SHA-2, only on versions with reduced amounts of rounds. Therefore, currently, all SHA-2 functions have a collision resistance level equal to the amount of hash bits divided by 2, which is the maximum possible.

SHA-256 and its modifications operate on *32-bit words*, while **SHA-512** and its modifications operate on *64-bit words*. Because of that, SHA-256 calculation is 2-4 times faster than SHA-512 on 32-bit CPUs, but SHA-512 is approximately 1.5 times faster than SHA-256 on 64-bit CPUs.

SHA-2 functions have an acceptable speed for modern hardware but are slower than their predecessor, the SHA-1 function. For example, the SHA-256 function is two times slower than SHA-1.

Modern x86_64 CPUs from Intel and AMD support **Intel SHA extensions**, which speed up the process of calculating SHA-256 and SHA-1. Some ARMv8 CPUs, such as Cortex A53, support **ARMv8 Cryptography Extensions**, which also speed up of the process of calculating SHA-256 and SHA-1, as well as SHA-224.

At the time of writing, SHA-2 functions are the most popular cryptographic hash functions, but the *SHA-2 family* already has a successor: the *SHA-3 family*.

Reviewing the SHA-3 family of hash functions

Unlike the in-house development of SHA-2, the **SHA-3** algorithms were chosen through an algorithm competition. This is similar to how the **Advanced Encryption Standard** (**AES**) algorithm was chosen through another competition. NIST organized such a competition because there were successful attacks on SHA-2's predecessors, namely **SHA-1**, **SHA-0**, and **MD5**, which were built on the same principles as SHA-2; there was a need for a hash function based on different principles. SHA-3 selection was a long process. NIST started to organize the competition in 2006 and officially announced it in 2007. The applicants submitted their algorithms until 2009. Then, there were two competition rounds in 2009 and 2010. After that, the winner was chosen in 2012, the standard was published in 2014, and finally it was approved in 2015.

Note that SHA-2 algorithms are not being deprecated or abandoned because of the standardization of SHA-3. The purpose of SHA-3 is to expand the diversity of good message digest algorithms and to provide a ready and easy replacement for SHA-2 if it will be needed.

The winner of the SHA-3 competition was the **Keccak** algorithm from a team of Belgian cryptographers. One of those cryptographers was Joan Daemen, who is also the co-author of the **Rijndael** algorithm (AES).

The SHA3 algorithm family consists of the following functions:

- SHA3-224
- SHA3-256

- SHA3-384

- SHA3-512

- SHAKE128

- SHAKE256

The first four functions are the main SHA-3 functions and are similar to the corresponding functions of the SHA-2 family. They output message digests of 224, 256, 384, and 512 bits, respectively. Similar to the SHA-2 family, those four functions have a collision resistance level that's half the amount of the message digest's size, meaning 112, 128, 192, and 256 bits, respectively, and a preimage resistance level of the same number of bits as the message digest's size, meaning 224, 256, 384 and 512 bits, respectively.

As we can see, these four SHA-3 functions *currently* provide the same level of security as the SHA-2 functions. But attacks on SHA-2 are advancing and this equality may end one day. Attacks on SHA-3 have currently advanced much less than they have on SHA-2.

The SHA-3 Keccak algorithm is slower than SHA-2 because it contains more sequential operations than SHA-2. The SHA3-256 function is approximately 1.5 times slower than SHA-256, while SHA3-512 is 2-4 times slower than SHA-512, depending on the CPU. CPU extensions such as **Intel SHA extensions** and **ARMv8 Cryptography Extensions** support SHA-2, but not SHA-3. However, some CPUs have instruction set extensions that can speed up the process of calculating SHA-3. Examples include **MMX, SSE, BMI2**, and **AVX2/AVX-512/AVX-512VL** on **x86/x86_64** CPUs, the **SVE/SVE2** and **ARMv8.2-SHA** crypto extension sets on **ARM** CPUs, and **Power ISA** on **POWER8** CPUs. It is worth mentioning that the ARMv8.4-A version of the ARMv8 CPU instruction set also supports SHA-3 acceleration.

As a response to the slowness of SHA-3, the authors of SHA-3 developed the **SHAKE128** and **SHAKE256** functions, which are noticeably faster than other SHA-3 functions. Strictly speaking, they are not hash functions, but **Extendable Output Functions** (XOFs). Extendable output functions can generate digests of an arbitrary size and serve as a basis for hash functions. You make a hash function from an XOF by choosing a particular digest size. The numbers in the names of SHAKE128 and SHAKE256 represent the functions' maximum collision attack resistance levels, which are 128 and 256 bits, respectively. Note that due to the birthday paradox, the variable-size digest must be long enough to reach the maximum security level, which is at least 256 bits for SHAKE128 and 512 bits for SHAKE256. SHAKE128 is approximately as fast as SHA-256, while SHAKE256 is 1.5 times slower than SHA-512 on modern x86_64 CPUs.

Later, the same authors presented the **KangarooTwelve** (**K12**) extendable output function, which is based on Keccak but has a reduced the number of rounds (from 24 to 12) and can exploit the availability of parallel execution on multi-core CPUs. The authors claim that KangarooTwelve is approximately 13 times faster than SHA3-256 (0.51 cycles per byte versus 6.4 cycles per byte on an Intel Skylake-X CPU) and still maintains the 128-bit security level. However, the independent benchmarks of real implementations show that KangarooTwelve is only 2-3 times faster than SHA3-256. So far, this security claim is true because the most well-known attack on the SHA-3 algorithm (at the time of writing) can only attack the reduced 6-round version of Keccak. However, KangarooTwelve has a smaller security margin than the full 24-round SHA-3. As a later development, KangarooTwelve is not considered part of the SHA-3 family and is not supported by OpenSSL.

Even though SHA-3 is slower than SHA-2 in software implementations, there are hardware implementations of SHA-3 that are faster than the hardware implementations of SHA-2 and even SHA-1. And with modern CPUs, the speed of SHA-3 is acceptable.

SHA-3 is currently not nearly as popular as SHA-2. SHA-3 support in cryptographic libraries is already good, but not many applications have started to use hash functions from that family. SHA-3 algorithms are not standardized for use in **TLS** or **X.509** yet and are not in use in popular cryptographic software such as **OpenSSH** and **GnuPG**. A notable use of SHA-3 is the **Ethereum** cryptocurrency, where it is used for proof-of-work checking. It is also worth mentioning that SHA-3 is now undergoing the NIST Post-Quantum Cryptography Standardization process for signature and key exchange. Migration to SHA-3 from SHA-2 is happening quite slowly, similar to how migrating SHA-2 from its predecessor, SHA-1, was.

Reviewing the SHA-1 and SHA-0 hash functions

SHA-1 is a cryptographic hash function that was developed by NSA in the 1990s. The SHA-1 specification was first published in 1993. However, the specification was shortly withdrawn because security flaws were found in the algorithm. The newly revised specification of SHA-1 was published in 1995 and the algorithm from 1993 has the unofficial name of SHA-0.

SHA-1 produces a 160-bit message digest. The algorithm is fast – approximately two times faster than **SHA-256**. **SHA-1** is also approximately as fast as its predecessor, the **MD5** algorithm, and on modern CPUs, it's even faster because of hardware acceleration.

Unfortunately, SHA-1 is not considered secure anymore. SHA-1's security level was originally claimed to be 80 bits, which is not secure by modern standards. The best attack sinks the security level further to 61 bits. In 2017, the first public SHA-1 collision was found. The **Centrum Wiskunde & Informatica** research center from the Netherlands and Google, published two PDF documents with different content but the same SHA-1 hash. If you could obtain an SHA-1 based digital signature of one document, the signature would be valid for the second document as well. This is just one example of why collisions in cryptographic hash functions are dangerous. In 2020, the cost of finding an SHA-1 collision dropped below 50,000 USD, which is easily affordable for large businesses, intelligence agencies, and even rich individuals.

SHA-1 was the most popular cryptographic hash algorithm before SHA-256 took over. It was used in the SSL, TLS, SSH, and IPsec protocols, X.509 certificates, **Pretty Good Privacy** (**PGP**) and **Secure Multipurpose Mail Extension** (**S/MIME**) implementations, **Digital Signature Algorithm** (**DSA**), and other areas. Source control management systems, such as Git and Mercurial, still use SHA-1 for object integrity and identification, though they are continuing to work on migrating to other hash algorithms.

Migration from SHA-1 to SHA-256 was a long process for the IT industry. The famous cryptographer *Bruce Schneier* recommended migrating from SHA-1 in 2005. NIST officially deprecated SHA-1 in 2011 and major web browsers stopped accepting SHA-1-based certificates in 2017. Microsoft stopped support for SHA-1-based signatures for Windows Updates in 2020. Many lesser-known applications have not been migrated yet.

The predecessor of SHA-1 is the MD5 hash function, from the MD hash function family.

Reviewing the MD family of hash functions

The MD family of hash functions consists of four functions: **MD2**, **MD4**, **MD5**, and **MD6**. There are no **MD1** and **MD3** functions. There is also no official information regarding why they don't exist, but rumor has it that MD1 was a proprietary algorithm that was never available to the general public, while MD3 was an experimental algorithm that was abandoned by its designer.

MD stands for **Message Digest**. A fun fact is that **MD5** (as well as **SHA-1** and **SHA-2**) is based on **Merkle-Damgård construction**, which can also be shortened to **MD**.

MD functions were designed by the famous cryptographer Ronald Rivest, the same person who invented **RC** symmetric ciphers, such as **RC2**, **RC4**, and **RC5**, which we reviewed in *Chapter 2, Symmetric Encryption and Decryption*.

OpenSSL supports the MD2, MD4, and MD5 hash functions. They all have a message digest size of 128 bits and an initial security level of 64 bits. Unfortunately, those functions are not secure anymore and it's not recommended that you use them. The best attacks reduce the security levels of MD2, MD4, and MD5 to 63, 1 (yes, only one bit!), and 18 bits, respectively. A collision attack on MD4 or MD5 can be performed in a fraction of a second on a typical PC.

MD5 is the most famous function of the MD family. MD5 is a predecessor of SHA-1 and shares a lot of math with SHA-1 and SHA-2. MD5 was very widespread before it was superseded by SHA-1. It was used in all popular cryptographic protocols, standards, and software. It was also very popular for **password hashing** in Unix and web systems. An interesting fact about **MD5** and **SHA-1** is that the **SSL 3.0**, **TLS 1.0**, and **TLS 1.1** protocols used a combination of **MD5** and **SHA-1** because it's hard to find a data block that produces both **MD5** and **SHA-1** collision simultaneously.

The **MD4** function is famous for being used for **password hashing** in Windows NT, 2000, and XP. MD4 has been disabled for password hashing by default since Windows Vista but still can be enabled, even under Windows 10.

Reviewing the BLAKE2 family of hash functions

The **BLAKE2** hash function family consists of several hash functions, two of which are supported by OpenSSL, namely **BLAKE2s** and **BLAKE2b**. **BLAKE2s** produces a 256-bit message digest, while **BLAKE2b** produces a 512-bit message digest. The functions still maintain the maximum collision resistance levels of 128 and 256 bits, respectively. **BLAKE2** functions have a larger security margin than **SHA-2** functions and are similar to **SHA-3** functions.

BLAKE2 functions are famous for their speed. **BLAKE2s** and **BLAKE2b** are faster than **MD5**, **SHA-1**, **SHA-2**, and **SHA-3** on older CPUs without hardware acceleration. On newer CPUs with hardware acceleration, such as Intel Skylake or newer, **SHA-1** is the fastest, but **BLAKE2s** and **BLAKE2b** are still faster than their **SHA-2** counterparts, **SHA-256** and **SHA-512**. **BLAKE2s** and **BLAKE2b** are also noticeably faster than **SHA3-256** and **SHA3-512** while having similar security margins.

The BLAKE2 cryptographic hash function family was developed by an international group of cryptographers in 2012. The BLAKE2 family is based on the BLAKE function family, which was released in 2008, participated in the SHA-3 hash function competition, and even reached the final of the competition, but lost to the Keccak algorithm in the end. The BLAKE function family is based on the **ChaCha** stream cipher, which we reviewed in the previous chapter.

The **BLAKE2** function family already has a successor: the **BLAKE3** function, which was released in 2020. The **BLAKE3** function supports message digests of an arbitrary size that's equal to or longer than 256 bits. **BLAKE3** is a few times faster than **BLAKE2** and can be heavily parallelized because it is based on the **Merkle tree structure**. Regarding BLAKE3 security, the authors claim 128-bit resistance against both collision and preimage attacks. But considerably less security analysis has been done on BLAKE3 than on other hash functions. Hence, it's currently hard to say how secure BLAKE3 is. **BLAKE3** is not included in OpenSSL 3.0.

Even though **BLAKE2** was not standardized for usage in *TLS*, *SSH*, or *PGP*, some software developers noticed the hash function family and decided to use it in their software. Certain BLAKE2 algorithms are used in popular software such as WhatsApp, 7-zip, WinRAR, Rsync, Chef, WireGuard, and cryptocurrencies such as Zcash and NANO.

Reviewing less popular hash functions supported by OpenSSL

OpenSSL also supports other message digest algorithms, but they are not as popular as the ones that we have already reviewed. Some of the less popular algorithms are the national standards of particular countries.

National cryptographic hash functions

GOST94 is a Russian cryptographic hash function that was declassified in 1994. It is based on the **GOST89** block cipher and produces a message digest of 256 bits. GOST94 has an initial security level of 128 bits. There is a theoretical attack that reduces the security level to 105 bits, at the cost of impossible memory requirements. GOST94 has a successor: the **Streebog** hash function, which was published in 2012, also known as **GOST2012** or **GOST12**. Both GOST94 and Streebog are national standards of the Russian Federation.

SM3 is a Chinese cryptographic hash function that was published in 2010. SM3 is similar to SHA-256 in terms of its structure and security. Its security level is 128 bits. SM3 has been a national standard of the People's Republic of China since 2016.

Other cryptographic hash functions

Whirlpool is a cryptographic hash function based on the AES block cipher. Whirlpool was designed by Vincent Rijmen (the co-designer of AES) and Paulo Barreto. The hash function generates a 512-bit message digest and still maintains a collision resistance level of 256 bits. Whirlpool is not a fast hash function; it is approximately 10% slower than SHA3-512. Whirlpool was published in 2000 but has not gained much popularity since then. Some notable uses of Whirlpool include the **TrueCrypt** disk-encryption program and its successor, **VeraCrypt**, which supports Whirlpool as one of its hashing algorithms.

RIPEMD-160 is a hash function that was designed by a group of Belgian cryptographers in 1996, the most popular function from the **RIPEMD family**. RIPEMD-160 is based on the original RIPEMD function from 1992, which, in turn, is based on MD4. RIPEMD-160 generates a 160-bit message digest and has a security level of 80 bits, which is not enough by today's standards. Therefore, it is not recommended to use it.

MDC-2 is a message digest function that uses a symmetric block cipher with a 64-bit block size to produce a 128-bit message digest. MDC-2 stands for **Modification Detection Code 2**. In the OpenSSL implementation, MDC-2 uses DES cipher. Unfortunately, 128-bit digests can have only a 64-bit security level at best, and that is not enough security nowadays. Hence, the MDC-2 function does not conform to modern security standards and is not recommended to use it. It is considered deprecated and is not compiled into OpenSSL by default, even though its source code remains in the library.

Which cryptographic hash function should you choose?

So, which message digest function should you use in your new project? If your project does not have special requirements, choose **SHA3-256**. This function provides good security, is well supported by crypto libraries, has acceptable performance, and is future-proof. Some cryptographers are already advising people to migrate from **SHA-2** to **SHA-3**. It is expected that **SHA-3** functions will get better support in the future versions of security standards and protocols, such as **TLS**, **SSH**, **PGP**, and **X.509**, as well as in popular software that uses cryptography, such as web browsers, PGP and GnuPG, various pieces of digital signing software, and the password hashing subsystems of operating systems and websites. It is also expected that newer CPUs and dedicated cryptography chips will gain better hardware acceleration for **SHA-3** algorithms.

If you need more compatibility and interoperability with existing software here and now, choose **SHA-256** from the **SHA-2** family. But be ready to migrate to an **SHA-3** function if your **SHA-2** security is broken.

If you want more speed and security, and interoperability is not a problem, then choose the **BLAKE2b** function with a 512-bit message digest. It has very good security and is noticeably faster than the **BLAKE2s**, **SHA-2**, and **SHA-3** functions on 64-bit CPUs.

With that, we have learned about the properties of the different cryptographic hash functions supported by OpenSSL, as well as recommendations on what hash function to use in which situation. But enough with theory! Let's do some practical message digest calculation.

How to calculate a message digest on the command line

Calculating a message digest with OpenSSL on the command line is easy. You need to use the `openssl dgst` subcommand of the `openssl` tool. The documentation for this subcommand is available on the `openssl-dgst` man page:

```
$ man openssl-dgst
```

Let's generate a sample file for further message digest calculation:

```
$ seq 20000 >somefile.txt
```

To check which message digest algorithms are supported in your version of OpenSSL, you can use the `-list` switch:

```
$ openssl dgst -list
Supported digests:
-blake2b512          -blake2s256          -md4
-md5                 -md5-sha1            -ripemd
-ripemd160           -rmd160              -sha1
-sha224              -sha256              -sha3-224
-sha3-256            -sha3-384            -sha3-512
-sha384              -sha512              -sha512-224
-sha512-256          -shake128            -shake256
-sm3                 -ssl3-md5            -ssl3-sha1
-whirlpool
```

Let's calculate the SHA3-256 digest:

```
$ openssl dgst -sha3-256 somefile.txt
SHA3-256(somefile.txt)= 658656e129914052546af527ba8cf573ab27f-
b47551a0682ffcf00eeaf56d32b
```

As you may recall, message digest calculation is a deterministic operation. No matter how many times we calculate the digest of the same data, the digest will always be the same.

That's how easy it is. Now, let's learn how to calculate the same digest in *C code*.

How to calculate the message digest programmatically

We are going to implement the `digest` program that will calculate SHA3-256 message digest of a file.

Our `digest` program will receive only one command-line argument: the name of the input file to be hashed.

As with symmetric encryption in the previous chapter, let's make a high-level plan for calculating the message digest:

1. First, we must initialize the message digest calculation context.

2. Then, we must feed data to the message digest calculation context chunk by chunk, reading chunks from the input file.

3. Next, we must finalize the calculation and get the message digest.

4. Finally, we must print the calculated message digest to *stdout*.

Similar to symmetric encryption, OpenSSL contains the new **EVP API** and the old, deprecated low-level API for message digest calculation. The functions of the EVP API start with the `EVP_` prefix, while the functions of the low-level API start with hash function-specific prefixes, such as `MD5_` or `SHA256_`. We discussed the disadvantages of the old, deprecated API in the previous chapter, so we will not discuss this again here. As with symmetric ciphers, we are going to use the EVP API for message digest calculation. Even if we wanted to use the low-level API functions, we wouldn't be able to use them for SHA3-256, since SHA-3 algorithms are relatively new and are not supported by the old API.

Implementing the digest program

Let's implement our `digest` program:

1. First, we must create and initialize the message digest calculation context:

```
EVP_MD_CTX* ctx = EVP_MD_CTX_new();
EVP_DigestInit(ctx, EVP_sha3_256());
```

2. Then, we must feed the data from the input file into the context:

```
while (!feof(in_file)) {
    size_t in_nbytes = fread(in_buf, 1, BUF_SIZE, in_
file);
    EVP_DigestUpdate(ctx, in_buf, in_nbytes);
}
```

3. Once all the data has been fed to the context, we must finalize the calculation and get the message digest into the unsigned char array:

    ```
    const size_t DIGEST_LENGTH = 256 / 8;
    unsigned char md[DIGEST_LENGTH];
    EVP_DigestFinal(ctx, md, NULL);
    ```

4. Once we have obtained the message digest, we don't need the EVP_MD_CTX object anymore. We have to free it to avoid memory leaks:

    ```
    EVP_MD_CTX_free(ctx);
    ```

5. The only thing left to do is print the calculated message digest. Let's print it in the same format that the openssl dgst subcommand does:

    ```
    printf("SHA3-256(%s)= ", in_fname);
    for (size_t i = 0; i < DIGEST_LENGTH; ++i) {
        printf("%02x", md[i]);
    }
    printf("\n");
    ```

Compared to symmetric encryption, message digest calculation does not need many parameters, such as keys, initialization vectors, or padding types. Cryptographic hashing only needs a hash function type and input data. There are no requirements about input data format, any bitstream can be hashed. Thus, it is difficult to fail to calculate a message digest. If your program experiences failures with hashing, the most probable reasons are input/output errors or initialization errors, such as a particular hash function not being compiled into your version of OpenSSL, which means that the message digest's calculation cannot be initialized.

The full source code for the digest program can be found on GitHub in the digest.c file: https://github.com/PacktPublishing/Demystifying-Cryptography-with-OpenSSL-3/blob/main/Chapter03/digest.c.

Running the digest program

Let's run our digest calculation program on the same somefile.txt file that we used in the previous section:

```
$ ./digest somefile.txt
SHA3-256(somefile.txt)= 658656e129914052546af527ba8cf573ab27f-
b47551a0682ffcf00eeaf56d32b
```

As we can see, that calculated digest is identical to the digest that was calculated by the openssl dgst subcommand. This confirms that our program works as expected.

Summary

In this chapter, we learned what cryptographic hash functions and message digests are. We also learned about the common attacks that are performed on hash functions and how to assess a hash function's security. Then, we reviewed the cryptographic hash functions supported by OpenSSL and how much security they provide. We finished our review by providing a practical piece of advice on which hash functions to use in which situations.

In the practical section, we learned how to calculate a message digest using the `openssl dgst` subcommand. Finally, we learned how to develop a C program that will use the OpenSSL library for message digest calculation. We compared a message digest that was generated by our program with one that was generated by `openssl dgst` and confirmed that our digest was generated correctly.

In the next chapter, we will learn about **Message Authentication Codes (MACs)** and **Hash-based Message Authentication Codes (HMACs)**. HMACs are based on cryptographic hash functions, which is one of the reasons why it was important to learn about hash functions and message digests in this chapter.

4

MAC and HMAC

In this chapter, we will learn about **message authentication codes (MACs)**, also known as **authentication tags**. MACs are used in popular secure network protocols, such as *TLS, SSH,* and *IPsec* in order to establish both the integrity and authenticity of the transmitted data. They are also used in proprietary network protocols, for example, in financial software, for the same purpose. Additionally, MACs can be used in non-networked authenticated encryption, as we demonstrated in *Chapter 2, Symmetric Encryption and Decryption.* Another application of MAC is as the basis of some key derivation functions, such as PBKDF2. Key derivation will be covered in more detail in *Chapter 5, Derivation of an Encryption Key from a Password.* We will learn how to calculate a MAC using both the command line and C code.

In this chapter, we are going to cover the following topics:

- What is a MAC?
- Understanding MAC function security
- HMAC – a hash-based MAC
- MAC, encryption, and the Cryptographic Doom Principle
- How to calculate HMAC on the command line
- How to calculate HMAC programmatically

Technical requirements

This chapter will contain commands that you can run on a command line along with C source code that you can also build and run. For the command-line commands, you will need the `openssl` command-line tool with OpenSSL dynamic libraries. To build the C code, you will need OpenSSL dynamic or static libraries, library headers, a C compiler, and a linker.

We will implement an example program in this chapter, in order to practice what we are learning. The full source code of that program can be found here: `https://github.com/PacktPublishing/Demystifying-Cryptography-with-OpenSSL-3/tree/main/Chapter04`.

What is a MAC?

A MAC is a short array of bits, for example, 256 bits, that **authenticates** a message. **Message authentication** means that the receiver of the message can verify that the message is coming from the stated sender and has not been changed during the transfer. In order to generate a MAC, the sender needs a message and a **secret key**. In order to verify the MAC, the receiver requires the message and the same secret key. A MAC is produced by a **MAC function**.

The difference between a MAC and a message digest is that a message digest is not protected against forgery; however, a MAC does have such protection. If both the message and its digest are transmitted over an unprotected network, an attacker can change the message and recalculate its digest so that the changed digest will match the changed message. On the other hand, if a message is transmitted with its MAC, an attacker cannot recalculate the MAC for the changed message in the same way. This is because they do not possess the secret key. Therefore, it is widely agreed that message digests only provide message **integrity**, but MACs provide both **integrity** and **authenticity**.

In addition, MACs are different from **digital signatures**. Digital signatures use asymmetric cryptography so that the signer and the verifier of the signature use different keys of the same keypair. Only the signer can produce the signature because only they possess the **private key**. Hence, digital signatures provide **non-repudiation**, meaning that the signer cannot deny that they possessed information that they signed. When using MACs, both the sender and the receiver use the same secret key. Therefore, both the sender and the receiver can generate a MAC for any information that they possess, and it is difficult for a third party to determine which of them has generated the MAC. Hence, MACs, unlike digital signatures, do not provide non-repudiation. More information about digital signatures is given in *Chapter 7*, *Digital Signatures and Their Verification*.

Being different from both hash functions and digital signature functions, MAC functions also have different security requirements.

Understanding MAC function security

A MAC function is considered secure if it can resist the list of forgery attacks described as follows, which have been listed from more difficult to less difficult. All of the attacks that are described suggest that an attacker does not possess a secret key:

- A **universal forgery attack** is successful if an attacker can create a valid MAC for any message given to them.

- A **selective forgery attack** aims to produce the correct MAC for a particular message. The message is chosen prior to the attack and, usually, has some value for the attacker if they can authenticate it.

- An **existential forgery attack** works by finding a pair of any kind of message and its respective MAC.

- An **existential forgery under a chosen-message attack** suggests that there is an oracle that can generate a MAC for any message chosen by the attacker. The attacker can feed messages to the oracle, obtain MACs, and analyze the behavior of the oracle and the MAC function that the oracle performs. The attack is successful if the attacker can find a pair of any kind of message that was not fed to the oracle and its corresponding MAC.

Of course, as with other cryptographic attacks, any attack on a MAC can only be considered successful if it is executed without infeasible amounts of computation.

The security of a MAC function is measured using the same measurement units as the security of other cryptographic functions – in security bits. It is important to note that, usually, a MAC function uses another underlying function that has its own security properties. The security of the MAC function depends on the security of its underlying function and the secret key that was used.

There are different types of MAC functions, and the one that is used most often in secure network protocols is HMAC.

HMAC – a hash-based MAC

Hash-based Message Authentication Code (HMAC) is a MAC that is generated by the **HMAC function**.

The HMAC function uses a cryptographic hash function and a secret key. The function is not overly complex and can be understood by many non-cryptographers. It is defined as follows:

```
HMAC(K, message) = H(K' XOR opad || H(K' XOR ipad || message))
```

Here, the following can be understood:

- `Message`: This is the message to be authenticated.
- `H`: This is the hash function, for example, SHA3-256.
- `K`: This is the secret key.
- `K'`: This is a block-sized key derived from K depending on the hash function's internal block size, B.
- `ipad`: This is the inner padding, consisting of byte `0x36`, which is repeated B times.
- `opad`: This is the outer padding, consisting of byte `0x5C`, which is repeated B times.
- `||`: This refers to a concatenation.

Note that K' is derived from K, as follows:

- If the length of K is less than or equal to B, then K' is K padded with 0x00 bytes up to the length of B.

- If the length of K is greater than B, then K' is H(K) padded with 0x00 bytes up to the length of B.

Note that the hash function's internal block size, B, is not the same as the produced hash length. As a rule, the hash length is less than B. For example, the hash length of the SHA-256 function is 256 bits, but its internal block size is 1088 bits.

It is worth mentioning that an HMAC function using a particular hash function is often called by a name consisting of the *HMAC-* prefix and the underlying hash function name. For instance, an *HMAC* function using the *SHA-256* function is called *HMAC-SHA-256*.

An HMAC function produces an HMAC value of the same length as the hash length of the underlying hash function. For example, the HMAC-SHA-256 function produces a 256-bit HMAC.

A curious reader might ask the following: why do we need to complicate the HMAC function so much with nested hashing and padding? Why can't we just assume that the HMAC implementation is the following?

```
H(K ∥ message)
```

Well, the short answer is that those complications are needed to counter various attacks on HMAC, which, first and foremost, includes the **length extension attack**. The length extension attack aims to produce a valid MAC by appending an attacker-controlled message to the original message, without knowing the original message and the secret key. Many cryptographic hash functions, including SHA-256, are vulnerable to the length extension attack. Newer hash functions families, such as SHA3, are not susceptible to the length extension attack and can be used with simpler MAC functions. For example, for SHA-3 functions, their own MAC function exists: **KECCAK Message Authentication Code (KMAC)**.

When it comes to security strength, the security level of an uncompromised HMAC function can be calculated as follows:

```
SecurityLevel = min(K_bits, L)
```

Here, the following can be understood:

- K_bits: This is the security strength of secret key K in bits.

- L: This is the hash length of the underlying hash function in bits.

For example, if a 256-bit strong secret key is used, the HMAC-SHA-256 function achieves its highest security level: 256 bits.

So, what is the security strength of a secret key? Essentially, it is the key's entropy. If a key is generated by a cryptographically secure random generator, its security strength is the same as its length. This means that a 256-bit long key has 256-bit security strength. If the random generator that was used is suspected to have weak randomness, for example, every 2 generated bits only have 1 bit of entropy, then it makes sense to generate a key that is two times longer (512 bits) to get the same security strength (256 bits). But what if the key is derived from a low-entropy data source, such as a password? Well, the key cannot have more entropy than its source, and the security level of the whole HMAC function with such a key is degraded to the amount of entropy in the password. More information about how to derive keys from passwords is given in *Chapter 5, Derivation of an Encryption Key from a Password*.

An HMAC function can take a key of any length. However, keys shorter than L, considering that they are obtained from a cryptographically secure random generator, are strongly discouraged because they weaken the security of the HMAC function. Keys longer than L can be used, but a longer key does not improve the security of the HMAC function very much. This is because the output of the HMAC function is still limited to L. Therefore, the most obvious key length is just L. When using HMAC in the TLS protocol, OpenSSL uses L-long secret keys.

A secret key for the HMAC function must be infeasible to guess, just like a key for symmetric encryption. This means that the key must have enough entropy. One way to achieve that is to generate the key using a cryptographically strong pseudorandom generator.

As mentioned earlier, HMAC security depends on the security of the underlying hash function. However, an HMAC function is often significantly more secure than its underlying hash function if the latter becomes compromised. For example, even though the *MD5* hash function is severely compromised, and its current security level is 18 bits, the security level of the *HMAC-MD5* function is believed to be 97 bits. But even though an HMAC function is cryptographically stronger than its hash function, it makes sense to avoid any unnecessary risks and to use an HMAC function based on a secure hash function, for instance, HMAC-SHA-256.

One of the practical values of HMAC is that HMAC is the type of MAC that is used in the TLS, SSH, and IPsec protocols. In the next section, we will explain how a MAC can be combined with encryption and used in secure network protocols.

MAC, encryption, and the Cryptographic Doom Principle

When combining a MAC with encryption, one of the following schemes is used:

- **Encrypt-then-MAC (EtM)**: Here, the plaintext is encrypted, then the MAC is calculated on the *ciphertext* and sent together with the ciphertext.

- **Encrypt-and-MAC (E&M)**: Here, the plaintext is encrypted, but the MAC is calculated on the *plaintext* instead of the ciphertext. The ciphertext and the MAC are then sent together.

- **MAC-then-Encrypt (MtE)**: Here, the MAC is calculated on the *plaintext*. Concatenation of the plaintext and the MAC is then encrypted.

On the receiving side, the EtM scheme allows you to check the authenticity of the encrypted message before the decryption operation. The other two schemes require decryption of the whole plaintext before the MAC can be verified.

Security researchers regard EtM as the most secure scheme, provided that a strong and unforgeable MAC function is used. From a security point of view, it makes sense to verify the data authenticity and discard bad messages as soon as possible, especially if the message is coming from an untrusted channel, such as the internet. If decryption must be done before the message authenticity is verified by the receiver, an attacker can change any messages in transmission and attack the encryption before the receiver can discard the message.

In 2011, a famous security researcher, Moxie Marlinspike, formulated the *Cryptographic Doom Principle*. Put simply, if you have to perform *any* cryptographic operation before verifying the MAC on a message you've received, it will *somehow* inevitably lead to doom. Moxie then mentions some examples when violating the Cryptographic Doom Principle makes it possible to mount successful attacks on encryption.

The principle sounds quite bold, especially the *any* and *inevitable* parts. In my opinion, it should be taken more as a general recommendation than a hard rule.

That being said, even though EtM is the most secure scheme, it is also possible to implement the other two schemes securely, albeit more care and attention are needed.

Until several years ago, authentication (MAC) and encryption could only be used as separate operations. However, recently, authenticated encryption modes, such as AES-GCM or ChaCha20-Poly1305, have become popular and are superseding non-authenticated encryption modes. Authenticated encryption modes provide authentication as one of their core features and do not require separate authentication operations, such as running an HMAC function on plaintext or ciphertext. If you are using authenticated encryption, you don't need to think about EtM versus MtE. There is no established term for it, but you could say that you are doing *MAC-while-Encrypt* when using authenticated encryption.

As you can see, there are different methods of combining authentication with encryption. But which methods are used in the popular security protocols?

Historically, *TLS* has been using the MtE scheme. The TLS protocol is based on the SSL protocol that was invented in 1995 when the superiority of the EtM scheme had not yet been proven. Later, the **EtM TLS protocol extension** was introduced, which allowed a TLS client and server to negotiate EtM instead of MtE. In TLS 1.2, authenticated encryption ciphers were added to the protocol. Finally, in TLS 1.3, only authenticated ciphers remained as the allowed ciphers. It's important to remember that even though authenticated ciphers do not require a separate MAC operation, HMAC is still used in TLS 1.3 as the basis for a **Pseudorandom Function** (**PRF**), which is needed for **key exchange**.

Similar to TLS, *SSH* is also an old protocol. The currently used version 2 of the SSH protocol was published in 1998. Historically, SSH has been using the E&Mscheme. However, the authentication scheme in SSH depends on the MAC algorithm, and newer MAC algorithms use the EtM scheme. The newer EtM algorithms are preferred over the older E&M algorithms. Also, the newer versions of the SSH implementations support authenticated ciphers that do not require a separate MAC.

IPsec has been using EtM since the beginning, as it was created in the 1990s. Later, authenticated ciphers were added to IPsec, similar to TLS and SSH.

We have now learned what MAC and HMAC are and how they are used. Let's do some practice and learn how to calculate HMAC on the command line.

How to calculate HMAC on the command line

Now we will learn how to calculate HMAC on the command line. To do this, we need to instruct the `openssl` tool on which type of MAC function to run and which underlying function to use. The MAC function will be HMAC, and for the underlying function, let's choose the SHA-256 hash function.

The `openssl` tool provides two methods of HMAC calculation:

- Using the `openssl dgst` subcommand. This is the same subcommand that we used to calculate a message digest in the previous chapter.
- Using the `openssl mac` subcommand. A new subcommand was introduced in OpenSSL 3.0.

We will learn how to use both methods.

As usual, first, let's generate a sample file that we will use as input for HMAC calculation:

```
$ seq 20000 >somefile.txt
```

HMAC calculation requires a secret key. So, let's generate it:

```
$ openssl rand -hex 32
df036c471b612f8ad099078d8e3bd9c64339e7aeab56ec-
75e2222c415db113de
```

Here is how you calculate HMAC using the `openssl dgst` subcommand. In order to calculate HMAC instead of the message digest, you have to add `-mac HMAC` to the command-line switches and supply the secret key via the `-macopt hexkey:` switch:

```
$ openssl dgst -sha-256 -mac HMAC -macopt \
hexkey:df036c471b612f8ad099078d8e3bd9c64339e7aeab56ec-
75e2222c415db113de \
```

```
somefile.txt
HMAC-SHA256(somefile.txt)= 55e18ba91be755133ab0f4dbca5d06f2e7d-
f0b6bb4cd5f16f9f2d2f7cf83372c
```

As you can see, HMAC calculation on the command line is almost as easy as message digest calculation.

The following shows you how to do the same HMAC calculation using the new `openssl mac` subcommand:

```
$ openssl mac -digest SHA-256 -macopt \ hexkey:df036c471b-
612f8ad099078d8e3bd9c64339e7aeab56ec75e2222c415db113de \
-in somefile.txt \
HMAC
55E18BA91BE755133AB0F4DBCA5D06F2E7DF0B6BB4CD5F16F9F2D2F-
7CF83372C
```

Note that we have got the same HMAC value, but the output format is slightly different.

Now, let's learn how to calculate HMAC programmatically in a C program.

How to calculate HMAC programmatically

We are going to implement the `hmac` program that will calculate HMAC-SHA-256.

Our `hmac` program will need two command-line arguments:

1. The input filename
2. The secret key, hex-encoded

When it comes to the **Application Programming Interface** (**API**) for HMAC calculations, OpenSSL 3.0 provides three whole APIs:

*   The deprecated legacy low-level API, consisting of functions with an `HMAC_` prefix. A fun fact about this API is that even though it's not an `EVP` API, it uses the `EVP_MD` API to access underlying message digest functions.
*   The `EVP_DigestSign` API. This API is mostly used for digital signatures. It is possible to use this API for MAC, but such usage is not very intuitive.
*   The `EVP_MAC` API. This new API was specially created for MAC and introduced in OpenSSL 3.0. We are going to use *this* API in our code.

The official documentation for the `EVP_MAC` API can be found on the man page of the same name:

```
$ man EVP_MAC
```

The following man pages could also be interesting:

```
$ man EVP_MAC-HMAC
$ man OSSL_PARAM
$ man OSSL_PARAM_int
```

As in the previous chapters, let's make a high-level implementation plan:

1. Fetch the HMAC algorithm implementation description as the EVP_MAC object.

2. Create MAC calculation parameters as an OSSL_PARAM array.

3. Create and initialize the MAC calculation context, EVP_MAC_CTX.

4. Read data from the input file, chunk by chunk, and feed the obtained data to the MAC calculation context.

5. Finalize the calculation and get HMAC.

6. Print HMAC to stdout.

Let's start coding!

Implementing the hmac program

Here is how we implement the hmac program:

1. First, we have to fetch the HMAC algorithm description from OpenSSL's default algorithm provider:

   ```
   EVP_MAC* mac = EVP_MAC_fetch(NULL, OSSL_MAC_NAME_HMAC,
   NULL);
   ```

   Pay attention to the OSSL_MAC_NAME_HMAC value passed to the function. That's how we specify that we want a particular HMAC algorithm, not another MAC algorithm, such as CMAC or GMAC.

2. Next, we have to create parameters for the MAC calculation context:

   ```
   OSSL_PARAM params[] = {
       OSSL_PARAM_construct_utf8_string(
           OSSL_MAC_PARAM_DIGEST,
           OSSL_DIGEST_NAME_SHA2_256,
           0),
       OSSL_PARAM_construct_end()
   };
   ```

Pay attention to the OSSL_MAC_PARAM_DIGEST and OSSL_DIGEST_NAME_SHA2_256 values. That's how we specify that we want to use SHA-256 as the underlying message digest function.

3. We have fetched the algorithm and created the parameters; let's use them to create and initialize the MAC calculation context:

```
EVP_MAC_CTX* ctx = EVP_MAC_CTX_new(mac);
EVP_MAC_init(ctx, key, key_length, params);
```

We have also set the secret key and its length into the context. We have got that secret key as a command-line argument and unhexified it.

4. The initialization is complete. Now we need to feed data from the input file to the context:

```
while (!feof(in_file)) {
    size_t in_nbytes = fread(in_buf, 1, BUF_SIZE, in_
file);
    EVP_MAC_update(ctx, in_buf, in_nbytes);
}
```

5. After all the data has been fed to the context, finalize the calculation and get the resulting HMAC:

```
const size_t HMAC_LENGTH = 256 / 8;
unsigned char hmac[HMAC_LENGTH];
size_t out_nbytes = 0;
EVP_MAC_final(ctx, hmac, &out_nbytes, HMAC_LENGTH);
```

6. Now we no longer need the EVP_MAC and EVP_MAC_CTX objects. Let's free them and avoid any memory leaks:

```
EVP_MAC_CTX_free(ctx);
EVP_MAC_free(mac);
```

7. Finally, let's print the calculated HMAC in the same format as the openssl mac subcommand:

```
for (size_t i = 0; i < HMAC_LENGTH; ++i) {
    printf("%02X", hmac[i]);
}
printf("\n");
```

The complete source code of our hmac program can be found on GitHub as a hmac.c file: https://github.com/PacktPublishing/Demystifying-Cryptography-with-OpenSSL-3/blob/main/Chapter04/hmac.c.

Running the hmac program

Let's run our HMAC calculation program and check whether it works:

```
$ ./hmac somefile.txt df036c471b612f8ad099078d8e3bd9c
64339e7aeab56ec75e2222c415db113de
55E18BA91BE755133AB0F4DBCA5D06F2E7DF0B6BB4CD5F16F9F2D2F-
7CF83372C
```

As you can see, the HMAC calculated by our small program is the same as the one calculated by the openssl tool in the previous section. Such an observation suggests that our program works correctly.

Summary

In this chapter, we learned what MACs are and how they differ from message digests and digital signatures. We also learned about MAC function security and attacks that a good MAC function must resist. Following this, we learned what an HMAC function is and what its security depends on. We finished the theoretical part with a review of several methods of combining a MAC function with encryption, discovered what the best method is, and discussed the Cryptographic Doom Principle.

In the practical part, we learned about two methods of HMAC calculation on the command line. Then, we also learned how to calculate HMAC programmatically in C code. We compared the resulting HMACs calculated by all the methods used and, to our satisfaction, confirmed that all the methods produced the same HMAC.

In the next chapter, we will learn about **Key Derivation Functions** (**KDFs**) and how to derive encryption keys from passwords.

5

Derivation of an Encryption Key from a Password

In this chapter, we will learn about deriving **symmetric encryption keys** from **passwords** or **passphrases**. As we have learned in *Chapter 2, Symmetric Encryption and Decryption*, symmetric encryption algorithms do not encrypt with a password, but with an encryption key. Hence, in order to use a password for encryption, an encryption key must be derived from the password and then used for encryption.

This chapter features an overview of the key derivation functions supported by OpenSSL. In the practical part of the chapter, we will learn how to derive an encryption key from a password, using both the command line and C code.

We are going to cover the following topics in this chapter:

- Understanding the differences between a password and an encryption key
- What is a key derivation function?
- Overview of key derivation functions supported by OpenSSL
- Deriving a key from a password on the command line
- Deriving a key from a password programmatically

Technical requirements

This chapter will contain commands that you can run on a command line and C source code that you can build and run. For the command-line commands, you will need the `openssl` command-line tool with OpenSSL dynamic libraries. To build the C code, you will need OpenSSL dynamic or static libraries, library headers, a C compiler, and a linker.

We will implement an example program in this chapter, in order to practice what we are learning. The full source code of that program can be found here: `https://github.com/PacktPublishing/Demystifying-Cryptography-with-OpenSSL-3/tree/main/Chapter05`.

Understanding the differences between a password and an encryption key

What is the difference between a symmetric encryption key and a password? A symmetric encryption key is a secret array of bits directly used by an encryption algorithm. As a rule, an encryption algorithm requires an encryption key of a specific length, for example, 256 bits. Some less popular ciphers allow variable-length encryption keys, but this is an exception rather than a rule. An encryption key is not very human-friendly: it looks like random data (and often is random data), it is long to write and read, and it is impossible to memorize, unless you are superhuman.

On the contrary, a password or a passphrase is often much more human-friendly. Many passwords and passphrases are readable by a human. Especially in movies, passwords are always short, simple, and readable. No wonder people prefer 8-character passwords or 4-word passphrases over 256-bit keys, and popular encryption software provides the possibility to encrypt data with passwords instead of raw encryption keys.

While a password is more human-friendly than an encryption key, it cannot be used directly by an encryption algorithm. We have to derive a key from the password first, and then use the derived key for encryption. But how do we do it? With the help of key derivation functions!

What is a key derivation function?

A **Key Derivation Function** (KDF) is a function that derives a secret key of the desired bit length from some other secret material, such as a password, a passphrase, another shared secret, or a combination of asymmetric private and public keys. That other secret material is also called **Input Key Material** (**IKM**), while the secret key produced is also called **Output Key Material** (**OKM**). IKM and OKM often have different lengths. A KDF typically uses a cryptographic hash function or block cipher operations under the hood.

A **Password-Based Key Derivation Function** (PBKDF) is a KDF designed to produce secret keys from low-entropy IKMs, such as passwords. Those secret keys can be used as symmetric encryption keys. Another popular application of PBKDFs is password hashing. PBKDFs provide more brute-force-resistant password hashing than cryptographic hash functions alone.

Some key derivation functions are used for key exchange in secure network protocols. Those KDFs are not secure enough to derive keys from low-entropy IKMs. Hence, we are not going to review such KDFs in this chapter. We are going to focus on key derivation from passwords.

A typical KDF takes the following parameters:

- An IKM, for example, a password.

- **Salt** – some amount of randomly generated data. It is used to add more randomness to the key derivation process and hinder precomputed hash attacks, also known as rainbow table-based attacks. It is technically possible to supply empty salt to a KDF, but it is not recommended. NIST recommends salt to be at least 128 bits long. The generation of salt must not depend on IKM. Salt can be public or secret.

- **Info** – Application-specific information. It does not add security but can be useful for binding key material to its usage. Application-specific information can, for example, include the protocol version, algorithm identifier, or the user or object ID. Using different "info" values for different purposes is called **domain separation**.

- An underlying **Pseudorandom Function** (**PRF**), such as an HMAC function or a block cipher function.

- Function-specific, brute-force-resistant parameter(s). For many KDFs, it is just an iteration count, but some functions, such as *scrypt*, take several parameters influencing both *CPU* and *memory* usage.

- Desired OKM length.

Not all parameters are supported by every KDF. IKM and OKM lengths are supported by every KDF. Every good PBKDF should support salt and brute-force-resistance parameters. Some KDFs allow you to parameterize the PRF and add info.

Of all the parameters mentioned, only the IKM parameter (password) is considered secret. Other parameters are not secret and are either stored in cleartext or implied by the solution that uses the KDF, such as an authentication module or encryption software.

A secure PBKDF has the following properties:

- It is *deterministic*, meaning that given the same input parameters, the function will always produce the same secret key.

- It is *irreversible*, meaning that it is computationally infeasible to obtain the original IKM from the OKM produced. This feature is especially important for the password hashing application of KDFs because the passwords should not be easily recovered from OKMs. However, irreversibility is also important for encryption key generation, because if the same password is used to generate several encryption keys and one of those keys becomes compromised, it is not desired that the password should be recovered and used to recover other encryption keys.

- It is *brute-force* resistant, meaning that the execution of a KDF should use significant computational and memory resources.

Let's talk a bit more about brute-force resistance. It is important to understand that a typical password has much less entropy than a randomly generated secret key. In the case of a good random bit generator, a randomly generated key has as many entropy bits as its length, typically 128 or 256 bits.

Passwords are different. Currently, most websites require passwords to be at least 8 characters long. Some sites have started to require a minimum of 12 characters. Many sites demand a mixture of uppercase and lowercase Latin letters, digits, and symbols. This gives us approximately 80 possible characters. Let's assume that the probabilities of all characters to be contained in a password are uniformly distributed. Then, the entropy of a password can be calculated using the following formula:

```
Entropy = log₂(nchar^plen)
```

Where:

- `nchar` – number of possible characters, in our case 80
- `plen` – password length

According to the formula, the entropy of an 8-character password will be approximately 51 bits. If we raise the password length to 12 characters, the entropy will be approximately 76 bits.

It is important to understand that a PBKDF cannot give you more entropy than its input. If a PBKDF outputs a 256-bit key from a password containing 76 bits of entropy, and the salt is public, the output key will still have only 76 bits of entropy.

As we can see, a typical password does not have very much entropy. Therefore, PBKDFs cannot rely only on password entropy to effectively resist brute-force attacks. Password-based KDFs should also require a lot of computational resources. Many PBKDFs solve this by running a lot of iterations of the underlying PRF. At the same time, PBKDFs should not be too slow because key derivation is often used during interaction with a human, for example, during the verification of the entered password, so a PBKDF should preferably still complete in a fraction of a second.

As we can see, security level, or security strength, is not necessarily equal to the number of entropy bits. You can increase the security strength of a PBKDF by iterating the underlying PRF many times. It should be noted though that security strength does not grow linearly but logarithmically, depending on the number of iterations. For example, to increase security strength by 8 bits, you will need only 256 (2^8) iterations, but to increase security strength by 16 bits, you will need a huge 65,536 (2^{16}) iterations.

Lately, however, it has become popular to crack passwords using heavy parallelization on fast **Graphical Processing Units (GPUs)**, **Application-Specific Integration Circuits (ASICs)**, or **Field-Programmable Gate Arrays (FPGAs)**, which happen to have a lot of processing power for simple computational operations. Hence, being computationally intensive is not enough for a good PBKDF. A secure PBKDF should also use a significant amount of memory, meaning that the parallelization of password cracking would be constrained by the available memory and full GPU/ASIC/FPGA processing power could not be utilized.

What PBKDFs are supported by OpenSSL? We will find out in the next section.

Overview of key derivation functions supported by OpenSSL

OpenSSL 3.0 supports several key derivation functions, but only two of them are suitable for deriving keys from passwords, namely, *scrypt* and *PBKDF2*.

PBKDF2 is a popular PBKDF, described and recommended by the PKCS #5 standard. It uses an HMAC function, such as HMAC-SHA-256, as an underlying PRF. PBKDF2 supports a tunable number of iterations and can be made computationally intensive, but not memory-intensive. In 2021, the **Open Web Application Security Project** (**OWASP**) recommended 310,000 iterations for PBKDF2 with the HMAC-SHA-256 PRF.

Scrypt is the best available choice for PBKDF in OpenSSL 3.0. Scrypt is a PBKDF that is not only computationally intensive but also memory-intensive. Scrypt uses PBKDF2 with HMAC-SHA-256 under the hood. Scrypt enables you to tune the volume of computations, memory usage, and parallelism. In 2021, OWASP recommended the following brute-force-resistant parameters for Scrypt: N=65,536, r=8, p=1. While Scrypt can be used to produce symmetric encryption keys, it is also one of the user password hashing methods on modern GNU/Linux systems. Another application of Scrypt is as a proof-of-work algorithm in some cryptocurrencies, such as Litecoin and Dogecoin.

Single-step KDFs and HKDF are not suitable as PBKDFs because they are not computationally intensive. They also do not take brute-force-resistant parameters.

ANSI X9.42, ANSI X9.63, and TLS1 PRFs are not computationally intensive and require TLS-specific parameters.

SSH KDF is also not computationally intensive and requires SSH-specific parameters.

Scrypt is our best choice as a PBKDF. Let's try it on the command line!

Deriving a key from a password on the command line

Producing an encryption key from a password on the command line can be done using the `openssl kdf` subcommand. This is a new subcommand that was added in OpenSSL 3.0. You can read its documentation on the `openssl-kdf` man page:

```
$ man openssl-kdf
```

Before deriving the key, let's generate 128-bit salt:

```
$ openssl rand -hex 16
cf0e0acf943629ecffea41c87bab94d4
```

Now we can derive a 256-bit key suitable for symmetric encryption. Let's use the *Scrypt* KDF. OWASP recommended brute-force-resistant settings and the password SuperPa$$w0rd:

```
$ openssl kdf \
  -keylen 32 \
  -kdfopt 'pass:SuperPa$$w0rd' \
  -kdfopt hexsalt:cf0e0acf943629ecffea41c87bab94d4 \
  -kdfopt n:65536 -kdfopt r:8 -kdfopt p:1 \
  SCRYPT
D0:3D:31:A1:A2:2A:F6:68:99:B3:02:22:60:3B:D7:21:5B:15:5B:80:2B:
85:33:36:E6:3B:AB:F9:EE:8F:FE:C7
```

Note that the command-line argument containing the password is enclosed in single quotes. This is to avoid the special interpretation of $ characters by the command interpreter. Another method of passing special characters in a password would be to pass a hex-encoded password using the -kdfopt hexpass: option instead of -kdfopt pass:.

We have learned how to produce an encryption key from a password on the command line. Now let's learn how to do it programmatically in C code.

Deriving a key from a password programmatically

We are going to implement the kdf program, which will derive a key from a password.

Our key derivation program will take two command-line arguments:

1. Password
2. Hex-encoded salt

We are not going to take the N, r, and brute-force-resistant Scrypt parameters because because we want to simplify our example program and its usage. Instead, we are going to use OWASP-recommended settings.

OpenSSL 3.0 provides the following APIs for key derivation:

- The PKCS5_PBKDF2_HMAC(), PKCS5_PBKDF2_HMAC_SHA1(), and EVP_PBE_scrypt() legacy functions, specific to particular KDFs.

- The EVP_PKEY API. This API is intended for use with asymmetric cryptography and contains the EVP_PKEY_derive() function. That function is mostly intended for non-password-based key derivation during key exchange operations in secure network protocols, such as **Diffie-Hellman key exchange**, but also supports password-based key derivation using the *Scrypt* algorithm.

- The EVP_KDF API. This is a new API specially created for KDF, available and recommended since OpenSSL 3.0. We are going to use this API.

Documentation for the EVP_KDF API and its usage with *Scrypt* can be found on these man pages:

```
$ man EVP_KDF
$ man EVP_KDF-SCRYPT
```

As usual, let's make a high-level implementation plan:

1. Fetch the key derivation algorithm implementation description as an EVP_KDF object.

2. Create the key derivation parameters as an OSSL_PARAM array.

3. Create the key derivation calculation context, EVP_KDF_CTX.

4. Derive the key.

5. Print the produced key to stdout.

Now, let's implement those ideas in the code.

Implementing the kdf program

Follow these steps to implement the kdf program according to our plan:

1. First, we have to fetch the *Scrypt* key derivation algorithm description from OpenSSL's default algorithm provider:

    ```
    EVP_KDF* kdf = EVP_KDF_fetch(
        NULL, OSSL_KDF_NAME_SCRYPT, NULL);
    ```

2. Next, we have to create key derivation parameters:

    ```
    uint64_t scrypt_n = 65536;
    uint32_t scrypt_r = 8;
    uint32_t scrypt_p = 1;
    OSSL_PARAM params[] = {
        OSSL_PARAM_construct_octet_string(
            OSSL_KDF_PARAM_PASSWORD,
            (char*)password, strlen(password)),
        OSSL_PARAM_construct_octet_string(
            OSSL_KDF_PARAM_SALT, (char*)salt, salt_length),
        OSSL_PARAM_construct_uint64(
            OSSL_KDF_PARAM_SCRYPT_N, &scrypt_n),
        OSSL_PARAM_construct_uint32(
            OSSL_KDF_PARAM_SCRYPT_R, &scrypt_r),
    ```

```
    OSSL_PARAM_construct_uint32(
        OSSL_KDF_PARAM_SCRYPT_P, &scrypt_p),
    OSSL_PARAM_construct_end()
};
```

Unfortunately, OSSL_PARAM_construct_*() functions only take non-const pointers, so we have to cast password and salt pointers, and create scrypt_n, scrypt_r, and scrypt_p variables as non-const as well.

3. Next, we have to create the key derivation context:

```
    EVP_KDF_CTX* ctx = EVP_KDF_CTX_new(kdf);
```

4. All the pieces are now in place, so it is time to derive the key:

```
    EVP_KDF_derive(ctx, key, KEY_LENGTH, params);
```

5. Now that we no longer require the EVP_KDF and EVP_KDF_CTX objects, let's free them and avoid memory leaks:

```
    EVP_KDF_CTX_free(ctx);
    EVP_KDF_free(kdf);
```

6. The key has been produced. Let's print it in the same format as the openssl kdf subcommand:

```
    for (size_t i = 0; i < KEY_LENGTH; ++i) {
        if (i != 0)
            printf(":");
        printf("%02X", key[i]);
    }
    printf("\n");
```

The complete source code for our kdf program can be found on GitHub as the kdf.c file: https://github.com/PacktPublishing/Demystifying-Cryptography-with-OpenSSL-3/blob/main/Chapter05/kdf.c.

Running the kdf program

Let's run our key derivation program and see whether it works:

```
$ ./kdf 'SuperPa$$w0rd' cf0e0acf943629ecffea41c87bab94d4
D0:3D:31:A1:A2:2A:F6:68:99:B3:02:22:60:3B:D7:21:5B:15:5B:80:2B:
85:33:36:E6:3B:AB:F9:EE:8F:FE:C7
```

As we can see, the encryption key derived by our small kdf program is the same as the key produced by the openssl kdf subcommand in the previous section, suggesting that our program works correctly.

Summary

In this chapter, we have learned about the concept of deriving an encryption key from a password. Then we learned about what key derivation functions are and what the requirements are for good PBKDFs. We finished the theoretical part with a review of key derivation functions supported by OpenSSL and a recommendation on which KDF to use for password-based key derivation.

In the practical part, we learned how to derive a symmetric encryption key from a password on the command line. Then we also learned how to derive the same key programmatically in C code. We compared the resulting keys derived by both methods and, to our satisfaction, confirmed that both methods produced the same secret key.

In the next chapter, we will start learning about asymmetric cryptography.

Part 3:
Asymmetric Cryptography and Certificates

In this part, we will learn about asymmetric cryptography, public and private encryption keys, digital signatures and their verification, and X.509 certificates. This part will compare asymmetric ciphers, such as RSA and Elliptic Curves. All the technologies mentioned will be illustrated using command-line and C code examples.

This part the following chapters:

- *Chapter 6, Asymmetric Encryption and Decryption*
- *Chapter 7, Digital Signatures and Their Verification*
- *Chapter 8, X.509 Certificates and PKI*

6

Asymmetric Encryption and Decryption

In this chapter, we will learn about **asymmetric encryption**, how it works, and how public and private keys are used to achieve encryption and decryption. In the practical part of this chapter, we will learn how to use asymmetric encryption and decryption on the command line and in C code.

We are going to cover the following topics in this chapter:

- Understanding asymmetric encryption
- Understanding a Man in the Middle attack
- What kind of asymmetric encryption is available in OpenSSL?
- Understanding a session key
- Understanding RSA security
- How to generate an RSA keypair
- How to encrypt and decrypt with RSA on the command line
- How to encrypt with RSA programmatically
- Understanding the OpenSSL error queue
- How to decrypt with RSA programmatically

Technical requirements

This chapter will contain commands that you can run on a command line and C source code that you can build and run. For the command line commands, you will need the `openssl` command-line tool with OpenSSL dynamic libraries. For building the C code, you will need OpenSSL dynamic or static libraries, library headers, a C compiler, and a linker.

We will implement some example programs in this chapter, in order to practice what we are learning. The full source code of those programs can be found here: `https://github.com/PacktPublishing/ Demystifying-Cryptography-with-OpenSSL-3/tree/main/Chapter06`

Understanding asymmetric encryption

As we learned in *Chapter 2, Symmetric Encryption and Decryption*, symmetric encryption algorithms use the same key for encryption and decryption. **Asymmetric encryption algorithms**, conversely, use two keys – **a public key** and **a private key**. A public key and its corresponding private key form a **keypair**. The public key is used for encryption and the private key is used for decryption.

Why do we need the complication with two keys? Why can't we just always use symmetric encryption with one key? In short, asymmetric encryption is needed when it is difficult or impossible to send a secret key and ensure that no one eavesdropped on the transferred key. Let's imagine that Alice wants to send a message to Bob over a non-secure channel – for example, over the internet. On the internet, transit hosts between Alice and Bob can eavesdrop on the passing traffic and even change it. Alice does not want anyone to eavesdrop on the message, therefore she decides to encrypt the message. But how to transfer the encryption key? If Alice and Bob had a freely available secure communication channel for sending the key, they could just send the actual message over that channel, without encryption. Thus, Alice and Bob decide to use asymmetric cryptography:

1. Bob generates a keypair and sends his public key to Alice.
2. Alice encrypts the message with Bob's public key and sends the encrypted message to Bob.
3. Bob decrypts the message with his private key.

If an attacker eavesdrops on the traffic and gets both Bob's public key and the message, they will not be able to decrypt the message. Only Bob's private key can decrypt the message. Therefore, Bob has to keep his private key secret and not share it with anyone.

It works well if a potential attacker can only passively eavesdrop on the traffic but cannot change it. But what if they can? Then, they can attempt a Man in the Middle attack.

Understanding a Man in the Middle attack

A **Man in the Middle** (**MITM**) attack is an attack where an attacker both listens in on the transit traffic and changes it, trying to impersonate the receiver to the sender and the sender to the receiver.

Let's demonstrate a possible attack for the scenario with Alice and Bob mentioned previously. Let's suppose that Mallory acts as a Man in the Middle in order to recover the plaintext of the encrypted message that Alice wants to send to Bob. Then, the attack scenario will be as follows:

1. Bob generates a keypair and sends his public key to Alice.

2. Mallory generates her own keypair. She intercepts Bob's public key sent to Alice and saves it for future use. Instead of Bob's public key, Mallory sends her own public key to Alice, disguised as Bob's key.

3. Alice encrypts her message with Mallory's public key, thinking that it is Bob's public key. Alice then sends the encrypted message to Bob.

4. Mallory intercepts Alice's message. Mallory decrypts the message with her private key. Then, she re-encrypts the message with Bob's public key and sends the encrypted message to Bob.

5. The outcome is that Alice thinks that she sent the message to Bob and no one else has read it. Bob thinks that he received the message from Alice and no one else has read it. Mallory got away with the secret information from the message, unnoticed.

How do we defend against an MITM attack? There are different methods, but each method requires a trusted communication channel available at least for a short time before the main communication happens.

Meeting in person

The two parties (Alice and Bob) can meet in person and exchange or verify their public keys. This method is trivial but often not very practical, especially if Alice and Bob live far away from each other. However, sometimes it is practical. For instance, some IT conferences include **key signing parties**. People who come to the conference from distant parts of the world gather and show each other IDs, such as passports or driving licenses, and their **Pretty Good Privacy** (**PGP**) key fingerprints. Participants of the party can also sign each other's keys; that's why it is called a key signing party.

Verifying a key fingerprint over the phone

A public key fingerprint is basically its full or partial cryptographic hash, hex- or base64-encoded. After exchanging the public keys over the internet – for example, via email – Alice and Bob have a phone call and verify each other's fingerprints. In such a case, Alice and Bob's voices serve as a form of authentication. Unfortunately, nowadays, this key verification method is less practical and reliable than before. Faster CPUs and advanced cryptanalysis methods force Alice and Bob to use longer fingerprints, and recent developments of deepfake technologies make it possible to falsify human voices in real time. Even so, verification by voice is still quite a good authentication method. In order to falsify the key exchange, an attacker needs to accomplish an MITM attack on two different communication channels and employ advanced deepfake technology.

Key splitting

The key can be split into several parts, and each part can be sent to the recipient using a different delivery method, such as email, instant messenger, publishing on a file exchange server, and sending a flash drive by physical mail. The idea is that it will be difficult for an attacker to intercept and falsify messages on all channels. After the recipient has reassembled the key, its fingerprint can additionally be verified over the phone.

Signing the key by a trusted third party

A third party – let's call him Thomas – who is trusted by both Alice and Bob can digitally sign Bob's public key, certifying that it really is Bob's key. Then, Alice can verify the signature. This method requires that Alice must first get Thomas' public key via some trusted channel. A similar but more complex model of key verification is used in PGP's **web of trust** and in **Public Key Infrastructure (PKI)**, based on X.509 certificates. More information about digital signatures is available in *Chapter 7, Digital Signatures and Their Verification*, and more details about X.509 certificates can be found in *Chapter 8, X.509 Certificates and PKI*.

Alice and Bob now know how to securely exchange the public keys. But what asymmetric encryption algorithm should they use in order to encrypt the messages that they want to securely send to each other? Let's learn about that in the next section.

What kind of asymmetric encryption is available in OpenSSL?

The OpenSSL library implements several asymmetric crypto algorithms, but only one of those algorithms allows you to *directly* encrypt data. It is the **Rivest-Shamir-Adleman (RSA)** algorithm.

Other available asymmetric crypto algorithms, such as **Digital Signature Algorithm (DSA)** and **Elliptic Curve Digital Signature Algorithm (ECDSA)**, can be used for digital signatures. **Diffie–Hellman (DH)** and **Elliptic Curve Diffie–Hellman (ECDH)** algorithms can be used for key exchange in the **Transport Layer Security (TLS)** protocol.

As we know, symmetric cryptography keys do not have structure; they are just arrays of random bits. Conversely, asymmetric crypto algorithms use structured keys, meaning that a key can have several components, and a component may have certain requirements – for example, it must be a prime number instead of a random bit array. Each asymmetric crypto algorithm has its own structure of public and private keys. Hence, there are different formats of asymmetric keys, such as RSA keys and ECDSA keys.

Why did we say previously that RSA is the only asymmetric crypto algorithm available in OpenSSL that can *directly* encrypt data? What does *directly* mean? It means that the RSA algorithm alone is enough for encryption. Can other algorithms be used *indirectly* for encryption? Yes, it is possible. There is the **ElGamal** algorithm, which can use a DH algorithm with DSA keys, or an ECDH algorithm with ECDSA keys, in order to do asymmetric encryption. ElGamal involves creating an ephemeral (temporary) DSA/ECDSA key in addition to the DSA/ECDSA key that you want to use for encryption, doing a DH/ECDH key exchange between the two keys in order to get the shared secret, deriving a symmetric encryption key from the shared secret, and finally, encrypting the data with that symmetric key. As we can see, it is more complicated than using RSA. There are also other schemes for deriving a symmetric key using a defined asymmetric key and an ephemeral asymmetric key, such as **Integrated Encryption Scheme** (**IES**) and **Hybrid Public Key Encryption** (**HPKE**). OpenSSL does not implement ElGamal, IES, HPKE, or similar algorithms. Therefore, for asymmetric encryption examples in this chapter, we will use RSA.

A symmetric encryption key used in an ElGamal algorithm is called a **session key**. The concept of using a session key is not specific to ElGamal. A session key is also used with RSA and in secure network protocols, such as TLS, SSH, and IPsec. Let's look at the session key in detail next.

Understanding a session key

It is important to understand how asymmetric encryption is used in practice. Asymmetric ciphers, such as RSA, are much slower than symmetric ciphers, such as AES. Therefore, usually, the actual data that a sender wants to encrypt is not encrypted by RSA. Instead, the sender generates a symmetric session key. Then, the actual data is encrypted by a symmetric algorithm, such as AES, with the session key, which is encrypted by RSA. When decrypting, the recipient first decrypts the session key by RSA and then decrypts the actual data by AES with the session key. Such an encryption scheme is often referred to as a **hybrid encryption scheme**.

In secure network protocols, such as TLS, SSH, and IPsec, the communication session begins with the **handshaking** operation, part of which is the **key exchange** operation. In the older versions of the protocols, the key exchange operation involved the generation of the session key by one party of the communication, encrypting it by RSA, and sending it encrypted to the other party. In the current versions of the protocols, the communication parties use the DH or ECDH key exchange methods, where both communication parties derive the same session key, which they then use for encryption of the useful data. More information about TLS handshaking will be available in *Chapter 9, Establishing TLS Connections and Sending Data over Them*.

For the hybrid encryption to be secure, both symmetric encryption by the session key and asymmetric encryption by the RSA key must be secure. The next section gives an insight into RSA security.

Understanding RSA security

The security of RSA relies on the difficulty of the integer factorization problem. As a reminder, the factorization operation is breaking a positive integer number into a multiplication of prime numbers. Currently, there is no polynomial-time algorithm for integer factorization that can be run by a classical computer, and hence, this problem remains very computationally expensive. And how big are the integer numbers used in RSA? Typically, they are hundreds or thousands of decimal digits, or thousands or tens of thousands of bits. Apparently, usual integer types in C language are not large enough to perform mathematics with big numbers used in RSA. Hence, OpenSSL includes a big-number sub-library in order to deal with big numbers. Types and functions of that big-number sub-library have a BN_ prefix.

An RSA public or private key consists of several big or small integer numbers called a modulus, an exponent, and, optionally, primes and coefficients. As mentioned, one of those numbers is a modulus. The RSA key size is considered to be the size of the modulus. For instance, if an RSA key contains a 2,048-bit modulus, then the size of that RSA key is also 2,048 bits.

It's important to remember that the security level of an RSA key is much lower than the key size. For example, a 2,048-bit RSA key has a security level of only 112 bits. The security level of an RSA key does not grow linearly depending on the key size. The key size must be increased substantially in order to gain only a few security bits.

Here is a table that lists security levels estimated by the National Institute of Standards and Technology (NIST) for RSA keys of different sizes:

RSA key size in bits	Security level in bits
1,024	80
2,048	112
3,072	128
4,096	152
7,680	192
8,192	200
15,360	256

Table 6.1: Security levels for different RSA key sizes

As we can see, in order to reach the same security level as AES-256, we need an RSA key of 15,360 bits! Are there any disadvantages with long RSA keys? Unfortunately, there are:

- There is slower performance for both encryption and decryption, and signing and signature verification. Performance drops faster than linear with the growth of the key size. When doubling the key size in the range of 1024–4096 bits – for example, increasing the key size from 1,024 to 2,048 bits – encryption and signing becomes approximately 7 times slower, and decryption and signature verification becomes approximately 3 times slower. To give a rough idea about RSA speed, a PC with anIntel i5 CPU can do thousands of RSA encryptions or hundreds of RSA decryptions with a 4,096-bit key per second. As we can see, RSA encryption is much faster than RSA decryption. If you're curious, you can check speeds on your machine using the openssl speed rsa command.

- RSA outputs encrypted data in blocks equal to the key size. Considering that RSA is usually used for the encryption of a symmetric key and possibly an initialization vector, RSA encryption will expand the input data several times – for example, a 256-bit symmetric key and a 128-bit initialization vector encrypted by a 2,048-bit RSA key will produce 2,048-bit-long ciphertext. The longer the RSA key, the more length expansion during the RSA encryption will happen. Technically, the result of the RSA encryption is a very long integer, thus it is possible to strip leading zeros from it and shorten the ciphertext a little bit. But the benefit is not worth the hassle, and no popular encryption software implements such shortening.

- The RSA signature size in the standard PKCS #1 format is also equal to the RSA key size. Longer signatures are inconvenient.

- Longer RSA keys take a longer time to be generated – for example, on a PC with Intel i5 CPU, a 4,096-bit RSA key is generated in less than a second, but the generation of a 15,360-bit key can take 2 minutes.

As we can see, we have a trade-off between security and performance. The amount of space that an RSA key, encrypted block, or signature takes is much less of a concern. Unfortunately, in order to get only a few more bits of security, we have to increase the key size by many more bits, and we have to pay a significant performance penalty. Fortunately, CPUs, including those in mobile and embedded devices, are becoming faster and faster.

But what is the acceptable compromise? What RSA key size do we choose? NIST recommends using the following sizes for RSA keys:

- At least 2,048 bits until 2030

- At least 3,072 bits after 2030

At the time of writing, 2,048 bits is both the most popular and minimally acceptable size for RSA keys. Most RSA-based web server TLS certificates on the web use 2,048-bit keys. The next step will likely be 4,096-bit certificates. Many old articles on the internet advocated a compromise of 3,072-bit keys and certificates, but that idea didn't really take off. Current articles usually compare 2,048-bit and 4,096-bit certificates.

I personally think that it is nice to have some security margin, thus I prefer 4,096 bits as the RSA key size. Why not less? Because computers that I use work comfortably fast with such RSA keys. Why not more? Because 4,096 bits provide enough of a security margin and because some software, especially old software, does not support RSA keys longer than 4,096 bits. For example, even modern GnuPG does not allow you to create an RSA keypair longer than 4,096 bits. Also, for what it's worth, 4,096 is a nice number, because it is a power of 2, unlike 3,072.

I also think that it is even better to use **Elliptic Curve Cryptography** (**ECC**) instead of RSA in cases where the usage of ECC is as easy as the usage of RSA – for example, in TLS certificates and SSH keys. But for encryption, RSA is much more straightforward to use than ECC. We will learn more about ECC in *Chapter 7, Digital Signatures and Their Verification*.

What will happen with RSA security when **quantum computing** arrives? Unfortunately, asymmetric cryptography as we know it, both RSA and ECC, will be completely broken by quantum computing, and we don't have a standardized and practice-proven replacement yet. The good news is that many cryptographers are actively working on post-quantum cryptographic algorithms. At the time of this writing, NIST is running post-quantum cryptography standardization, which is a competition for quantum-resistant crypto algorithms, similar to AES and SHA-3 competitions. The winners of the competition will be standardized as the standard post-quantum cryptography algorithms. The most optimistic predictions are that quantum computers capable of breaking the current asymmetric cryptography will be created in the 2030s. Thus, we have a good hope that post-quantum crypto algorithms will be standardized and included in popular crypto libraries, such as OpenSSL, before powerful quantum computers become available even to big players, such as governments and corporations.

Quantum computing and OpenSSL support for post-quantum crypto algorithms are things that we expect in the future. But what can we do now? Learn how to use RSA. Let's start with generating our first RSA keypair.

How to generate an RSA keypair

The `openssl` tool provides two subcommands for generating RSA keypairs – `genrsa` and `genpkey`. The former can generate only an RSA keypair, while the latter is a more generic subcommand that can generate any type of keypair supported by OpenSSL. `genrsa` is declared deprecated since OpenSSL 3.0, thus we will use `genpkey`.

Documentation for the `openssl genpkey` subcommand can be found on the `openssl-genpkey` man page:

```
man openssl-genpkey
```

Why such a name, `genpkey`? OpenSSL has a concept of a **Public or Private Key** (**PKEY**). Here, it is important to clear up one confusion. Throughout the OpenSSL documentation, you will find mentions about public and private keys. Very often when mentioning a private key, the documentation really means a keypair. It applies to both command-line tools documentation and OpenSSL API documentation. For example, the `description` part of the `openssl-genpkey` man page says, *The genpkey command generates a private key*. If only a private key is generated, how would I generate the complementary public key? The OpenSSL documentation suggests that I can extract a public key from a private key, which can be quite confusing for inexperienced OpenSSL users. More specifically, what OpenSSL and PKCS standards usually call a private key is a data structure, holding information sufficient for constructing both private and public keys. Some of that information is shared between the public and the private key, particularly the modulus part for RSA. A public key is a similar data structure, containing only public key information. Therefore, for simplicity, we can assume that when mentioning a private key, OpenSSL means a keypair, and when mentioning a public key, OpenSSL means what it says – a public key.

I hope I was able to clear up more confusion than I created! Now, let's generate our first RSA keypair:

```
$ openssl genpkey \
    -algorithm RSA \
    -pkeyopt rsa_keygen_bits:4096 \
    -out rsa_keypair.pem
```

Using the -pkeyopt rsa_keygen_bits:4096 switch, we have specified that we want to generate a 4,096-bit keypair. After the generation, the keypair has been written into the file named rsa_keypair.pem.

The keypair file can be opened with a text editor and will contain something like this:

```
-----BEGIN PRIVATE KEY-----
MIIJQwIBADANBgkqhkiG9w0BAQEFAASCCS0wggkpAgEAAoICAQDC2/
sxiM72yGgy
... a lot of base64-encoded data ...
FZTCpfZK4ecBXkHHaVnHBmdS1OEyngU=
-----END PRIVATE KEY-----
```

The keypair is saved in the **Privacy Enhanced Mail** (PEM) format. PEM is the default format used by OpenSSL for storing keys or certificates. Even though *mail* is mentioned in the PEM format name, the format is not just used for mail. PEM format is really a Base64 wrapping around some binary data, with a text header (the BEGIN line) and a text footer (the END line). If you remove the header and the footer from the keypair PEM file and Base64-decode it, you will get the keypair in the **Distinguished Encoding Rules** (DER) format. DER is another popular format for storing keys and certificates supported by OpenSSL. DER is a binary representation for data structures described by **Abstract Syntax Notation One** (ASN.1). ASN.1 is a notation that allows you to describe data structures for serialization in a platform-independent way – for example, an RSA keypair described by ASN.1 is an ASN.1 sequence of ASN.1 integers.

We can inspect the structure of the generated keypair using the openssl pkey subcommand. Documentation for the openssl pkey subcommand can be found on the openssl-pkey man page:

```
man openssl-pkey
```

There is also a similar RSA-specific subcommand, openssl rsa. It has been deprecated since OpenSSL 3.0, together with openssl genrsa, openssl rsautl, and other key type-specific subcommands.

Here is how we inspect the keypair structure:

```
$ openssl pkey -in rsa_keypair.pem -noout -text
Private-Key: (4096 bit, 2 primes)
```

```
modulus:
    …

publicExponent: 65537 (0x10001)
privateExponent:
    …

prime1:
    …

prime2:
    …

exponent1:
    …

exponent2:
    …

coefficient:
    …
```

It is very good that we have generated a keypair. Now, we have to extract the public key out of it in order to share the public key with a person that will encrypt data for us, because we should never share our keypair; we should only share the public key.

This is how we extract the public key from the keypair:

```
$ openssl pkey \
    -in rsa_keypair.pem \
    -pubout \
    -out rsa_public_key.pem
```

Note the -pubout switch. That's how we specified that we want only the public key in the output, not the whole keypair.

The resulting rsa_public_key.pem file does not contain secret information and can be freely shared. We can inspect the structure of our public key file:

```
$ openssl pkey -pubin -in rsa_public_key.pem -noout -text
Public-Key: (4096 bit)
Modulus:
    …

Exponent: 65537 (0x10001)
```

Note the -pubin switch. That's how we specified that the openssl pkey subcommand must treat the input as a public key, not as a keypair.

As we can observe, the public key file contains much less information than the keypair file – only the modulus and the public exponent.

We have spent enough time on key generation. Now, let's put those keys to some use.

How to encrypt and decrypt with RSA on the command line

The openssl tool provides two subcommands for encrypting with RSA – pkeyutl and the deprecated, RSA-specific rsautl subcommand. We will, of course, use pkeyutl. Documentation for that subcommand can be found on the openssl-pkeyutl man page:

```
man openssl-pkeyutl
```

As explained previously, RSA is usually used for encrypting a session key, which will then be used to encrypt useful data. Let's generate a 256-bit session key:

```
$ openssl rand -out session_key.bin 32
```

Now, let's use openssl pkeyutl with our public RSA key for encrypting the session key:

```
$ openssl pkeyutl \
    -encrypt \
    -in session_key.bin \
    -out session_key.bin.encrypted \
    -pubin \
    -inkey rsa_public_key.pem \
    -pkeyopt rsa_padding_mode:oaep
```

Note the -pkeyopt rsa_padding_mode:oaep switch. It instructs openssl pkeyutl to use the PKCS #1 v2.0 **Optimal Asymmetric Encryption Padding (OAEP)** padding type for the RSA encryption. It is strongly recommended to use that padding type because it is the most secure one. If you use the default PKCS #1 v1.5 padding, your ciphertext may be vulnerable to a Bleichenbacher padding oracle attack.

Let's check the files that we have created:

```
$ cksum session_key.bin*
186975932 32 session_key.bin
2324953448 512 session_key.bin.encrypted
```

Note that the input session key file is only 32 bytes (256 bits) long, but its encrypted version is a whole 512 bytes (4,096 bits) long. It is because the RSA's output ciphertext block is the same size as the RSA key size used.

Try to encrypt several times and note that the encrypted file will have the same size but a different checksum after every encryption. Though RSA encryption *as such* is deterministic, the used OAEP padding is not deterministic, which leads to non-deterministic ciphertext.

We have successfully encrypted a small file. But what will happen if we try to encrypt a bigger file? Let's try. First, let's generate a bigger file:

```
$ seq 20000 >somefile.txt
```

We have got a file approximately 100 KB in size. Let's try to encrypt it:

```
$ openssl pkeyutl \
    -encrypt \
    -in somefile.txt \
    -out somefile.txt.encrypted \
    -pubin \
    -inkey rsa_public_key.pem \
    -pkeyopt rsa_padding_mode:oaep
Public Key operation error
C011FAE8677F0000:error:0200006E:
rsa routines:ossl_rsa_padding_add_PKCS1_OAEP_mgf1_ex:
data too large for key size:crypto/rsa/rsa_oaep.c:87:
```

We have got an error, telling us that our input data is too large for the key size. It is because RSA cannot encrypt data any longer than its key length during one operation. If padding is used, the maximum accepted plaintext length is even shorter. When OAEP padding is used, the maximum input data length is key size – 42 – in our case, 4096 – 42 = 4054 bytes. If you need to encrypt longer data, you should encrypt it with a symmetric session key.

It's time to decrypt what we encrypted and compare it to the original. In order to decrypt, we need to provide the keypair to openssl pkeyutl, not just the public key:

```
$ openssl pkeyutl \
    -decrypt \
    -in session_key.bin.encrypted \
    -out session_key.bin.decrypted \
    -inkey rsa_keypair.pem \
    -pkeyopt rsa_padding_mode:oaep
```

Let's check the checksums:

```
$ cksum session_key.bin*
186975932 32 session_key.bin
186975932 32 session_key.bin.decrypted
2324953448 512 session_key.bin.encrypted
```

As we can see, the sizes and checksums of `session_key.bin` and `session_key.bin.` `decrypted` match, meaning that the decrypted file is equal to the original file. It is absolutely great that decryption is always deterministic!

We have learned how to encrypt and decrypt on the command line. Now, let's learn how to encrypt with RSA programmatically.

How to encrypt with RSA programmatically

OpenSSL 3.0 provides the following APIs for RSA encryption:

- A legacy API with the `RSA_` prefix and the `RSA_public_encrypt()` function. This API has been deprecated since OpenSSL 3.0, so we are not going to use it.

- The `EVP_PKEY` API, particularly the `EVP_PKEY_encrypt()` function. We are going to use this API.

- The `EVP_Seal` API. This is a hybrid encryption API that generates a session key, encrypts the session key with RSA, and then encrypts the user data with the session key. This API contains the `EVP_SealInit()`, `EVP_SealUpdate()`, and `EVP_SealFinal()` functions, which work similarly to `EVP_EncryptInit()`, `EVP_EncryptUpdate()`, and `EVP_EncryptFinal()`. `EVP_SealUpdate()` is just #define for `EVP_EncryptUpdate()`. There are also the corresponding `EVP_Open` functions for decrypting the *seals* – `EVP_OpenInit()`, `EVP_OpenUpdate()`, and `EVP_OpenFinal()`. Unfortunately, the `EVP_Seal` API is rather inflexible. It supports only RSA encryption of the session key. The API does not provide a method to specify padding or other properties for RSA encryption, thus RSA encryption will always use the default PKCS #1 v1.5 padding instead of OAEP padding. It is a bit difficult to understand how to call the `EVP_SealInit()` function; you will likely spend several minutes looking at the documentation before you understand it. I think that the `EVP_Seal` API is badly designed in general and should be replaced by a better hybrid encryption API. Therefore, I do not recommend using the `EVP_Seal` API.

We are going to develop the `rsa-encrypt` program that encrypts a small portion of data – for example, a session key, using RSA, similar to how we encrypted with `openssl pkeyutl` in the previous section. Our program is going to be interoperable with `pkeyutl`, meaning that `pkeyutl` will be able to decrypt the ciphertext produced by our program.

As mentioned, we are going to use the `EVP_PKEY` API. Here is the list of the relevant man pages for the functions that we are going to use:

```
$ man PEM_read_PUBKEY
$ man EVP_PKEY_CTX_new_from_pkey
$ man EVP_PKEY_encrypt_init
$ man EVP_PKEY_CTX_set_rsa_padding
$ man EVP_PKEY_get_size
$ man EVP_PKEY_encrypt
$ man provider-asym_cipher
```

Our program will take three command-line arguments:

1. The input filename
2. The output filename
3. The RSA public key filename

Let's make a high-level implementation plan, as we usually do. Our program will need to perform the following steps:

1. Load the RSA public key from the RSA public key file.
2. Create the `EVP_PKEY` context from the key.
3. Initialize the `EVP_PKEY` context for encryption and set the OAEP padding mode.
4. Read the plaintext from the input file.
5. Encrypt the plaintext.
6. Write the produced ciphertext into the output file.

Implementing the rsa-encrypt program

Let's proceed with the implementation:

1. First, load the RSA public key:

   ```
   const char* pkey_fname = argv[3];
   FILE* pkey_file = fopen(pkey_fname, "rb");
   EVP_PKEY* pkey = PEM_read_PUBKEY(
       pkey_file, NULL, NULL, NULL);
   ```

2. Next, create the EVP_PKEY context from the loaded key:

```
EVP_PKEY_CTX* ctx = EVP_PKEY_CTX_new_from_pkey(
    NULL, pkey, NULL);
```

3. Then, initialize EVP_PKEY_CTX and set the padding mode:

```
EVP_PKEY_encrypt_init(ctx);
EVP_PKEY_CTX_set_rsa_padding(ctx, RSA_PKCS1_OAEP_
PADDING);
```

You can also initialize in the new OpenSSL 3.0 style, using OSSL_PARAM with parameters:

```
int rsa_padding = RSA_PKCS1_OAEP_PADDING;
OSSL_PARAM params[] = {
    OSSL_PARAM_construct_int(
        OSSL_ASYM_CIPHER_PARAM_PAD_MODE, &rsa_padding),
    OSSL_PARAM_construct_end()
};
    EVP_PKEY_encrypt_init_ex(ctx, params);
```

It's interesting that the OpenSSL 3.0 documentation (on the provider-asym_cipher man page) defines the OSSL_ASYM_CIPHER_PARAM_PAD_MODE parameter as an integer, but in the OpenSSL source code (in the rsa_enc.c file), the same parameter is defined as a UTF-8 string. The code accepts both integer and string values and calls the legacy pad mode number integer value. When setting the padding mode with the string, the context initialization code will look like this:

```
OSSL_PARAM params[] = {
    OSSL_PARAM_construct_utf8_string(
        OSSL_ASYM_CIPHER_PARAM_PAD_MODE,
        OSSL_PKEY_RSA_PAD_MODE_OAEP,
        0),
    OSSL_PARAM_construct_end()
};
    EVP_PKEY_encrypt_init_ex(ctx, params);
```

I prefer the old initialization style because it's the most readable, concise, and type-safe, even though it is less generic. OpenSSL also prefers the old style. OpenSSL 3.0 source code contains some EVP_PKEY_CTX_set_rsa_padding() calls but no calls involving OSSL_ASYM_CIPHER_PARAM_PAD_MODE, except in the RSA implementation code.

4. The next thing we should do is read the input data. But how much should we read? We know that RSA with padding can encrypt slightly less than the key size bytes in one encryption operation. We can try to read and encrypt the key size bytes. If the encryption operation fails because the input was too long, we will discover it from the encryption error.

Let's discover the key size, allocate input and output buffers of the appropriate size, and read the input data:

```
size_t pkey_size = EVP_PKEY_get_size(pkey);
unsigned char* in_buf  = malloc(pkey_size);
unsigned char* out_buf = malloc(pkey_size);
size_t in_nbytes = fread(in_buf, 1, pkey_size, in_file);
```

5. Asymmetric encryption of the input data is done using the EVP_PKEY_encrypt() function:

```
size_t out_nbytes = pkey_size;
EVP_PKEY_encrypt(
    ctx, out_buf, &out_nbytes, in_buf, in_nbytes);
```

6. The encrypted data should be written into the output file:

```
fwrite(out_buf, 1, out_nbytes, out_file);
```

7. After the work is done, we have to deallocate the used buffers and objects:

```
free(out_buf);
free(in_buf);
EVP_PKEY_CTX_free(ctx);
EVP_PKEY_free(pkey);
```

The complete source code of our rsa-encrypt program can be found on GitHub as the rsa-encrypt.c file: https://github.com/PacktPublishing/Demystifying-Cryptography-with-OpenSSL-3/blob/main/Chapter06/rsa-encrypt.c.

Running the rsa-encrypt program

Let's run the rsa-encrypt program and encrypt the 32-byte session key file that we created before:

```
$ ./rsa-encrypt \
    session_key.bin \
    session_key.bin.encrypted \
    rsa_public_key.pem
Encryption succeeded
```

Our program reported success; let's check the files:

```
$ cksum session_key.bin*
186975932 32 session_key.bin
390548196 512 session_key.bin.encrypted
```

So far so good – our program has created the `session_key.bin.encrypted` file of the right size. I promised that our program would be interoperable with `openssl pkeyutl`. Let's check it:

```
$ openssl pkeyutl \
    -decrypt \
    -in session_key.bin.encrypted \
    -out session_key.bin.decrypted \
    -inkey rsa_keypair.pem \
    -pkeyopt rsa_padding_mode:oaep
```

No errors are reported.

Let's check the files and their checksums:

```
$ cksum session_key.bin*
186975932 32 session_key.bin
186975932 32 session_key.bin.decrypted
2324953448 512 session_key.bin.encrypted
```

As we can observe, the sizes and checksums of `session_key.bin` and `session_key.bin.decrypted` match, meaning that `openssl pkeyutl` can successfully decrypt the file encrypted by the `rsa-encrypt` program.

I have mentioned error handling but have not shown any error handling code so far. I do so because I do not want the error handling code to clutter the code fragments, although the full complete source code on GitHub contains error handling. Error handling for OpenSSL is a topic in its own right and deserves a whole section in this chapter. Let's advance to this section, where we will also discuss the OpenSSL error queue.

Understanding the OpenSSL error queue

When running the `rsa-encrypt` program, many things can go wrong, such as the following:

- The public key file may be corrupted or not contain a key. In this case, key loading will fail.
- The public key file may contain a non-RSA key. In this case, key loading will succeed, but encryption will fail.
- The input file may be too big. In this case, encryption will also fail but for another reason.

How do we handle such errors? Those OpenSSL functions that can fail usually indicate so by returning NULL, 0, or a negative number. Success is usually indicated by returning 1. Some functions also add an error to the OpenSSL error queue on failure.

The OpenSSL error queue is a container for errors that the OpenSSL library wants to report. *Every thread of the process has its own OpenSSL error queue.* The error queue does not require initialization or uninitialization; OpenSSL automatically handles it. Every thread starts with an empty error queue. The error queue stores errors until they are taken out of the queue or the thread finishes execution. Therefore, it is a good idea to check the error queue, handle the errors, and if needed, clear the queue after calls to OpenSSL.

Not all functions put errors into the error queue on failure – for example, I was unable to get any errors into the OpenSSL error queue on symmetric decryption failure and HMAC calculation initialization failure. But OpenSSL functions handling asymmetric cryptography, X.509 certificates, or TLS usually support the error queue and put errors there on failure. Some functions, especially those that verify X.509 certificates, can put several errors into the error queue during one call.

Here are some popular functions for interacting with the OpenSSL error queue:

- ERR_get_error(): Get the code of the earliest error in the queue and remove that error from the queue.

- ERR_peek_error(): Get the code of the earliest error in the queue but leave that error in the queue.

- ERR_GET_LIB() and ERR_GET_REASON(): Get components of the code returned by ERR_get_error() or ERR_peek_error().

- ERR_error_string_n(): Make a human-readable error string from the error code.

- ERR_clear_error(): Clear the queue and remove all the errors from it.

- ERR_print_errors_fp(): Print the error queue to a FILE stream and clear the queue. Note that while this function is very convenient for debugging, it cannot indicate failure if it fails to print the error queue – for example, if the FILE stream writes to a filesystem and the disk is full. The ERR_print_errors_fp() function neither returns an error code nor puts an error into the error queue because its task is to also clear the queue.

- I find this failure to report failures in a failure handling function a bit ironic, even though I find the behavior of this function logical.

It is important to understand that exit codes returned by OpenSSL functions are not the same as error codes contained in the errors that are put into the error queue – for example, if input for RSA encryption is too long, the EVP_PKEY_encrypt() function returns the 0 *exit code* and puts an error into the error queue with the 0x200006E *error code*, which consists of the following components:

- A library number provided by ERR_GET_LIB(): 4, which is ERR_R_RSA_LIB

- A reason code provided by ERR_GET_REASON(): 0x6E, which is 110, which is RSA_R_DATA_TOO_LARGE_FOR_KEY_SIZE

Here is sample code for getting the earliest error from the error queue and printing the error information:

```
unsigned long error_code = ERR_get_error();
printf("Error code: %lX\n", error_code);
printf("Library number: %i\n", ERR_GET_LIB(error_code));
printf("Reason code: %X\n", ERR_GET_REASON(error_code));
```

The sample code provided will print the library number and the reason code as numbers. But where can we find their symbolic representations, such as ERR_R_RSA_LIB and RSA_R_DATA_TOO_LARGE_FOR_KEY_SIZE? Unfortunately, I could not find the answer in the OpenSSL documentation, but I could find the answer in the OpenSSL library headers. The list of library numbers can be found in the err.h header, and the list of library-specific reason codes can be found in the library-specific error header file – for example, for the RSA sub-library, the library-specific error header file is rsaerr.h.

The ERR_get_error(), ERR_peek_error(), ERR_GET_LIB(), and ERR_GET_REASON() functions provide a way for sophisticated error handling of OpenSSL calls. But what if we want something quick and easy for debugging? Then, we can use the ERR_print_errors_fp() function. We can do it just like this:

```
ERR_print_errors_fp(stderr);
```

The error queue will be printed to stderr and cleared.

That's how the ERR_print_errors_fp() function is used in the source code of our rsa-encrypt program:

```
if (ERR_peek_error()) {
    exit_code = 1;
    if (error_stream) {
        fprintf(
            error_stream,
            "Errors from the OpenSSL error queue:\n");
        ERR_print_errors_fp(error_stream);
    }
}
```

Let's try to run `rsa-encrypt` with an input that is too long:

```
$ seq 20000 >somefile.txt
$ ./rsa-encrypt \
    somefile.txt \
    somefile.txt.encrypted \
    rsa_public_key.pem
EVP_API error
Errors from the OpenSSL error queue:
806B3E2A797F0000:error:
  0200006E:rsa routines:
  ossl_rsa_padding_add_PKCS1_OAEP_mgf1_ex:
  data too large for key size:
  crypto/rsa/rsa_oaep.c:87:
Encryption failed
```

We have got the same printout from the OpenSSL error queue that `openssl pkeyutl` prints on the same error. There is a lot of information for one error, but some part of the long error string is human-readable:

```
    data too large for key size
```

You can find more information on OpenSSL call error handling on the OpenSSL man pages:

```
$ man ERR_get_error
$ man ERR_GET_LIB
$ man ERR_error_string_n
$ man ERR_print_errors_fp
$ man ERR_clear_error
```

It is, of course, up to you how you are going to handle errors from the OpenSSL calls. But as a responsible programmer, you should not forget to process and clear the OpenSSL error queue after failures.

Imagine that you performed several operations with OpenSSL. For most operations, function exit codes were enough for you, and you forgot to clear the error queue, but for the last failed operation, you want to get the error from the queue. The queue, however, now contains errors from all your performed operations. How are you going to find the errors for the last operation among all the other errors? There is no good way. Therefore, you should start your operation with an empty error queue. By *operation* here, I don't necessarily mean a single call to OpenSSL. An operation may contain several calls, but it should represent a logical piece of work so that you are comfortable with processing all the operation's errors at once.

When is it better to clear the OpenSSL error queue – before or after the operation? Different people have different opinions on it. One opinion is that the error queue should be cleared after the operation because a responsible programmer should clean after themselves and not *leak* errors. Another opinion is that clearing the error queue before the operation is better because it ensures an empty error queue before the operation. I prefer to clear the queue both before and after the operation – after because it is responsible, and before because in complex projects where many people are contributing, one or more persons will sometimes forget to clear the error queue after themselves. Humans make mistakes; it's the sad truth of life and software development.

Alright, enough with philosophy. It's now time to learn how to decrypt with RSA using C code.

How to decrypt with RSA programmatically

In this section, we are going to develop a small rsa-decrypt program, so that we can learn how to do RSA decryption.

Our program will take three command-line arguments similar to those taken by `rsa-encrypt`, but note that the third argument is the name of a file containing a keypair, not just a public key:

1. The input filename
2. The output filename
3. The RSA keypair filename

Of course, now the input file is expected to contain ciphertext, which will be decrypted, and the resulting plaintext will be written into the output file.

Our high-level implementation plan for `rsa-decrypt` will contain the sequence of actions opposite to that of `rsa-encrypt`, listed as follows:

1. Load an RSA keypair from the RSA keypair file. We need an RSA private key for decryption; a public key will not be enough.
2. Create the EVP_PKEY context from the key.
3. Initialize the EVP_PKEY context for decryption and set the OAEP padding mode.
4. Read ciphertext from the input file.
5. Decrypt the ciphertext.
6. Write the produced plaintext into the output file.

Implementing the rsa-decrypt program

Let's implement the `rsa-decrypt` program according to our plan, step by step:

1. First, load the RSA keypair:

    ```
    const char* pkey_fname = argv[3];
    FILE* pkey_file = fopen(pkey_fname, "rb");
    EVP_PKEY* pkey = PEM_read_PrivateKey(
        pkey_file, NULL, NULL, NULL);
    ```

    Note that the same type, EVP_PKEY, is used for holding either a public key or a whole keypair.

2. Next, create the EVP_PKEY context from the loaded keypair:

    ```
    EVP_PKEY_CTX* ctx = EVP_PKEY_CTX_new_from_pkey(
        NULL, pkey, NULL);
    ```

3. Then, initialize EVP_PKEY_CTX and set the padding mode:

    ```
    EVP_PKEY_decrypt_init(ctx);
    EVP_PKEY_CTX_set_rsa_padding(ctx, RSA_PKCS1_OAEP_
    PADDING);
    ```

4. Find out the key size, allocate input and output buffers of the appropriate size, and read the input data:

    ```
    size_t pkey_size = EVP_PKEY_get_size(pkey);
    unsigned char* in_buf  = malloc(pkey_size);
    unsigned char* out_buf = malloc(pkey_size);
    size_t in_nbytes = fread(in_buf, 1, pkey_size, in_file);
    ```

5. Decrypt the obtained ciphertext using the EVP_PKEY_decrypt() function:

    ```
    size_t out_nbytes = pkey_size;
    EVP_PKEY_decrypt(
        ctx, out_buf, &out_nbytes, in_buf, in_nbytes);
    ```

6. Write the decrypted data into the output file:

    ```
    fwrite(out_buf, 1, out_nbytes, out_file);
    ```

7. After the work is done, we have to deallocate the used buffers and objects:

    ```
    free(out_buf);
    free(in_buf);
    ```

```
EVP_PKEY_CTX_free(ctx);
EVP_PKEY_free(pkey);
```

The complete source code of our `rsa-decrypt` program can be found on GitHub as the `rsa-decrypt.c` file: `https://github.com/PacktPublishing/Demystifying-Cryptography-with-OpenSSL-3/blob/main/Chapter06/rsa-decrypt.c`.

Running the rsa-decrypt program

Let's run the `rsa-decrypt` program and decrypt the previous encrypted session key file that we created before:

```
$ ./rsa-decrypt \
    session_key.bin.encrypted \
    session_key.bin.decrypted \
    rsa_keypair.pem
Decryption succeeded
```

Our program reported success. Let's check the files and their checksums:

```
$ cksum session_key.bin*
186975932 32 session_key.bin
186975932 32 session_key.bin.decrypted
2324953448 512 session_key.bin.encrypted
```

As we can see, the sizes and checksums of `session_key.bin` and `session_key.bin.decrypted` match, meaning that our `rsa-decrypt` can successfully decrypt the session key file.

Summary

In this chapter, we learned about the concept of asymmetric cryptography. Then, we learned about the concept of an MITM attack and also how to mitigate that attack. After that, we learned what a session key is. We finished the theoretical part by learning about RSA security, the trade-off between security and performance, and what RSA key size to choose.

In the practical part, we learned how to encrypt and decrypt with RSA on the command line. Then, we learned how to encrypt and decrypt with RSA programmatically in C code. We also learned about the OpenSSL error queue and how to check it for errors.

In the next chapter, we will continue learning about asymmetric cryptography. Particularly, we will learn about digital signatures and their verification.

7

Digital Signatures and Their Verification

In this chapter, we will learn about **digital signatures** and how to sign content and verify the signature later. Digital signatures have many important practical applications, such as signing documents, certificates, software, and network requests and responses, including financial transactions. Digital signatures are also important for the security of cryptocurrencies, such as Bitcoin and others. Digital signature algorithms are a necessary building block for client and server identity verification in secure network protocols, such as *TLS*, *SSH*, and *IPsec*. Digital signatures are used both in the *TLS* protocol handshake and for signing **X.509 certificates**, which are used for identity presentation and verification in *TLS*. More information about X.509 certificates will be provided in *Chapter 8, X.509 Certificates and PKI*. The TLS protocol will be covered in *Part 4, TLS Connections and Secure Communication*. Digital signatures are also used in secure messaging standards, such as **Pretty Good Privacy (PGP)** and **Secure Multipurpose Mail Extensions (S/MIME)**. For example, OpenSSL releases are signed by *PGP* digital signatures.

We will also provide an overview of the digital signature algorithms that are supported by OpenSSL and recommendations on which digital signature schemes to use and which to avoid. In the practical part of this chapter, we will learn how to digitally sign content and verify the produced signature on the command line and programmatically using C code.

In this chapter, we are going to cover the following topics:

- Understanding digital signatures
- Overview of digital signature algorithms supported by OpenSSL
- How to generate an elliptic curve keypair
- How to sign and verify a signature on the command line
- How to sign programmatically
- How to verify a signature programmatically

Technical requirements

This chapter will contain commands that you can run on a command line and C source code that you can build and run. For the command-line commands, you will need the `openssl` command-line tool, as well as some OpenSSL dynamic libraries. To build the C code, you will need OpenSSL dynamic or static libraries, library headers, a C compiler, and a linker.

We will implement some example programs in this chapter, in order to practice what we are learning. The full source code of those programs can be found here: `https://github.com/PacktPublishing/Demystifying-Cryptography-with-OpenSSL-3/tree/main/Chapter07`

Understanding digital signatures

A digital signature is an array of bits that provides cryptographically strong guarantees of authenticity, integrity, and non-repudiation of a digital message. What do those guarantees mean? Let's take a look:

- **Authenticity** means that the message is coming from the claimed sender, provided that only the claimed sender possesses the private key that was used to produce the signature.

- **Integrity** means that the message has not been changed by a third party during transmission, for example.

- **Non-repudiation** means that the sender cannot deny that they produced the signature, provided that no one else has had access to the private key that was used to produce the signature.

A digital signature is produced using a *private key* that can be verified using the corresponding *public key*. Hence, digital signature and verification algorithms are considered **asymmetric cryptography algorithms**, even though they are not **asymmetric encryption algorithms**.

It is important to know that when a message is signed, usually, the digital signature algorithm is not applied to the message itself. Instead, the signature algorithm is applied to the *message digest*, which is produced by some cryptographic hash functions, such as SHA-256. Cryptographers say that such signature schemes are based on the **hash-and-sign** paradigm.

A notable and arguable exception is the EdDSA signature algorithm. It's notable because it is the only popular signature algorithm that takes the whole message instead of its digest as the input. It's arguable because EdDSA internally hashes the input message anyway, albeit in a more sophisticated manner than hashing is done for other signature algorithms.

So, why is a message digest signed instead of the message itself? The reasons are the same as why a session key is used for asymmetric encryption. Asymmetric crypto algorithms are relatively slow – much slower than cryptographic hash functions. A fast hashing algorithm transforms a potentially very long input message into a short message digest of known length so that a slow digital signature algorithm would not need to process a lot of input. Such separation of work improves performance, compared to if the whole long message needs to be processed by the signature algorithm. Another reason is that a digital signature algorithm can only sign a limited volume of data in one block. It is inconvenient to split the message into several blocks with several signatures and invent a secure method of chaining the produced signatures and resisting various order-changing attacks.

Note how *effective and performant* asymmetric cryptography builds on top of symmetric cryptography. Asymmetric encryption uses symmetric session keys, while digital signatures use message digests. Therefore, it is important to learn about *symmetric* cryptography before *asymmetric* cryptography.

Difference between digital signatures and MACs

As we can see, digital signatures have something in common with **Message Authentication Codes** (**MACs**). Both digital signatures and MACs can provide authentication and integrity. However, there are some important differences:

- Digital signatures are produced using asymmetric private keys and verified using public keys. MACs use the same symmetric key to produce an authentication tag and its verification.

- It is possible to verify a digital signature without the signer giving away its secret private key. Anyone possessing the public key can verify the signature. With a MAC, the same secret key must be possessed by both the signer and the verifier. Only the verifier can verify that the message is coming from the claimed sender and only if the verifier did not authenticate the same message. A third party cannot verify the message. If there are several verifiers, it becomes even more difficult to verify the origin of the message, not only because of the claimed sender but also because any verifier possessing the same secret key could authenticate the message.

- Unlike digital signatures, MACs do not provide non-repudiation. For any message that the sender authenticated, they can claim that it was the verifier who authenticated it.

Now that we understand what a digital signature is, let's find out what kind of digital signature algorithms are provided by OpenSSL.

Overview of digital signature algorithms supported by OpenSSL

In this section, we will review the digital signature algorithms that are supported by OpenSSL and give some recommendations on which algorithms to use.

Reviewing RSA

The **Rivest-Shamir-Adleman** (**RSA**) algorithm was invented by Ronald Rivest, Adi Shamir, and Leonard Adleman. Ronald Rivest is the same person who invented symmetric encryption algorithms from the **RC** family and message digest algorithms from the **MD** family. The RSA algorithm was first published in 1977. It was the first popular asymmetric crypto algorithm.

RSA is quite a universal algorithm since it can both encrypt and sign messages. RSA is the slowest algorithm to sign but the fastest to verify for the same security level among the digital signature algorithms provided by OpenSSL.

The speed of both signing and verification depends on the key size. The signing speed quickly drops with the growth of the key size. The verification speed also drops, but not as quickly. Verification is 30-70 times faster than signing, depending on the key size.

RSA produces the largest signatures. An RSA signature is the same size as the key size that was used to produce the signature. For example, a signature that was produced by a 4,096-bit key will have a size of 4,096 bits or 512 bytes. Signatures produced by other algorithms are significantly smaller.

Another disadvantage of RSA is that RSA keys are much longer than keys of more modern **Elliptic Curve (EC)**-based algorithms. Also, to gain just a few bits of security, the size of an RSA key must be increased substantially.

RSA is quite an old algorithm. OpenSSL supports another old algorithm, DSA.

Reviewing DSA

The **Digital Signature Algorithm (DSA)** was invented by David W. Kravitz while he was working for the **National Security Agency (NSA)** of the United States. The DSA was first published in 1991 when NIST proposed the DSA for use in their **Digital Signature Standard (DSS)**.

The security of the DSA relies on the computational difficulty of the discrete logarithm problem. Like RSA, the DSA uses long keys, such as 2,048-bit keys. As with RSA, the security level of a DSA key is much lower than its length. DSA keys happen to have the same security level as RSA keys of the same lengths. Hence, a table that maps RSA key length to its security level, as shown in *Chapter 6, Asymmetric Encryption and Decryption*, can also be used to find out DSA key security. For example, a 2,048-bit DSA key would have a security level of 112 bits.

The first DSS, adopted as FIPS-186 in 1994, only allowed DSA to be used with the SHA-1 hash function and key lengths up to 1,024 bits. The latest DSS, FIPS 186-4 from 2013, also allows us to use DSA with the SHA-224 and SHA-256 hash functions and key lengths up to 3,072 bits. OpenSSL supports DSA via all three aforementioned hash functions and keys with very long lengths. In my opinion, however, you should not need a DSA key that's longer than 4,096 bits.

Even though DSA keys are long, like RSA keys, they produce a signature much shorter than the key length. A DSA's signature length, in bits, is *approximately* 4*K_bits, where K_bits is the security strength of the used DSA key. For example, a 4,096-bit RSA key produces a 512-byte signature, but a DSA key of the same length produces a 70- or 71-byte signature.

Currently, the DSA is not a very popular algorithm and is being superseded by ECDSA.

Reviewing ECDSA

The **Elliptic Curve Digital Signature Algorithm** (**ECDSA**) is a variant of the DSA algorithm that uses **Elliptic Curve Cryptography** (**ECC**). ECC is a form of public key cryptography that is based on the algebraic structure of elliptic curves over finite fields. ECC was invented by Neal Koblitz and Victor Miller in 1985. ECDSA was proposed by Scott Vanstone in 1992 as a comment on the first DSS standard.

ECDSA's advantage over DSA is that it has a shorter key size for the same security level. The security level of an elliptic curve key is approximately half of the key length. For example, a 224-bit key has a 112-bit security level. For comparison, a DSA key with the same security level must be as long as 2,048 bits. As with DSA, the ECDSA signature length, in bits, is *approximately* 4*K_bits, where K_bits is the security strength of the used ECDSA key.

When you're generating an ECDSA key, you have to choose a curve. A curve has a name and defines how long an EC key will be when the key is generated based on that curve. For instance, a key generated based on the NIST P-256 curve will have a length of 256 bits. OpenSSL supports NIST curves and Brainpool curves. NIST curves are developed by NSA and standardized by NIST. Brainpool curves are proposed by the Brainpool workgroup, a group of cryptographers that were dissatisfied with NIST curves because NIST curves were not verifiably randomly generated, so they may have intentionally or accidentally weak security. Brainpool curves are standardized and used by the Federal Office for Information Security of Germany (Bundesamt für Sicherheit in der Informationstechnik, BSI). The Brainpool workgroup defined a method of verifiably randomly generating elliptic curves and claimed that the workgroup generated Brainpool curves using that method. However, a research group led by Daniel J. Bernstein tried to verify the Brainpool workgroup method and could not generate the same Brainpool curves using the described method. Bernstein's group later proposed their own elliptic curves and own EC signature algorithm called EdDSA. More details on EdDSA curves will be provided in the next section.

Despite these doubts, NIST curves are currently the most popular curves for ECDSA. The NIST curve suite includes two very fast curves: the P-256 curve and the P-224 curve. The NIST P-256 curve is 16 times faster than the Brainpool P256r1 curve when signing and five times faster when verifying a signature. The NIST P-224 curve, comparable in security to 2,048-bit DSA, is approximately five times faster than DSA-2048 when signing and two times faster when verifying. Other NIST curves have speeds comparable to Brainpool curves of similar security, meaning that sometimes, NIST curves are faster, while other times, Brainpool curves are faster.

It is important to mention that the standard implementation of ECDSA needs a good **Random Number Generator** (**RNG**) both for key generation and during the signing process. There is also an alternative implementation of ECDSA that does not need random data generation when signing that uses the hash of the private key instead of random data. A faulty RNG during signing may result in leaking the private key via the signature. Care should be taken while implementing ECDSA properly; otherwise, an implementation may be vulnerable to a timing attack that may also reveal the private key. OpenSSL once had an implementation that was vulnerable to a timing attack, but the vulnerability was fixed in 2011.

ECDSA is quite a popular algorithm, but it has a competitor: another EC-based signature algorithm, called EdDSA.

Reviewing EdDSA

Edwards-curve Digital Signature Algorithm (EdDSA) is another signature algorithm that uses elliptic curves. It was published in 2011 by a group of cryptographers led by Daniel J. Bernstein, the same person that developed the ChaCha symmetric stream cipher family and the Poly1305 MAC algorithm.

EdDSA is based on **twisted Edwards curves** and aims to be both faster and easier to implement securely than ECDSA. Unlike ECDSA, EdDSA does not need RNG during signing and thus cannot leak private keys because of bad RNG.

EdDSA supports two curves: the 253-bit Curve25519 and the 456-bit Curve448. Those curves are designed for good security, attempting to make it difficult to make implementation mistakes that may weaken security. The curves are also immune to timing attacks.

As with ECDSA, the security level of EdDSA signatures is half of the key length, meaning 126.5 bits for Curve25519 and 228 bits for Curve448. The signature length for Curve25519 is 64 bytes, while for Cruve448, it is 114 bytes.

Even though Curve25519 and Ed448 are designed for speed, they are not faster than the NIST P-256 curve. NIST P-256 is approximately two times faster than Curve25519, both for signing and signature verification. The NIST P-224 curve has about the same speed as Curve25519. However, Curve25519 is 8-13 times faster than other NIST and Brainpool curves of comparable security for signing, and 2-9 times faster than them for verification. Curve448 is approximately two times faster than NIST and Brainpool curves of comparable security for signing and 1.5-3 times faster for verification.

EdDSA is an unusual digital signature algorithm. Usual signature algorithms expect input in the form of a cryptographic hash of the input data. For clarity, the input data is the data to be signed. On the contrary, EdDSA expects the whole input data as input but allows the algorithm's user to provide a so-called prehash function that will be applied to the input data before further processing.

A prehash function can be an actual cryptographic hash function, such as SHA-256. Such a variant of EdDSA is called **HashEdDSA**. The HashEdDSA variant is the most similar to traditional signature algorithms because it feeds the input data hash to further processing. A prehash function can also be the identity function, the function that just returns its input. Such a variant of EdDSA is called **PureEdDSA**.

It's worth noting that the EdDSA algorithm internally uses the SHA-512 hash function when using Curve25519 and the SHAKE256 function when using Curve448. Hence, in the case of HashEdDSA, the input data will be hashed twice. Should PureEdDSA always be used, then? No, it's not that easy – please read on.

Another difference between EdDSA and the traditional signature algorithms is that EdDSA is a two-pass algorithm, which means it processes the input data twice. This means, in turn, that PureEdDSA does not support streamed input data, unlike traditional signature algorithms. If the input data is long and coming from slow storage or requested via an expensive network connection, PureEdDSA may not be the best choice.

OpenSSL 3.0 only supports the PureEdDSA variant of EdDSA and requires all the data to be put into memory for hashing. This can be problematic if the input data is very long, and memory is scarce. On the other hand, even though HashEdDSA is not directly supported by OpenSSL yet, the programmer can hash the input data themself first and then use PureEdDSA for further processing.

Now, let's look at the last signature algorithm we will review – SM2.

Reviewing SM2

Shang Mi 2 (**SM2**) is another elliptic curve-based digital signature algorithm. It is a national standard of the People's Republic of China. SM2 was invented by Xiaoyun Wang et al. and standardized by the Chinese Commercial Cryptography Administration Office in 2012.

SM2 only supports one curve: the 256-bit CurveSM2. CurveSM2's speed for signing and verifying is about the same as that of 256-bit Brainpool curves. The signature length for CurveSM2 is 71 bytes.

The SM2 signature algorithm is usually used with a 256-bit SM3 hash function. OpenSSL also supports combining SM2 only with SM3 in its high-level APIs.

As we can see, OpenSSL supports several digital signature algorithms. But which should you choose? Let's talk about it in the next subsection.

Which digital signature algorithm should you choose?

Recently, the EdDSA algorithm and Curve25519 have become quite popular. Curve25519 appears to be trusted by many security experts. If your data to be signed always fits into memory and you do not need compatibility with old software, choose EdDSA. It is worth mentioning that, at the time of this writing, major **Certificate Authorities** do not issue EdDSA-based X.509 certificates yet. Hence, if you need a TLS certificate for a server on the internet, you will need to choose a certificate that's been signed with another algorithm, for the time being.

If you want a more traditional signature algorithm or want to support streaming, then choose ECDSA, which is also very popular.

If you need interoperability with old software, or if you need very fast signature verification, then choose RSA.

With that, we have learned about different digital signature algorithms supported by OpenSSL and recommendations on which algorithm to use in which situation. That concludes the theoretical part of this chapter. The next section will be practical. There, we will learn how to generate an EC keypair and how to sign some data on the command line.

How to generate an elliptic curve keypair

I want to demonstrate the traditional approach to digital signatures when a message digest of the input data is signed. Hence, we will use ECDSA, not EdDSA, in our examples.

As we already know, a new keypair can be generated using the `openssl genpkey` subcommand. We will generate an EC keypair of the longest length available in OpenSSL, 570 bits, based on the NIST B-571 curve:

```
$ openssl genpkey \
    -algorithm EC \
    -pkeyopt ec_paramgen_curve:secp521r1 \
    -out ec_keypair.pem
```

Here, we have used the `-pkeyopt ec_paramgen_curve:secp521r1` switch to specify that we want to use the NIST B-571 curve. Which other curve names could be used instead of `secp521r1`? The full list of supported curves can be obtained using the following command:

```
$ openssl ecparam -list_curves
```

Once the keypair has been generated and written into the `ec_keypair.pem` file, we can inspect its structure:

```
$ openssl pkey -in ec_keypair.pem -noout -text
Private-Key: (570 bit)
priv:
    … hex values …
pub:
    … hex values …
ASN1 OID: sect571r1
NIST CURVE: B-571
```

As we can see, an EC keypair's structure is simpler than an RSA keypair's structure. It's just two long values – a private part and a public part.

Extracting the public key from the keypair can be done similarly to how we did it for RSA in *Chapter 6, Asymmetric Encryption and Decryption*:

```
$ openssl pkey \
    -in ec_keypair.pem \
    -pubout \
    -out ec_public_key.pem
```

Let's inspect the structure of the extracted public key:

```
$ openssl pkey -in ec_public_key.pem -pubin -noout -text
Public-Key: (570 bit)
pub:
    … hex values …
ASN1 OID: sect571r1
NIST CURVE: B-571
```

Here, we can see that the public key contains the same pub value as in the keypair and, naturally, does not contain the priv part.

To digitally *sign*, you need a *private key*, and to *verify* the signature, you need a *public key*. As a reminder, you should never share your private key or keypair. You should only distribute your public key.

As we explained in *Chapter 6, Asymmetric Encryption and Decryption*, when OpenSSL documentation mentions a private key, usually, it means a keypair. Also, there is no command-line command to extract the private part from a keypair. This can only be done programmatically by knowing how an EC key is constructed in the C code and picking up the right data. But extracting the private key from a keypair does not make much sense in practice because when OpenSSL needs a private key, it can use the whole keypair. If you need to sign something using OpenSSL, either on the command line or programmatically, just supply the whole keypair to OpenSSL – do not bother extracting the private key.

With that, we have generated our elliptic curve keypair. Now, let's sign something.

How to sign and verify a signature on the command line

OpenSSL provides several subcommands for signing and verifying signatures. Let's take a look:

- The deprecated RSA-specific openssl rsautl subcommand.

- The openssl dgst subcommand: This is usually used for message digest calculation but can also be used to sign the produced digests. This means that it cannot be used to sign PureEdDSA because that signature algorithm does not sign digests.

- The openssl pkeyutl subcommand: This subcommand can be used to sign with any signature algorithm supported by OpenSSL. Before OpenSSL 3.0, openssl pkeyutl did not support signing long inputs; the user had to make the message digest before signing. Since OpenSSL 3.0, openssl pkeyutl supports both "raw input," as it is called in the documentation, and a message digest as input.

We are going to use the openssl pkeyutl subcommand for our examples. Its documentation can be found on the openssl-pkeyutl man page:

```
man openssl-pkeyutl
```

Follow these steps to sign and verify a signature on the command line:

1. First, let's generate a file with sample data that we are going to sign:

```
$ seq 20000 >somefile.txt
```

2. Now, let's sign the sample file using the SHA3-512 hash function and the EC keypair that we have already generated:

```
$ openssl pkeyutl \
    -sign \
    -digest sha3-512 \
    -inkey ec_keypair.pem \
    -in somefile.txt \
    -rawin \
    -out somefile.txt.signature
```

3. Let's check the filesystem:

```
$ cksum somefile.txt*
3231941463 108894 somefile.txt
2915754802 151 somefile.txt.signature
```

The output of this operation is a 151 bytes long signature written to the somefile.txt. signature file.

4. Now, if we share the original somefile.txt file, the signature in somefile.txt. signature, and our public key in ec_public_key.pem, anyone can verify the signature. That's how it is done on the command line:

```
$ openssl pkeyutl \
    -verify \
    -digest sha3-512 \
    -inkey ec_keypair.pem \
    -in somefile.txt \
    -rawin \
    -sigfile somefile.txt.signature
Signature Verified Successfully
```

Note that we used the -sign switch for signing and the -verify switch for signature verification.

5. What if the signed data was modified during transmission? Let's simulate such a situation by appending some data to the signed data and trying to verify it again:

```
$ echo "additional data" >> somefile.txt
$ openssl pkeyutl \
    -verify \
    -digest sha3-512 \
    -inkey ec_keypair.pem \
    -in somefile.txt \
    -rawin \
    -sigfile somefile.txt.signature
Signature Verification Failure
```

As we can see, the signature verification failed in this case. We have observed that if the signed data remains intact – that is, the signature verification succeeds, but the signed data has been altered – the signature verification procedure detects it and reports a failure.

Now that we've learned how to digitally sign and verify the produced signature on the command line, let's learn how to do it programmatically.

How to sign programmatically

OpenSSL 3.0 provides the following APIs for digital signatures:

- Legacy low-level APIs that consist of functions with algorithm-specific prefixes, such as RSA_, DSA_, and ECDSA_. These APIs have been deprecated since OpenSSL 3.0.

- The EVP_PKEY API: This API is not deprecated but is still low level. It is more convenient to use a high-level API.

- The EVP_Sign API: This API is high level but has some disadvantages. This API uses the key argument only after the whole input data has been read and hashed. Therefore, if there is a problem with the key, it will be discovered later rather than sooner. Another disadvantage is that this API is inflexible and does not allow you to set signing parameters to PKEY_CTX if the signature algorithm supports them. The OpenSSL documentation does not recommend this API.

- The EVP_DigestSign API: This is a high-level API where drawbacks of the EVP_Sign API have been fixed. The OpenSSL documentation recommends this API, so we are going to use it here.

We are going to develop a small ec-sign program that signs a file using the ECDSA algorithm, similar to how we signed with openssl pkeyutl in the previous section. Our program is going to be interoperable with pkeyutl, meaning that pkeyutl will be able to verify the signature that's produced by our program.

Here are some relevant manual pages for the API that we are going to use:

```
$ man PEM_read_PrivateKey
$ man PEM_read_PUBKEY
$ man EVP_DigestSignInit_ex
$ man EVP_DigestVerifyInit_ex
```

Our program will take three command-line arguments:

1. The name of the input file containing the data to be signed
2. The name of the output file where the signature will be written
3. The name of the file containing the signing keypair

Our high-level implementation plan will be as follows:

1. Load the keypair from the keypair file.
2. Create an EVP_MD_CTX object that will be used as the signing context.
3. Initialize the signing context with the hash function name and the loaded keypair.
4. Read the data to be signed chunk by chunk and feed it to the signing context.
5. Discover the signature length and allocate memory for the signature.
6. Finalize the signing and get the signature.
7. Write the signature into the output signature file.

Now it's time to implement our plan by writing the necessary code.

Implementing the ec-sign program

Let's get started with the implementation:

1. First, load the keypair:

```
const char* pkey_fname = argv[3];
FILE* pkey_file = fopen(pkey_fname, "rb");
EVP_PKEY* pkey = PEM_read_PrivateKey(
    pkey_file, NULL, NULL, NULL);
```

2. Then, create the EVP_MD_CTX signing context and initialize it with the SHA3-512 hash function and the loaded keypair:

```
EVP_MD_CTX* md_ctx = EVP_MD_CTX_new();
EVP_DigestSignInit_ex(
        md_ctx,
        NULL,
        OSSL_DIGEST_NAME_SHA3_512,
        NULL,
        NULL,
        pkey,
        NULL);
```

3. Then, the signing context initialization is created. Let's feed the input data to the context:

```
const char* in_fname = argv[1];
FILE* in_file = fopen(in_fname, "rb");
while (!feof(in_file)) {
    size_t in_nbytes = fread(in_buf, 1, BUF_SIZE, in_
file);
    EVP_DigestSignUpdate(md_ctx, in_buf, in_nbytes);
}
```

Once all the data has been fed to the context, we have to finalize the signing process and get the signature. But we don't know how much memory to allocate for the signature buffer!

4. Fortunately, the EVP_DigestSignFinal() function will give us the signature length if we supply NULL as the signature buffer pointer:

```
size_t sig_len = 0;
EVP_DigestSignFinal(md_ctx, NULL, &sig_len);
```

Note that EVP_DigestSignFinal() is not the only OpenSSL function that can indicate the desired output buffer length this way. Many other OpenSSL functions will also write the wanted buffer length at the supplied length pointer if the supplied buffer pointer is NULL.

5. Now, we know the signature length and can allocate memory for the signature:

```
unsigned char* sig_buf = malloc(sig_len);
```

6. With that, we have a place to store the signature and can finally get it:

    ```
    EVP_DigestSignFinal(md_ctx, sig_buf, &sig_len);
    ```

    Note that this time, we supply `sig_buf` instead of NULL as the target signature buffer into the `EVP_DigestSignFinal()` function.

    Instead of using the `EVP_DigestSignInit_ex()`, `EVP_DigestSignUpdate()`, and `EVP_DigestSignFinal()` functions, we could use a one-shot function called `EVP_DigestSign()`, if all our data to be signed can be loaded into one contiguous buffer. We don't have to do it with ECDSA, but it would be the only way to make a PureEdDSA signature in OpenSSL 3.0.

7. Now that we have got the signature, let's write it into the output file:

    ```
    const char* sig_fname = argv[2];
    sig_file = fopen(sig_fname, "wb");
    fwrite(sig_buf, 1, sig_len, sig_file);
    ```

8. Finally, let's free buffers and objects to avoid memory leaks:

    ```
    free(sig_buf);
    free(in_buf);
    EVP_MD_CTX_free(md_ctx);
    EVP_PKEY_free(pkey);
    ```

The complete source code for our `ec-sign` program can be found on GitHub in the `ec-sign.c` file: `https://github.com/PacktPublishing/Demystifying-Cryptography-with-OpenSSL-3/blob/main/Chapter07/ec-sign.c`.

Running the ec-sign program

Let's run our `ec-sign` program and see how it works:

```
$ ./ec-sign \
    somefile.txt \
    somefile.txt.signature \
    ec_keypair.pem
Signing succeeded
```

The program has been reported as a success. Let's use `openssl pkeyutl` to check whether our program has produced a good signature:

```
$ openssl pkeyutl \
    -verify \
    -digest sha3-512 \
    -inkey ec_keypair.pem \
    -in somefile.txt \
    -rawin \
    -sigfile somefile.txt.signature
Signature Verified Successfully
```

It is very good that our program has been able to produce the correct signature. But what's even better is that we have learned how to write such a program. Our next adventure is to learn how to verify signatures programmatically.

How to verify a signature programmatically

To learn how to verify signatures programmatically, let's develop a small `ec-verify` program that can verify signatures produced by `ec-sign` or `openssl pkeyutl`.

Our program will take three command-line arguments:

1. The name of the input file containing the signed data
2. The name of the file containing the signature
3. The name of the file containing the verifying public key

Here is our high-level implementation plan for the program:

1. Load the signature.
2. Load the verifying public key.
3. Create an `EVP_MD_CTX` object that will be used as the verifying context.
4. Initialize the verifying context with the hash function's name and the loaded public key.
5. Read the signed data chunk by chunk and feed it to the verifying context.
6. Finalize the verification and find out whether the verification has succeeded or failed.

Now it's time to implement our plan.

Implementing the ec-verify program

Follow these steps for implementing the ec-verify program according to our plan:

1. First, we must load the signature. However, we don't know how much memory to allocate for it. So, let's open the signature file and find out its length:

```
const char* sig_fname = argv[2];
FILE* sig_file = fopen(sig_fname, "rb");
fseek(sig_file, 0, SEEK_END);
long sig_file_len = ftell(sig_file);
fseek(sig_file, 0, SEEK_SET);
```

Such a seek-based method of finding out the file length may not be optimal, but it uses only the standard C library and thus is very cross-platform.

2. Now, when we know the signature length, we can allocate memory for the signature and load it from the signature file:

```
unsigned char* sig_buf = malloc(sig_file_len);
size_t sig_len = fread(sig_buf, 1, sig_file_len, sig_
file);
```

3. Next, load the verifying public key:

```
const char* pkey_fname = argv[3];
FILE* pkey_file = fopen(pkey_fname, "rb");
EVP_PKEY* pkey = PEM_read_PUBKEY(
    pkey_file, NULL, NULL, NULL);
```

4. Then, create the verifying context and initialize it with the SHA3-512 hash function and the loaded public key:

```
EVP_MD_CTX* md_ctx = EVP_MD_CTX_new();
EVP_DigestVerifyInit_ex(
    md_ctx,
    NULL,
    OSSL_DIGEST_NAME_SHA3_512,
    NULL,
    NULL,
    pkey,
    NULL);
```

5. Now that the verifying context has been initialized, let's feed it with the signed data:

```
while (!feof(in_file)) {
    size_t in_nbytes = fread(in_buf, 1, BUF_SIZE, in_
file);
    EVP_DigestVerifyUpdate(md_ctx, in_buf, in_nbytes);
}
```

6. Once all the signed data has been processed by the context, we can find out the verification status:

```
int status = EVP_DigestVerifyFinal(md_ctx, sig_buf, sig_
len);
```

The EVP_DigestVerifyFinal() function returns 1 if the signature verification is successful. Any other returned value indicates a failure.

Like the signing API, the verifying API also has a one-shot verification function called EVP_DigestVerify() that does not take data chunk by chunk but requires the whole signed data to be placed in a contiguous memory block. Using EVP_DigestVerify() is, as of OpenSSL 3.0, the only way to verify signatures for algorithms that do not support streaming, such as PureEdDSA.

7. Once we have got the verification status from the EVP_DigestVerifyFinal() function, we don't need our used buffers and objects anymore and can free them:

```
free(in_buf);
EVP_MD_CTX_free(md_ctx);
EVP_PKEY_free(pkey);
free(sig_buf);
```

The complete source code for our ec-verify program can be found on GitHub in the ec-verify.c file: https://github.com/PacktPublishing/Demystifying-Cryptography-with-OpenSSL-3/blob/main/Chapter07/ec-verify.c.

Running the ec-verify program

Let's run our ec-verify program and try to verify the signature that's been produced by the ec-sign program:

```
$ ./ec-verify \
    somefile.txt \
    somefile.txt.signature \
    ec_public_key.pem
Verification succeeded
```

Good – our `ec-verify` program has successfully verified a valid signature.

Let's try to change the signed data and check whether verification will fail:

```
$ echo "additional data" >> somefile.txt
$ ./ec-verify \
    somefile.txt \
    somefile.txt.signature ec_public_key.pem
EVP_API error
Verification failed
```

As we can see, our `ec-verify` program can distinguish a valid signature from an invalid one.

This section concludes the practical part of this chapter. Let's proceed to the summary.

Summary

In this chapter, we have learned about the concept of digital signatures, how they use message digest, and how digital signatures differ from message authentication codes. We also learned about the cryptographical guarantees that digital signatures provide. Then, we reviewed the digital signature algorithms supported by OpenSSL, discussed their technical merits, and mentioned a little bit of their history. We finished the theoretical part with recommendations on which digital signature algorithm to choose in which situation.

In the practical part, we learned how to sign with ECDSA and verify signatures on the command line. Then, we learned how to sign and verify signatures programmatically using C code.

In the next chapter, we will learn about X.509 certificates and **Public Key Infrastructure** (**PKI**) based on X.509 certificates.

X.509 Certificates and PKI

In this chapter, we will learn about **X.509 certificates**. Certificates are data structures used for identity presentation and verification. X.509 certificates are crucial for the functioning of TLS and TLS-based protocols, such as HTTPS, where certificates are used to prove the identities of websites. Certificates are also used in secure messaging standards, such as S/MIME; VPN solutions, such as OpenVPN; smart cards, software signing, and so on. X.509 certificates can also optionally be used in IPsec.

We will learn about what certificates consist of, how certificate verification chains are built, and how **Public Key Infrastructure** (**PKI**) works. In the practical part of this chapter, we will learn how to generate certificates and verify certificate chains on the command line and programmatically using C code.

We are going to cover the following topics in this chapter:

- What is an X.509 certificate?

- Understanding certificate signing chains

- How are X.509 certificates issued?

- What are X509v3 extensions?

- Understanding X.509 Public Key Infrastructure

- How to generate a self-signed certificate

- How to generate (issue) a non-self-signed certificate

- How to verify a certificate on the command line

- How to verify a certificate programmatically

Technical requirements

This chapter will contain commands that you can run on a command line and C source code that you can build and run. For the command-line commands, you will need the `openssl` command-line tool with OpenSSL dynamic libraries. For building the C code, you will need OpenSSL dynamic or static libraries, library headers, a C compiler, and a linker.

We will implement an example program in this chapter, in order to practice what we are learning. The full source code of that program can be found here: `https://github.com/PacktPublishing/Demystifying-Cryptography-with-OpenSSL-3/tree/main/Chapter08`.

What is an X.509 certificate?

An X.509 certificate is a data structure that is used for identity presentation and identity verification. A certificate may be saved to a file or transmitted via a network, and also as a part of a secure network protocol, such as TLS. An X.509 certificate binds an identity to a public key using a digital signature.

Here is an example text representation of an X.509 certificate:

```
Certificate:
    Data:
        Version: 3 (0x2)
        Serial Number: ... hex bytes ...
        Signature Algorithm: sha256WithRSAEncryption
        Issuer: C = US, O = Let's Encrypt, CN = R3
        Validity
            Not Before: Mar  4 12:43:52 2022 GMT
            Not After : Jun  2 12:43:51 2022 GMT
        Subject: CN = www.openssl.org
        Subject Public Key Info:
            Public Key Algorithm: rsaEncryption
                RSA Public-Key: (2048 bit)
                Modulus: ... hex bytes ...
                Exponent: 65537 (0x10001)
        X509v3 extensions:
            X509v3 Key Usage: critical
                Digital Signature, Key Encipherment
            X509v3 Extended Key Usage:
                TLS Web Server Authentication,
                TLS Web Client Authentication
            X509v3 Basic Constraints: critical
                CA:FALSE
            X509v3 Subject Key Identifier:
                ... hex bytes ...
            X509v3 Authority Key Identifier:
```

```
    ... hex bytes ...
... more X509v3 extensions ...
```

As we can observe, an X.509 certificate contains the following fields:

- **X.509 version**: Modern X.509 certificates have version 3.

- **Serial number**: The unique number of the certificate among certificates signed by the same issuer.

- **Signature algorithm**: Denotes the cryptographic hash function and digital signature algorithm used to sign the certificate.

- **Issuer**: The entity that signed the current certificate or, according to the X.509 terminology, issued it. The issuer is presented in the **Distinguished Name** (**DN**) format, which will be explained later.

- **Validity**: This is two timestamp fields, Not Before and Not After, defining when the certificate is valid.

- **Subject**: This is the entity that the certificate identifies. It can be a person, a website, an organization, or something else. The Subject field is also represented in the Distinguished Name format.

- **The certificate's public key**: The public key is very important for the identity verification that the certificate provides. Different key types are supported, such as RSA, DSA, ECDSA, and EdDSA. It's important to remember that an X.509 certificate does not contain a private key, only a public key.

- **X509v3 extensions**: They contain additional optional information.

- **The certificate signature**: This is produced by the certificate issuer.

Similar to public and private keys, X.509 certificates are encoded using **Abstract Syntax Notation One** (**ASN.1**) into **Distinguished Encoding Rules** (**DERs**) or **Privacy-Enhanced Mail** (**PEM**) format.

X.509 certificates' Subject and Issuer fields are represented in the DN format. A Distinguished Name looks like this: C = US, O = Let's Encrypt, CN = R3. As we can observe, a DN consists of key-value pairs. The keys have defined meanings, for example, C means Country and O means Organization. The most important key is CN, which means Common Name. It is the main name of the entity identified by the certificate. It can be a website name, such as www.openssl. org; a person's name, such as John Doe; or, if a certificate is needed for a technical purpose, the name of the certificate itself, for example, Technical certificate 123 or just R3.

Every X.509 certificate has the corresponding private key. That private key is not included in the certificate but matches the public key that is included in the certificate, meaning that a digital signature produced by that private key can be verified by the public key from the certificate. That private key is often called the certificate's private key. The owner of the certificate needs the certificate's private key in order to prove that they really own the certificate and haven't just copied it. Such proof can be established by the owner signing some data using the private key and the verifying party verifying the signature using the public key extracted from the certificate.

An X.509 certificate is usually not secret information and can be freely distributed, similar to a public key. The certificate's private key, on the contrary, is secret information that only the certificate owner should possess, because whoever possesses the private key can claim the identity of the certificate owner and cryptographically prove such an identity. Theft of the private key can lead to identity theft. For example, if someone steals the www.openssl.org website certificate's private key and also performs a **DNS poisoning** or **Man in the Middle (MITM)** attack, they could set up a false www.openssl.org website that will pass the certificate verification. There are ways to mitigate the identity theft described, such as **Certificate Revocation Lists (CRLs)** and **Online Certificate Status Protocol (OCSP)**, but an attacker may still have a time window for their attacks before the compromised certificate is revoked. Here's another example: if a certificate's private key is used for signing email messages, whoever steals the private key will be able to sign emails on behalf of the certificate owner.

When some data is signed by the certificate's private key, it is often said that the data is signed by the certificate. Certificates themselves can also be signed. In fact, each X.509 certificate is signed by some certificate, meaning by that certificate's private key. That signing certificate is specified in the Issuer field in the DN format. A certificate can be signed by its own private key. Such a certificate is called a self-signed certificate. Self-signed certificates have the same DN in both the Subject and Issuer fields. A certificate can also be signed by another certificate, and that other certificate can be signed by a third certificate, and so on. In such a case, we have a certificate signing chain.

Understanding certificate signing chains

A **certificate signing chain**, also known as a **certificate verification chain**, simply a **certificate chain**, or a **chain of trust**, is an ordered collection of certificates where each certificate is signed by the next certificate in the collection. All except the last certificate, of course. The last certificate is self-signed.

Why are certificate signing chains needed? In order to verify the certificate validity. A curious reader might ask, doesn't the certificate's private key solve this problem? No, it's not so easy. When verifying identity using an X.509 certificate, we have to verify two claims:

1. **That whoever presents the certificate for identification owns the certificate**: This claim is proven using the certificate's private key.
2. **That the presented certificate is valid**: This claim is proven using the certificate signing chain.

It is similar to how you identify yourself with a passport. You can identify yourself only with your own passport, and your passport must be valid.

How does certificate verification work? In order to understand that, we need to learn how certificates are produced or, according to X.509 terminology, *issued*.

Most website certificates on the internet are issued by organizations called **Certificate Authorities (CAs)**. A CA is an organization that issues certificates and usually charges money for them. Some CAs, for example, Let's Encrypt, issue certificates for free. CAs present themselves as **trusted third parties**. The idea is that you trust CAs to issue certificates and consider certificates issued by those CAs valid. You trust that the CA will check the identities of those who order a certificate from the CA and issue certificates only to those whose identities match the identity written in the certificate's Subject field.

Why should you trust some CA organization that you haven't met, have barely heard of, and when you do not know the people working there? CAs give arguments that trust is their business; they cannot issue rogue certificates that do not match the identities of the subjects, otherwise, no one will trust the CAs, and they will go bankrupt. And therefore, you have to trust them. I personally find such argumentation questionable. But you do not have a lot of choice. You (or rather your OS, or your browser) either trust the certificates issued by those CAs, or pretend to trust them, or you cannot access HTTPS sites that use certificates issued by those CAs, which are the majority of the websites on the internet. That's how the modern World Wide Web works.

In order to verify a certificate, you have to build a certificate signing chain finished with a trusted certificate. Let's consider a popular case of website certificate verification. In this case, the first certificate in the chain will be the certificate that identifies the website. That certificate did not sign or issue any other certificates. Certificates that do not sign other certificates are called **leaf certificates**. The website certificate will be signed by the second certificate in the chain. In most cases, that second certificate will not be a self-signed certificate and thus will not finish the certificate chain. Certificates that both sign other certificates and aren't self-signed are called **intermediate CA certificates**. A typical certificate chain starting with a website certificate will have one or two intermediate CA certificates. After all the intermediate CA certificates, the last certificate in the chain will be self-signed. Self-signed certificates that sign other certificates are called **root CA certificates**.

The certificate chain will look like this:

Figure 8.1 – Certificate signing chain, horizontal representation

In various articles on the internet, it is also popular to draw certificate chains vertically, like this:

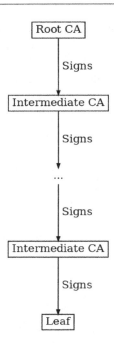

Figure 8.2 – Certificate signing chain, vertical representation

Note that the horizontal representation looks like a linked list, having a certificate to be verified as the first element and a trusted certificate as the last element. That is also how OpenSSL represents certificate signing chains.

In our descriptions and diagrams, we have mentioned intermediate CA certificates. But why are they needed? Why not just sign all leaf (end-entity) certificates with root certificates? There are several reasons for that:

- If an intermediate certificate is compromised, it can be revoked without revocation of the root certificate and other intermediate certificates of the same CA. Hence, the impact of the certificate compromise is limited.

- Many CAs support the automatic issuing of certificates online. This means that the private key of the signing certificate must reside on a server that is directly or indirectly accessible from the internet. Such accessibility is a risk. It is better to put an intermediate certificate at risk than the root certificate. As the root certificate does not sign other certificates very often, its private key can be stored in a safe offline place, for example, on a flash drive in a steel safe, in a locked and guarded room.

- Certificate revocation lists of large CAs can also be large. I have seen CRLs of 50 MB in size. By having several intermediate certificates, a CA can split its pool of issued certificates among intermediate certificates and issue smaller per-intermediate certificate CRLs.

As we have just learned, certificate chains are needed for certificate verification and may contain leaf (end-entity), intermediate, and root certificates. But who verifies those certificate chains and how do verifiers get all the certificates? Anyone who can get the needed certificates and build up a certificate signing chain can verify a certificate. Let's get back to the popular case of website certificate verification. In such a case, it is a browser or another HTTPS client that verifies the certificate. The browser gets the server certificate from the server during the TLS handshake. How does the browser get the root CA certificate? From the browser certificate store or the operating system certificate store. Most operating systems have an OS-wide certificate store that stores certificates and divides them into categories, such as trusted CA certificates, untrusted CA certificates, or client certificates with private keys. Those certificate stores are regularly updated via OS update mechanisms. Some web browsers also have their own certificate stores that can be used in addition to or as a replacement for the OS certificate store. The browser stores are updated by the corresponding browsers, not necessarily when a new browser version is released, but store updates can just be downloaded periodically.

Who decides which certificates are considered trusted? Whoever maintains the certificate store decides how the store is originally populated and which changes to the store (these can be both additions and deletions) are included in the updates. For the OS store, the maintainer is the OS vendor and for the browser store, it is the browser vendor. The OS and browser user can also add and delete certificates from the store. However, not so many users have enough knowledge, need, and desire to change the contents of their certificate stores. Hence, in most cases, the certificate store contains just the certificates that the OS or browser vendor decided to include in it. As a result, the list of trusted CA certificates will consist of certificates that the store vendor chose for you to trust.

The contents of most OS and browser certificate stores are the same or almost the same. The stores are populated by root CA certificates of well-known CAs. If you are visiting a website that has a certificate issued by one of those CAs, your browser will be able to verify the site certificate and will happily show you the web page. If, however, you are visiting an amateur website that uses a certificate not issued by a well-known CA, your browser will not be able to verify the certificate and will show you a warning that can be scary for non-tech-savvy people. In order to avoid the warning, you will have to add the CA certificate that directly, or via intermediate CA certificates, signed the website certificate to the OS or browser certificate store as a trusted certificate. This task can be difficult for a non-tech-savvy person. Therefore, most HTTPS sites on the internet have certificates issued by well-known CAs whose root CA certificates are present in OS or browser certificate stores and are considered trusted. For small amateur sites, it can be too much of a burden to pay money for a site certificate. Fortunately, since 2015, it is possible to get free site certificates from the uncommercial Let's Encrypt CA. Some big commercial CAs sometimes also issue free HTTPS certificates, usually as a trial.

Curious readers may have noticed that certificate stores have a special category for untrusted CA certificates. Why is it needed? The answer is simple. The untrusted CA certificates are intermediate CA certificates that can be used to build a certificate signing chain from a website certificate up to the trusted CA certificate. However, it is quite rare that an OS or browser certificate store contains untrusted CA certificates. How does the browser get the intermediate certificates needed then? Usually, the web server sends the intermediate CA certificates together with the site certificate.

When a certificate is being verified, how is the certificate signing chain built? It is obvious that the first certificate in the chain will be the certificate to be verified, for example, a website certificate. But how do you decide which certificate to put into the chain next? The next certificate can be looked up using two methods. The first method is to use the current certificate's `Issuer` field and look for a certificate with the same DN in the `Subject` field. The `Issuer` field always exists in the certificate, but sometimes several certificates with the same subject can be found. Therefore, searching by the `Issuer` field is ambiguous. The second method is to use the *Authority Key Identifier*" X509v3 extension, which contains the cryptographic hash of the issuer certificate public key. However, X509v3 extensions are optional, hence that extension may be missing from the certificate. Also, sometimes, when a certificate is renewed, it is renewed with the same key but another validity period. Therefore, the second method is also ambiguous. Thus, due to ambiguity, sometimes, in order to build a valid certificate signing chain, it is necessary to analyze several certificate signing paths. If at least one path allows us to build a certificate chain up to a trusted certificate, and all constraints, such as a validity period and constraints imposed by X509v3 extensions, are satisfied, then we can consider the certificate to be successfully verified. OpenSSL supports such an analysis of several signing paths when building a certificate signing chain.

In most cases, the certificate chain finishes with a self-signed root CA certificate. But, strictly speaking, it is not mandatory. OpenSSL supports certificate signing chains that finish with non-self-signed certificates. Using such signing chains, however, is considered a bad practice.

We have now learned a lot about certificate verification. But how are X.509 certificates issued?

How are X.509 certificates issued?

The X.509 certificate generation procedure consists of several stages:

1. The applicant (future certificate owner) generates the certificate's private and public keys.

2. The applicant generates a **Certificate Signing Request (CSR)**. The CSR contains the subject, the public key of the future certificate, the X509v3 extensions requested by the applicant, and the CSR signature. The CSR is signed by the certificate's private key.

3. The applicant sends the CSR to a CA for signing.

4. The CA checks the applicant's identity.

5. The CA makes a certificate based on information from the CSR. The CA also adds other information to the certificate, such as the issuer, validity fields, and X509v3 extensions. Finally, the CA signs the certificate.

6. The CA sends the certificate back to the applicant, who then becomes the certificate owner or holder.

Note that no one exposes the private key to another party in the process.

Let's say a few words about how the CA verifies the identity of the applicant in a popular case of issuing a certificate for a website. Some people believe that CAs *always* do a thorough check of the website and its owners, scan the website for malware, visit the website's owners in person, check a lot of their documents, and so on. Usually, it is not so. The identity of most certificates issued to websites is checked automatically and online, without any interaction between the people owning the website and people working in the CA organization. No documents are checked, such as the passports of the owners, contracts for web or DNS hosting, or other documents. What is checked then? It is checked that the applicant controls the website and the DNS of the website domain. The checks are automatic and can be something like this:

- Place a specific file at a specific URL on the website.
- Add a specific DNS record to the website domain.
- Create an email address in the site domain and receive a password at that email.

That's why usual HTTPS certificates are called **Domain-Validated (DV)** certificates.

What does such a DV certificate certify when used on a website? That the user's browser is connected to a website with the domain name specified in the certificate, such as www.openssl.org – no more, no less. A DV certificate does not assert that a website represents a specific organization, such as the OpenSSL Project. Some people believe in the myth that if a website has a certificate, it is certified and is thus a good site that cannot represent a bad organization, cannot contain malware, cannot attack its users, and all information on that website is true. Unfortunately, it is not so. Sites that are phishing, distributing malware, or doing other criminal activities can also have valid HTTPS certificates, and connections to those sites will be considered "secure" by browsers. It is important to understand that it is only the connection that is secure. The site itself could be very insecure.

Why are DV certificates still useful? Because they protect web browser users from MITM and DNS poisoning attacks. The users can be sure with a high probability that they are really visiting the site that they see in their browser's address line and that it is not a fake site mimicking the original site.

Are there certificates that certify that a website represents a specific organization, not only a specific domain name? Fortunately, yes. Such certificates are called **Extended Validation (EV)** certificates. When issuing an EV certificate, the CA does many more checks on the **CSR**. The CA checks that the CSR has come from the organization that owns the domain, the organization name in the CSR Subject field matches the real organization name, the organization exists and is properly registered in the government organization register, the organization's address and phone number are real, the person requesting the certificate has authority to do so on behalf of the organization, and so on. EV certificates are only issued to organizations, not to individuals.

EV certificates are significantly more expensive than DV certificates. For example, at the time of writing, one well-known CA sells DV certificates for 8 USD/year and EV certificates for 90 USD/year. Most sites on the internet use DV certificates. EV certificates are used by sites whose identity is especially important, such as the sites of banks.

The EV status of the issued certificate is signaled by an X509v3 extension. Unfortunately, there is currently no standardized X509v3 extension for EV status indication; different CAs use different X509v3 extensions. Therefore, browsers have to implement support for several EV-indicating X509v3 extensions.

Previously, major web browsers indicated that a website had an EV certificate by having a green background in the address bar and showing the site-owning company's name in the address bar. Since 2019, major web browsers stopped using such a strong visual indication. There is no green bar anymore and the company name is only shown if the browser user clicks on the padlock icon in the address bar. Most other software, not web browsers, have never had a strong visual indication of an EV certificate.

There are also **Organization Validation (OV)** and **Individual Validation (IV)** certificates. They are intermediate solutions between DV and EV certificates. When issuing such certificates, the CA verifies the identity of an organization or an individual and the issued certificate contains the name of the organization or the individual in the certificate's `Subject` field. The difference from EV certificates is that when a CA issues an OV or IV certificate, the CSR does not go through as thorough a validation process as for EV – fewer checks are made. OV and IV certificates are less popular than EV certificates. If an organization wants a higher-rank certificate than DV, it usually chooses an EV certificate rather than OV.

We have already mentioned X509v3 extensions several times. Let's learn a bit more about them.

What are X509v3 extensions?

X509v3 extensions are additional fields that can be added to an X.509 certificate. X509v3 extensions can impose constraints on certificate usage or provide additional information on the certificate. As an example, let's go through the X509v3 extensions found in the `www.openssl.org` website certificate:

- **Key Usage and Extended Key Usage**: These extensions are constraints that limit certificate usage to certain purposes. It is up to the software that verifies the certificate to enforce X509v3 constraints. If the verifying software does not recognize or enforce certain X509v3 constraints, they will be ignored.

- **The CA:FALSE basic constraint**: This extension asserts that the certificate must not be used to issue other certificates, meaning that the verification software must not consider such a certificate as an intermediate or root CA certificate.

- **Subject Key Identifier and Authority Key Identifier**: Informational extensions that help to look up the issuer certificate from the issued certificate.

- **Authority Information Access**: Informational extensions that help to locate CA resources, such as the OCSP server or CA certificates useful for verification of the current certificate.

- **Subject Alternative Name**: An informational extension that lists alternative domain names of websites that can use this certificate. In addition to `www.openssl.org`, other names could be listed, allowing the certificate owner to use the certificate on sites with other domain names, for example, `mail.openssl.org` or just `openssl.org`.

- **CT Precertificate SCTs**: Information about the certificate entry in the **Certificate Transparency** (**CT**) logs. CT is a monitoring solution that helps to discover the issuing of rogue X.509 certificates.

X509v3 extensions are not mandatory parts of the X.509 certificate format, but their addition makes the usage of certificates more convenient. Also, some software that verifies certificates, such as web browsers, may expect certain X509v3 extensions in the certificate and change the certificate verification result based on the extensions or their absence.

X.509 certificates are useful, but they would not be very useful alone. The certificates are a part of a bigger infrastructure, called Public Key Infrastructure.

Understanding X.509 Public Key Infrastructure

X.509 **PKI** is a combination of standards, algorithms, data structures, software, hardware, organizations, and procedures needed to create, store, transfer, use, revoke, and otherwise manage X.509 certificates and certificate keys.

Sounds complicated, but we have just learned how X.509 PKI works on the World Wide Web. CAs issue certificates that are used by websites and verified by web browsers. That's how millions of people using the web every day automatically verify the identity of websites. Some websites support the authentication of users using client certificates. In such cases, not only does the website present its certificate but also, the user's web browser presents a client certificate to the site so that the site can verify the client certificate, authenticate, and authorize the user.

X.509 PKI is not only used for the web. X.509 certificates are used for mail transfer, communication of automated computer systems, software signing, and so on.

Some people think that PKI is something mysterious and incomprehensible, but in reality, it's not. It's just managing keys and identities.

We have now learned about X.509 certificates, certificate signing chains, CAs, and PKI. The theoretical part of this chapter is finished. Let's proceed to the practical part and generate some certificates.

How to generate a self-signed certificate

In order to generate a certificate, we have to generate a key pair, a CSR, and finally, a certificate. The `openssl` tool can generate a self-signed certificate in several ways. One of the ways is to use a single command to generate a key pair and a self-signed certificate. But we will use separate commands because it is a more generic way.

We are going to use the following `openssl` subcommands: `genpkey`, `pkey`, `req`, and `x509`. Their documentation is available on the following man pages:

```
$ man openssl-genpkey
$ man openssl-pkey
$ man openssl-req
$ man openssl-x509
```

This is how we generate a self-signed certificate:

1. First, let's generate a key pair. This time let's use `ED448` as the key type:

    ```
    $ openssl genpkey -algorithm ED448 -out root_keypair.pem
    ```

    We have got no output, meaning that we have got no error.

2. Let's inspect our newly created key:

    ```
    $ openssl pkey -in root_keypair.pem -noout -text
    ED448 Private-Key:
    priv:
        e2:62:21:f0:32:25:20:ca:84:f9:b8:4f:0a:9f:51:
        51:3b:68:d0:0d:3a:91:c9:68:38:b4:2f:d0:53:af:
        62:5a:06:9d:b0:f5:86:11:73:f5:be:39:9a:78:be:
        ec:a2:53:d8:91:ad:8b:e5:2e:e2:b3:a3
    pub:
        70:3c:22:d9:9f:f8:d6:76:e0:4f:46:e8:74:7b:5f:
        98:98:ee:90:49:af:07:ba:05:a4:3b:b3:2c:e3:20:
        1a:00:cf:11:5c:76:93:32:0a:91:14:98:fa:dd:83:
        7b:9c:00:46:c8:d3:df:67:23:ea:e1:80
    ```

    Looks good!

3. Next, let's generate a CSR. To keep things simple, we will not add many X509v3 extensions. We will learn about more sophisticated certificate generation in *Chapter 12, Running a Mini-CA*:

    ```
    $ openssl req \
        -new \
        -subj "/CN=Root CA" \
        -addext "basicConstraints=critical,CA:TRUE" \
        -key root_keypair.pem \
        -out root_csr.pem
    ```

    Note that we added the `CA:TRUE` extension. We have to add it for CA certificates.

4. We have got no output and a new file, root_csr.pem, containing our CSR. Let's inspect it:

```
$ openssl req -in root_csr.pem -noout -text
Certificate Request:
    Data:
        Version: 1 (0x0)
        Subject: CN = Root CA
        Subject Public Key Info:
            Public Key Algorithm: ED448
                ED448 Public-Key:
                pub:
                    ... hex bytes ...
        Attributes:
            Requested Extensions:
                X509v3 Basic Constraints: critical
                    CA:TRUE
    Signature Algorithm: ED448
    Signature Value:
        ... hex bytes ...
```

5. Now let's generate a self-signed certificate using the CSR and the key pair. Our new certificate will have a validity period of 3,650 days, which is approximately 10 years:

```
$ openssl x509 \
    -req \
    -in root_csr.pem \
    -copy_extensions copyall \
    -key root_keypair.pem \
    -days 3650 \
    -out root_cert.pem
```

Note the -copy_extensions copyall switch. It is important to add that switch because the openssl x509 command, by default, would not copy X509v3 extensions from the CSR to the produced certificate.

6. We have got no output and a new file, root_cert.pem, containing our new self-signed certificate. Let's inspect it:

```
$ openssl x509 -in root_cert.pem -noout -text
Certificate:
```

```
    Data:
        Version: 3 (0x2)
        Serial Number:
            ... hex bytes ...
        Signature Algorithm: ED448
        Issuer: CN = Root CA
        Validity
            Not Before: Mar 27 22:25:17 2022 GMT
            Not After : Mar 24 22:25:17 2032 GMT
        Subject: CN = Root CA
        Subject Public Key Info:
            Public Key Algorithm: ED448
                ED448 Public-Key:
                pub:
                    ... hex bytes ...
        X509v3 extensions:
            X509v3 Basic Constraints: critical
                CA:TRUE
            X509v3 Subject Key Identifier:
                ... hex bytes ...
    Signature Algorithm: ED448
    Signature Value:
        ... hex bytes ...
```

Note that the Issuer and Subject fields are the same in the certificate. It is an indication of a self-signed certificate.

We have now successfully generated a self-signed certificate, which we will use as a root CA certificate. Let's now generate a couple of non-self-signed certificates.

How to generate a non-self-signed certificate

When generating a self-signed certificate, we used a generic approach instead of long combined commands. Therefore, the generation of non-self-signed certificates will be very similar. We will now generate a couple of non-self-signed certificates. We will use one as an intermediate CA certificate and another as an end-entity leaf certificate.

Let's proceed with the certificate generation:

1. First, let's generate a key pair for the intermediate CA certificate:

```
$ openssl genpkey \
    -algorithm ED448 \
    -out intermediate_keypair.pem
```

2. Next, generate a CSR:

```
$ openssl req \
    -new \
    -subj "/CN=Intermediate CA" \
    -addext "basicConstraints=critical,CA:TRUE" \
    -key intermediate_keypair.pem \
    -out intermediate_csr.pem
```

Note that we used a different Subject for the intermediate CA certificate.

3. Now we will issue the intermediate CA certificate, signing it with the private key of the root certificate:

```
$ openssl x509 \
    -req \
    -in intermediate_csr.pem \
    -copy_extensions copyall \
    -CA root_cert.pem \
    -CAkey root_keypair.pem \
    -days 3650 \
    -out intermediate_cert.pem
```

Note that we used -CA and -CAkey switches instead of the -key switch. The -CA switch is needed for copying the CA certificate's Subject value into the issued certificate's Issuer field, and also for taking other necessary information from the issuing certificate, for example, the *Authority Key Identifier*, if the corresponding X509v3 extension is used.

4. Let's inspect the issued intermediate CA certificate:

```
$ openssl x509 -in intermediate_cert.pem -noout -text
Certificate:
    Data:
        Version: 1 (0x0)
        Serial Number:
```

```
            ... hex bytes …
      Signature Algorithm: ED448
      Issuer: CN = Root CA
      Validity
          Not Before: Mar 27 23:11:35 2022 GMT
          Not After : Mar 24 23:11:35 2032 GMT
      Subject: CN = Intermediate CA
      Subject Public Key Info:
          Public Key Algorithm: ED448
              ED448 Public-Key:
              pub:
                  ... hex bytes ...
      X509v3 extensions:
          X509v3 Basic Constraints: critical
              CA:TRUE
          X509v3 Subject Key Identifier:
              ... hex bytes ...
          X509v3 Authority Key Identifier:
              ... hex bytes ...
  Signature Algorithm: ED448
  Signature Value:
      ... hex bytes ...
```

Note that this certificate has different `Issuer` and `Subject` fields, indicating that it is not a self-signed certificate.

5. Now let's issue a leaf certificate and sign it with the private key of the intermediate CA certificate. We will do it very similarly to issuing the intermediate CA certificate:

```
$ openssl genpkey -algorithm ED448 -out leaf_keypair.pem
$ openssl req \
    -new \
    -subj "/CN=Leaf" \
    -addext "basicConstraints=critical,CA:FALSE" \
    -key leaf_keypair.pem \
    -out leaf_csr.pem
$ openssl x509 \
    -req \
    -in leaf_csr.pem \
    -copy_extensions copyall \
```

```
    -CA intermediate_cert.pem \
    -CAkey intermediate_keypair.pem \
    -days 3650 \
    -out leaf_cert.pem
```

Note that this time we set CA:FALSE instead of CA:TRUE because leaf certificates are not supposed to issue other certificates.

6. Let's inspect the produced leaf certificate:

```
$ openssl x509 -in leaf_cert.pem -noout -text
Certificate:
  Data:
      Version: 1 (0x0)
      Serial Number:
          ... hex bytes ...
      Signature Algorithm: ED448
      Issuer: CN = Intermediate CA
      Validity
          Not Before: Mar 27 23:34:19 2022 GMT
          Not After : Mar 24 23:34:19 2032 GMT
      Subject: CN = Leaf
      Subject Public Key Info:
          Public Key Algorithm: ED448
              ED448 Public-Key:
              pub:
                  ... hex bytes ...
        X509v3 extensions:
            X509v3 Basic Constraints: critical
              CA:FALSE
            X509v3 Subject Key Identifier:
                ... hex bytes ...
            X509v3 Authority Key Identifier:
                ... hex bytes ...
  Signature Algorithm: ED448
  Signature Value:
      ... hex bytes ...
```

Looks good, the leaf certificate is issued by the intermediate CA certificate.

Now let's verify the leaf certificate using the other two certificates.

How to verify a certificate on the command line

Certificate verification on the command line can be done using the `openssl verify` command. Its documentation can be found on the `openssl-verify` man page.

Let's verify the leaf certificate that we have just generated. We will consider our root CA certificate a trusted certificate. Our intermediate CA certificate will be considered untrusted, but it will help us to build the certificate signing chain.

Here is how we can verify the leaf certificate on the command line:

```
$ openssl verify \
    -verbose \
    -show_chain \
    -trusted root_cert.pem \
    -untrusted intermediate_cert.pem \
    leaf_cert.pem
leaf_cert.pem: OK
Chain:
depth=0: CN = Leaf (untrusted)
depth=1: CN = Intermediate CA (untrusted)
depth=2: CN = Root CA
```

Note the `-trusted` and `-untrusted` switches. The `-trusted` switch is used to specify a file containing one or more trusted certificates. In order to successfully verify a certificate, `openssl verify` has to build a certificate signing chain from the certificate being verified up to a trusted certificate. The `-untrusted` switch is used to specify a file with one or more untrusted certificates. Untrusted certificates are useful as intermediate certificates in the certificate chain. Both `-trusted` and `-untrusted` switches can be used several times to specify several files.

`openssl verify` has reported `OK`, meaning that the certificate verification has succeeded. `openssl verify` has also printed the certificate chain that it has built in order to verify the certificate.

We have successfully verified a certificate on the command line. Let us now learn how to verify a certificate programmatically.

How to verify a certificate programmatically

OpenSSL 3.0 provides only one API for certificate verification. The API consists of functions starting with the `X509_` prefix.

We are going to develop a small program that verifies the leaf certificate that we have just generated, similar to how `openssl verify` does so.

Here are some relevant manual pages for the API that we are going to use:

```
$ man X509_STORE_new
$ man X509_STORE_load_file
$ man DEFINE_STACK_OF
$ man PEM_read_x509
$ man X509_STORE_CTX_new
$ man X509_verify_cert
$ man X509_STORE_CTX_get_error
$ man X509_free
```

Our program will take three command-line arguments:

1. The name of the file containing trusted certificates

2. The name of the file containing untrusted certificates

3. The name of the file containing the target certificate that is going to be verified

Our high-level implementation plan will be as follows:

1. Load trusted certificates.

2. Load untrusted certificates.

3. Load the target certificate.

4. Create and initialize the certificate verification context.

5. Verify the certificate.

Now it's the time to implement the plan.

Implementing the x509-verify program

Let's develop our x509-verify program according to the plan:

1. First, we have to load trusted certificates. We will need to supply a collection of trusted certificates to the verification function as an X509_STORE container. Fortunately, OpenSSL provides a convenient function, X509_STORE_load_file(), for loading certificates from a PEM file to X509_STORE:

    ```
    const char* trusted_cert_fname = argv[1];
    X509_STORE* trusted_store = X509_STORE_new();
    X509_STORE_load_file(trusted_store, trusted_cert_fname);
    ```

2. Next, we must load untrusted certificates. We will need to supply untrusted certificates to the verification function as a STACK_OF(X509) object. X509 is an OpenSSL type that represents an X.509 certificate. STACK_OF is a macro that constructs an OpenSSL stack type. The STACK_OF macro is similar to the std::stack template type in C++. The macro takes the stack element type as a parameter. OpenSSL uses STACK_OF stacks a lot in its API and internal code. STACK_OF(X509) objects are often used as certificate signing chains or just as certificate lists. OpenSSL functions that work with stacks, such as sk_X509_new_null() and sk_X509_push(), are also macros. They have the sk_ prefix and their names are parameterized with the stack element type name. For example, sk_ functions working with STACK_OF(X509) have the X509 substring in their names. In other words, the names of those functions start not just with sk_ but with sk_X509_. As the X509 substring is, in this case, just a parameter in a stack function name, you will not find a man page called sk_X509_push. But you will find the sk_TYPE_push man page, which is an alias for the DEFINE_STACK_OF man page.

3. Unfortunately, there is no convenient function in OpenSSL that would load certificates to STACK_OF(X509) in one operation. Therefore, we must load certificates one by one using the PEM_read_X509() function. First, let's find out the length of the file containing the untrusted certificates:

```
const char* untrusted_cert_fname = argv[2];
FILE* untrusted_cert_file =
    fopen(untrusted_cert_fname, "rb");
fseek(untrusted_cert_file, 0, SEEK_END);
long untrusted_cert_file_len = ftell(untrusted_cert_
file);
fseek(untrusted_cert_file, 0, SEEK_SET);
```

4. Then, let's load certificates one by one into a STACK_OF(X509) structure:

```
STACK_OF(X509)* untrusted_stack = sk_X509_new_null();
while (ftell(untrusted_cert_file) < untrusted_cert_file_
len){
    X509* untrusted_cert =
        PEM_read_X509(untrusted_cert_file, NULL, NULL,
NULL);
    sk_X509_push(untrusted_stack, untrusted_cert);
}
```

We cannot just use the `while (!feof (untrusted_cert_file))` loop condition because the `feof ()` function only detects the end of the file when there is an attempt to read beyond the end of the file. And if we call the `PEM_read_X509 ()` function at the end of the file before the end of the file condition is detected, the `PEM_read_X509 ()` function will fail. Therefore, we rely on the file position in the loop.

5. After the trusted and untrusted certificates are loaded, it is time to load the target certificate that has to be verified. It is just one certificate; thus, we can conveniently load it using one `PEM_read_X509 ()` function call:

```
const char* target_cert_fname = argv[3];
FILE* target_cert_file = fopen(target_cert_fname, "rb");
X509* target_cert =
    PEM_read_X509(target_cert_file, NULL, NULL, NULL);
```

6. All the certificates are loaded. Now it's time to create and initialize the certificate verification context, which is an object of the `X509_STORE_CTX` type:

```
X509_STORE_CTX* ctx = X509_STORE_CTX_new();
X509_STORE_CTX_init(
    ctx, trusted_store, target_cert, untrusted_stack);
```

7. The decisive moment – certificate verification using the verification context:

```
int err = X509_verify_cert(ctx);
```

The function returns 1 if the certificate has been verified successfully. Other return values indicate failure.

8. If a failure happened, the exact error can be obtained using the `X509_STORE_CTX_get_error ()` and `X509_verify_cert_error_string ()` functions:

```
if (err != 1) {
    int error_code = X509_STORE_CTX_get_error(ctx);
    const char* error_string =
        X509_verify_cert_error_string(error_code);
    fprintf(
        stderr,
        "X509 verification error: %s\n",
        error_string);
}
```

9. After the finished verification, the objects that were in use must be freed:

```
X509_STORE_CTX_free(ctx);
X509_free(target_cert);
sk_X509_pop_free(untrusted_stack, X509_free);
X509_STORE_free(trusted_store);
```

The complete source code of our x509-verify program can be found on GitHub in the x509-verify.c file: https://github.com/PacktPublishing/Demystifying-Cryptography-with-OpenSSL-3/blob/main/Chapter08/x509-verify.c

Running the x509-verify program

Let's run our x509-verify program and verify the leaf certificate, using the generated root CA certificate as a trusted certificate and the intermediate CA certificate as an untrusted certificate:

```
$ ./x509-verify \
    root_cert.pem \
    intermediate_cert.pem \
    leaf_cert.pem
Verification succeeded
```

As we can observe, certificate verification has succeeded, as we expected.

Let's also check a failing case. This time, we will not provide the intermediate CA certificate to our program so it won't be able to build a certificate signing chain up to the trusted certificate. We still have to provide three arguments to the program; thus, we will just provide the leaf_cert.pem argument two times:

```
$ ./x509-verify \
    root_cert.pem \
    leaf_cert.pem \
    leaf_cert.pem
X509 verification error: unable to get local issuer certificate
Verification failed
```

We observe verification failure in this case, just as expected.

As we can see, our x509-verify program supports both successful and failing cases.

This section concludes the practical part of the chapter. Let's proceed to the summary.

Summary

In this chapter, we learned about the concept of X.509 certificates, why are they needed, and what kind of information they contain. We also learned about certificate signing chains and their role in certificate verification. Then we learned about CAs, as well as the differences between root and intermediate CA certificates. We also learned about the process of issuing X.509 certificates and several types of certificates, such as domain validation and EV types. Then we learned about X509v3 extensions. We finished the theoretical part of the chapter by learning about the concept of PKI.

In the practical part of the chapter, we learned how to generate self-signed and non-self-signed certificates. Then, we learned how to verify certificates, both on the command line and programmatically using C code.

In the next chapter, we will learn about setting up TLS connections and sending data over them.

Part 4:
TLS Connections and
Secure Communication

In this part, we will learn about the TLS protocol, the successor of the SSL protocol, why it is needed, and why it is used so much on the modern internet. Then, we will learn how to establish secure communication channels using TLS, send and receive data, and shut them down. We will also learn why X.509 certificates are important for TLS connections and how they counter Man in the Middle attacks. Then, we will find out how to supply a certificate for a TLS connection and how to verify the certificate of a remote party. Working with TLS and certificates will be illustrated using command-line and C code examples.

This part contains the following chapters:

- *Chapter 9, Establishing TLS Connections and Sending Data over Them*
- *Chapter 10, Using X.509 Certificates in TLS*
- *Chapter 11, Special Usages of TLS*

9
Establishing TLS Connections and Sending Data over Them

In this chapter, we will learn about the **Transport Layer Security (TLS)** protocol. The TLS protocol is the successor of the **Secure Sockets Layer (SSL)** protocol and is used for secure network communication and serves as the basis for higher-level protocols, such as **Hypertext Transfer Protocol Secure (HTTPS)** and **Simple Mail Transfer Protocol Secure (SMTPS)**. The TLS protocol is most visible on the World Wide Web but is also used in other applications, such as file transfer, email, instant messaging, Voice over IP, remote access, connection to databases, financial data transmission, and many other applications that require encrypted communication.

We will learn about the basics of the TLS protocol and take a quick look at its history. In the practical part of this chapter, we will learn how to establish TLS connections, send data over them, and shut them down correctly. There will be both command-line and C code examples that illustrate how to communicate over TLS.

We are going to cover the following topics in this chapter:

- Understanding the TLS protocol
- The history of the TLS protocol
- Establishing a TLS client connection on the command line
- Preparing certificates for a TLS server connection
- Accepting a TLS server connection on the command line
- Understanding OpenSSL BIOs
- Establishing a TLS client connection programmatically
- Accepting a TLS server connection programmatically

Technical requirements

This chapter will contain commands that you can run on a command line and C source code that you can build and run. For the command-line commands, you will need the `openssl` command-line tool with OpenSSL dynamic libraries. For building the C code, you will need OpenSSL dynamic or static libraries, library headers, a C compiler, and a linker.

We will implement some example programs in this chapter, in order to practice what we are learning. The full source code of those programs can be found here: `https://github.com/PacktPublishing/Demystifying-Cryptography-with-OpenSSL-3/tree/main/Chapter09`.

Understanding the TLS protocol

TLS is a general-purpose protocol that provides secure communication. The latest version of the TLS protocol at the time of writing is 1.3. TLS provides the following aspects of security:

- Privacy or confidentiality of transmitted user data, using **symmetric encryption**. It is computationally infeasible to decrypt and read the transmitted user data. Using the term *user data* here and later, I mean data that the users of the TLS protocol, the sender, and the receiving party exchange with each other, as opposed to service data of the TLS protocol needed for the protocol to function.

- Integrity and authenticity of transmitted user data, protection against tampering, using **authenticated encryption** or **Message Authentication Code** (MAC). It is computationally infeasible to alter the transmitted user data without the receiving party detecting it. Starting from TLS 1.3, authenticated encryption is mandatory.

- Peer identity proof and protection against **Man in the Middle** (MITM) attacks, using **X.509 certificates**.

- **Perfect Forward Secrecy** (PFS), using **Ephemeral Diffie-Hellman** (DHE) or **Ephemeral Elliptic Curve Diffie-Hellman** (ECDHE) **key exchange**. It is computationally infeasible to decrypt a recorded TLS session even if the server certificate's private key becomes compromised in the future. Starting from TLS 1.3, PFS key exchange is mandatory.

What is PFS? To understand what PFS is, we have to understand key exchange. Key exchange or **key agreement** in TLS is a process of agreeing on a symmetric encryption key that will be used for encrypting user data in a TLS session. The oldest key exchange method is **RSA key exchange**, where the client generates a symmetric key and encrypts it with the server certificate public key. The newer methods are variants of **Diffie-Hellman** (DH) key exchange, where both the client and the server have an asymmetric keypair and derive a symmetric key from their own private key and the peer's public key. Earlier TLS versions allowed non-PFS key exchange methods, such as RSA key exchange and static DH/ECDH key exchange. When a non-PFS key exchange method is used, the server certificate keypair is used for both authentication and key exchange. In such a case, if an attacker has recorded a TLS session and later stolen the server certificate private key, then the attacker can use it to recover the symmetric session key used in the TLS session and subsequently decrypt the user data sent during the TLS session. When a PFS key exchange method, such as DHE or ECDHE, is used, the client and the server generate temporary (ephemeral) keypairs for key exchange. Those ephemeral keypairs are only needed for the key exchange and can be destroyed after that. In such a case, even if the server certificate key gets stolen, the attacker will not be able to decrypt the TLS session, because they will not have any ephemeral private key from that TLS session. As we can see, when a PFS key exchange method is used, the certificate keypair is used for authentication and the ephemeral keypair is used for key exchange. We can conclude that PFS in TLS is a property of a key exchange method that prevents an attacker from decrypting a recorded TLS session even if the server certificate key gets compromised.

TLS usually runs on top of a reliable transport protocol, such as **Transmission Control Protocol (TCP)**. TLS is typically used with an application-layer protocol, such as **Hypertext Transfer Protocol (HTTP)**, running on top of TLS. The protocol layers for this typical use case can be visually represented as follows:

HTTP
TLS
TCP
IP

Figure 9.1 – The protocol layers

It is common to think about an application protocol running on top of TLS as a secure variant of that application protocol. For example, HTTPS protocol is a secure variant of the HTTP protocol. HTTPS is HTTP running on top of TLS, while SMTPS is SMTP running on top of TLS. As we can observe, secure variants of application protocols have the S suffix in their names. Ordinary and TLS-enabled variants of application protocols usually listen on different ports. For example, by default, HTTP listens on port 80 and HTTPS listens on port 443. However, some protocols support non-TLS and TLS variants on the same ports. For example, SMTP supports the STARTTLS command, which *upgrades* the current TCP connection to SMTPS. This method of starting a TLS session explicitly is called **opportunistic TLS**.

There is also a modification of the TLS protocol called **Datagram Transport Layer Security (DTLS)**, designed for running on top of an unreliable transport protocol, such as **User Datagram Protocol (UDP)**. It's worth mentioning that TLS over TCP is much more widely used than DTLS over UDP. However, popular software that uses DTLS does exist. A notable example is OpenVPN. OpenVPN can use both DTLS over UDP and, as usual, TLS over TCP.

As with TCP, TLS is a client-server protocol. To start sending data over TLS, the client and the server must establish a TCP connection first and perform TLS handshaking.

Understanding a TLS handshake

The client usually starts TLS handshaking right after establishing the TCP connection, but, in the case of opportunistic TLS, the client and the server exchange some data in an unencrypted form first.

How exactly the TLS handshaking takes place depends on the TLS protocol version, but here are the important actions that are performed during the handshaking:

- The client sends the list of TLS protocol versions and cipher suites that the client supports. A TLS 1.3 cipher suite name is a compound value that looks similar to TLS_AES_256_ GCM_SHA384 or TLS_CHACHA20_POLY1305_SHA256. As we can see, a cipher suite name identifies a symmetric encryption algorithm such as AES_256 or CHACHA20, a block cipher operation mode such as GCM or an encryption authentication method such as POLY1305, and a cryptographic hash function such as SHA384. Older TLS versions use a different naming convention for cipher suite names that results in longer names – for example, TLS_DHE_RSA_WITH_AES_256_CBC_SHA256. A cipher suite name in this case also includes a key exchange method such as DHE and a certificate signature algorithm such as RSA. The older naming convention was abandoned, as it causes a combinatorial explosion because of too many categories of algorithms and modes, such as a key exchange algorithm, certificate signature algorithm, symmetric cipher, symmetric key length, block cipher operation mode, and message digest algorithm. TLS 1.3 only supports **Authenticated Encryption with Associated Data** (**AEAD**) modes. Older TLS versions support non-authenticated encryption modes, in which case the **Hash-Based Message Authentication Code** (**HMAC**) algorithm is used to authenticate the encrypted data.

- The server chooses the highest protocol version and the preferred TLS cipher suite that both the client and the server support. If there is no mutually supported protocol version or cipher suite, the handshake fails.

- The server sends its X.509 certificate, possibly with other certificates that will help to build the certificate signing chain. The client verifies the server certificate using a possessed trusted certificate of a **Certificate Authority** (**CA**). The client also checks that the certificate Subject field matches the server hostname. More information about using X.509 certificates in TLS will be given in *Chapter 10, Using X.509 Certificates in TLS*.

- The server signs a small amount of data received from the client with the server's private key, which corresponds to the public key contained in the server certificate. The client verifies the signature. This way, the server proves that it owns the certificate. In older versions of the TLS protocol, there was an alternative method of proving the certificate ownership: the client encrypts some data with the public key from the server certificate and the server decrypts it using its private key. But that alternative method, which involves encryption and decryption, only works with RSA server keys and certificates.

- Optionally, the client sends its own certificate and the server verifies it.

- If the client has sent its certificate, the client also proves that it owns the certificate by signing or decrypting some data with its private key.

- The client and the server negotiate the symmetric session key and the **initialization vector (IV)** to be used for the encryption of the user data that will be sent over the TLS protocol. The client and the server use a key exchange and key agreement algorithm, such as *ECDHE*, for agreeing on a **handshake secret**, also known as a **pre-master secret** in the older TLS versions. Then, both the client and the server use a **pseudorandom function (PRF)**, for example, the **HMAC-based key derivation function (HKDF)**, for generating the **master secret** and then the session key and the IV. Alternatively, instead of using a key agreement algorithm, the client can request the reuse of the saved handshake secret from an earlier TLS session. Reuse of the handshake secret saves computational resources because asymmetric cryptography used for the key agreement process is rather computationally expensive.

- The client and the server exchange data for TCP extensions that they would like to use. An example of a popular TCP extension is **Server Name Indication (SNI)**, which selects a particular website on a shared hosting, where many websites can be served on the same host and port. Another example of a useful TCP extension is the `pre_shared_key` extension, which allows the use of pre-shared secrets and reuse of the handshake secret from an earlier TCP session, as mentioned previously.

- Finally, the client and the server authenticate all previously sent handshaking messages with HMAC. The other party of the connection verifies the authentication. If the HMAC verification fails, the handshake is considered to have failed, and the connection is aborted. This measure mitigates handshake tampering by a malicious third party – for example, intending to use a weaker cipher when the connection is not properly protected yet.

The TLS handshake is quite important, but it is not the only part of a TLS connection. Let's learn what happens after the handshake.

What happens after the TLS handshake?

After the TLS handshake has succeeded, the client and the server can send data to each other, encapsulated into *TLS records*. The transmitted data is encrypted with the session key and authenticated either by an authenticated encryption tag or by HMAC if an older TLS protocol is used with a non-authenticated encryption mode. The receiving party checks the authentication of each TLS record and aborts the connection if an authenticity verification error is detected.

When one party of the TLS connection detects an error, it should communicate the error to the other party using a TLS alert message. Alert messages can indicate a fatal error or a warning. On receiving a fatal error, the receiving party must stop sending and receiving more data through the connection.

One of the possible alert messages is `close_notify`. This alert message is used for a proper shutdown of the TLS connection. With this warning-level message, one party of the connection notifies another party that the first party is closing its writing part of the TLS connection and will not send more data.

The connection party that sent the `close_notify` alert may still read data from the TLS connection in TLS 1.3. Older TLS versions mandated the other party that received the `close_notify` alert to discard its pending writes and also send the `close_notify` alert, leading to the closure of the TLS connection. The TLS protocol specification mandates both the client and the server to send `close_notify` messages when the TLS connection has come to its logical end and no more data should be sent or received. This requirement mitigates a truncation attack on the connection. If both have received a `close_notify` message from each other, they can be sure that no MITM has truncated the connection. Note that the closing of a TLS connection does not automatically mean closing the underlying TCP connection. The TCP connection must be closed separately after the TLS connection closure – of course, only if no more data is going to be sent on it.

Note how various cryptographic concepts that we learned before are used to build up the TLS protocol. Symmetric encryption is needed for user data encryption. Cryptographic hash functions serve as a basis for HMAC, digital signatures, and certificates. Authenticated encryption and HMAC are used to authenticate both user and service data. Key derivation functions are used for generating secrets, session keys, and IVs. Digital signatures are used to confirm X.509 certificate validity and ownership. X.509 certificates are used for identity verification and mitigating MITM attacks. The TLS protocol as we know it now is the result of research and experience on the part of many people over many years and combines a lot of cryptographic technologies to provide us with the means of secure network communications.

In this section, we mentioned several times the differences between TLS 1.3 and older versions of the protocol. Let's talk a bit more about the differences between TLS versions and the TLS protocol history in the next section.

The history of the TLS protocol

The TLS protocol is the successor of the SSL protocol. The SSL protocol was originally developed at Netscape Communications Corporation in the 1990s.

The SSL version 1.0 specification was never released to the public or used in a known software product because of security flaws in the protocols. SSL 1.0 was only used inside Netscape.

SSL 2.0 was published in 1995. It supported DES, 3DES, RC2, RC4, and IDEA symmetric ciphers, MD5-based MAC (not HMAC), RSA key exchange, and RSA-based certificates. Security researchers quickly discovered numerous security flaws in the protocol. SSL 2.0 had weak MAC authentication, unprotected handshakes, and was found to be vulnerable to length extension, truncation, cipher downgrade, and MITM attacks. SSL 2.0 did not gain much popularity and was soon superseded by SSL 3.0, which appeared in the next year. Even though SSL 2.0 was not used very much, it was only officially deprecated in 2011.

SSL 3.0, published in 1996, was a response to the flaws discovered in SSL 2.0. It featured a complete redesign of the SSL protocol. All existing TLS protocol versions are still built on the foundation of SSL 3.0 and have a lot in common with SSL 3.0. SSL 3.0 fixed the design flaws of SSL 2.0 and introduced a lot of new features, including support for both ephemeral and non-ephemeral DH key exchange, SHA-1-

based MAC, DSA-signed certificates, compression, session reuse, session renegotiation, handshake authentication, and protocol version negotiation. Support for weak symmetric ciphers, such as single DES, RC2, and 40-bit RC4, was dropped. SSL 3.0 never officially supported the AES cipher, albeit some libraries, including OpenSSL, supported AES with SSL 3.0 as a non-standard extension. SSL 3.0 was popular for a long time, but over time, it was found to be vulnerable to certain attacks, such as **Browser Exploit Against SSL/TLS (BEAST)**, **Compression Ratio Info-Leak Made Easy (CRIME)**, and especially **Padding Oracle On Downgraded Legacy Encryption (POODLE)**. It is worth noting that SSL libraries could mitigate those SSL protocol flaws by record splitting and compression disabling. SSL 3.0 also used flawed MAC-then-encrypt construction. Yet another drawback of SSL 3.0 is that it did not support TLS extensions. It led to the practical issue that web browsers, when negotiating the SSL 3.0 protocol, could not use the important SNI extension to specify the web server's name on shared hosting. SSL 3.0 was finally deprecated in 2015.

TLS 1.0 protocol was published in 1999 as an upgrade to SSL 3.0. The TLS 1.0 specification was not developed by Netscape, but by the **TLS Working Group (TLS WG)** organized by the **Internet Engineering Task Force (IETF)**. The protocol was renamed from SSL to TLS to avoid legal issues with Netscape. TLS 1.0 introduced support for TLS extensions and enhanced various aspects of the protocol, such as the PRF, MAC, the *Finished* message, and alert messages. Unlike SSL, TLS 1.0 used HMAC for TLS record authentication. Later, TLS 1.0 was extended with more symmetric ciphers, such as AES, Camellia, SEED, and GOST89, as well as with elliptic curve support, particularly support for ECDSA-signed certificates and ECDH/ECDHE key agreement methods. TLS 1.0 was vulnerable to BEAST and CRIME attacks in the same way as SSL 3.0. The original POODLE attack did not work for TLS 1.0, but it was later found that some TLS 1.0 servers used TLS libraries with a bug that makes a modified POODLE attack possible. TLS 1.0 was deprecated in 2021.

TLS 1.1 was published in 2006 as a further development of TLS 1.0. It featured explicit encrypted IV instead of implicit IV in the earlier protocol versions and thus was not vulnerable to the BEAST attack. TLS 1.1 also included improved handling of padding errors for mitigating attacks related to CBC padding, better session reuse, and other enhancements. Despite all the enhancements, TLS 1.1 did not support newer cryptographic algorithms, such as AEAD encryption modes and SHA-2 hash functions. TLS 1.1 relied on CBC-based cipher suites susceptible to padding oracle attacks and now-deprecated MD5 and SHA-1 hash functions for MAC and PRF. TLS 1.1 was officially deprecated in 2021 together with TLS 1.0.

TLS 1.2 was published in 2008. It added support for AEAD encryption modes, such as GCM and CCM, and more secure hash functions, such as SHA-256 and SHA-384, for MAC and PRF. At the same time, TLS 1.2 removed support for older algorithms, such as DES, IDEA, MD5, and SHA-1. Later, TLS 1.2 was extended with support for ARIA, ChaCha20, and Poly1305 algorithms. AEAD encryption modes completely mitigated padding oracle attacks, such as POODLE. As usual, the new protocol version had many small enhancements for various aspects of the protocol. At the time of writing, TLS 1.2 is not deprecated.

TLS 1.3, published in 2018, is a major cleanup of the TLS protocol. Adding more and more features to the earlier TLS versions accumulated a lot of legacies. TLS 1.3 drops support for a lot of older insecure or obsolete algorithms and features, such as non-AEAD cipher suites, non-PFS key exchange methods such as RSA and non-ephemeral DH/ECDH, DSA-signed certificates, weak and less-used elliptic curves, elliptic curve point format negotiation, custom DHE groups, ChangeCipherSpec protocol, compression, and renegotiation. TLS 1.3 only supports AES-GCM, AES-CCM, ChaCha20-Poly1305 symmetric AEAD ciphers, SHA-256- and SHA-384-based HMACs, and DHE/ECDHE key exchange methods. HKDF is used as the PRF. RSA-, ECDSA-, and PureEdDSA-based certificates are supported. RSA, and ECDSA-based certificates should be signed using a SHA-256, SHA-384, or SHA-512 hash function; however, as a special backward-compatibility measure, certificates signed using a SHA-1 message digest are still supported. As a result of the old feature dropping, TLS 1.3 is immune to both CRIME and POODLE attacks. Handshaking in TLS 1.3 is faster than in the former TLS versions because handshaking now only requires one data roundtrip instead of two as in the earlier versions. As a major speedup feature, TLS 1.3 also supports the **zero round-trip time** (**0-RTT**) handshaking mode, which allows the TLS client to send encrypted user data in the first data flight from the client to the server if an earlier TLS session can be reused. TLS 1.3 has a new session reuse mechanism that supports both earlier session resumption and pre-shared keys. TLS 1.3 also contains other improvements that are less important than those mentioned.

Which TLS version is the best? Of course, the latest one! But you may need to keep support for older versions for compatibility with the parties using older communication software. This is often the case with hardware that does not receive software updates anymore, such as old mobile phones, tablets, router boxes, or **Internet-of-Things** (**IoT**) devices.

We have now learned about the basics of TLS and the history of the protocol. Let us continue to the practical part of this chapter where we will learn how to make TLS connections on the command line and programmatically.

Establishing a TLS client connection on the command line

To establish a TLS client connection, we will use the s_client subcommand of the openssl tool. Its documentation can be found on its man page:

```
$ man openssl-s_client
```

There is an HTTPS server on the internet to use as an example, https://example.org/. Let's connect to it via TLS and get its home page:

```
$ openssl s_client -connect example.org:443
```

The openssl tool will output a lot of information about how the TLS handshaking has gone, which cryptographic algorithms were used, and even the base64-encoded server certificate will be printed.

We can also request verification of the server certificate and its hostname by adding the `-verify_return_error` and `-verify_hostname` command-line options:

```
$ openssl s_client \
    -connect example.org:443 \
    -verify_return_error \
    -verify_hostname example.org
```

If you want to verify the server certificate, you need to have trusted CA certificates in the directory where OpenSSL expects to find them. For example, on my Ubuntu Linux system, the system-installed OpenSSL looks for the trusted certificates in the `/etc/ssl/certs` directory. If you installed your own version of OpenSSL, for example, into the `/opt/openssl-3.0.0` directory, that version of OpenSSL will look for certificates in the `/opt/openssl-3.0.0/ssl/certs` directory. In such a case, you can provide trusted CA certificates to OpenSSL using any of the following methods:

- Copy all files, including the symlinks, from the system OpenSSL certs directory, such as `/etc/ssl/certs` to `/opt/openssl-3.0.0/ssl/certs`
- Make `/opt/openssl-3.0.0/ssl/certs` a symlink to `/etc/ssl/certs`
- Set the `SSL_CERT_DIR` environment variable to `/etc/ssl/certs`
- Add a `-CApath /etc/ssl/certs` switch to the `openssl s_client` command

If you are using an OS that does not have a system OpenSSL certificate store, such as Windows, you can download Mozilla's trusted CA certificate bundle from the `curl` utility website. At the time of writing, the certificate bundle URL is `https://curl.se/ca/cacert.pem`. You can download it, for example, using the `curl` utility itself:

```
$ curl --remote-name https://curl.se/ca/cacert.pem
```

Then, you can provide the downloaded certificate bundle to OpenSSL using any of the following methods:

- Set the `SSL_CERT_FILE` environment variable to the absolute or relative path of the downloaded `cacert.pem` file
- Add the `-CAfile path/to/cacerts.pem` switch to the `openssl s_client` command

After successfully establishing the TLS connection, we can type or copy and paste any data into the connection. Any data sent by the server will be printed to your terminal. Let's type the following to make an HTTP request for getting the server home page:

```
GET / HTTP/1.1
Host: example.org
```

```
Connection: close
(empty line, just press Enter here)
```

We will get an HTTP response containing HTTP headers and the HTML code of the server home page. The server will close the connection because we have specified the `Connection: close` header in the HTTP request. You will return to the command line. If you omit that request header, the server will not close the connection and you will remain in the connection. If you want to finish the connection with proper TLS and TCP connection shutdown, you type Q followed by *Enter* or execute an **End of File (EOF)** on your terminal by pressing *Ctrl + D* on Unix-like systems or *Ctrl + Z + Enter* on Windows systems. If you want to forcibly exit `openssl s_client` without proper connection shutdown, you can press *Ctrl + C*.

That's how easy it was. Let's now try establishing a TLS server connection. The TLS server connection will require a server certificate and its corresponding private key. Therefore, we have to generate a couple of certificates first.

Preparing certificates for a TLS server connection

To accept a TLS server connection, we will need to generate two keypairs and certificates: the server certificate and the self-signed **CA** certificate, which signs the server certificate. Why can't we just generate a self-signed server certificate, a curious reader may ask? Because using a self-signed certificate as a server certificate is considered an error by most TLS clients and libraries, including the OpenSSL library. Another question you may have is: why can't we reuse certificates from the OS certificate store for our TLS server? Because we don't possess private keys for those certificates.

As in *Chapter 8, X.509 Certificates and PKI*, we will use the `openssl req` and `openssl x509` subcommands for keypairs and certificate generation. But, this time, we will use combined generation commands to demonstrate them too.

We have to generate the CA certificate first. This time, we will use a command that combines the generation of a keypair, **Certificate Signing Request (CSR)**, and certificate in one command. This kind of command, combining the three mentioned actions, is only possible for generating a self-signed certificate:

```
$ openssl req \
    -newkey ED448 \
    -x509 \
    -subj "/CN=Root CA" \
    -addext "basicConstraints=critical,CA:TRUE" \
    -days 3650 \
    -noenc \
    -keyout ca_keypair.pem \
    -out ca_cert.pem
```

Now, we have the CA keypair and certificate and can create and sign the server certificate. This time, we will also use a combined command, but we cannot combine all three operations. We can only combine two operations, namely the generation of the server keypair and the CSR:

```
$ openssl req \
    -newkey ED448 \
    -subj "/CN=localhost" \
    -addext "basicConstraints=critical,CA:FALSE" \
    -noenc \
    -keyout server_keypair.pem \
    -out server_csr.pem
```

The next command will create (or issue) the server certificate signed by the CA certificate:

```
$ openssl x509 \
    -req \
    -in server_csr.pem \
    -copy_extensions copyall \
    -CA ca_cert.pem \
    -CAkey ca_keypair.pem \
    -days 3650 \
    -out server_cert.pem
```

Note that we used the server hostname (localhost) in the server certificate Subject field. It is needed to pass the hostname validation of the certificate if the TLS client decides to perform it.

Now that our certificates are ready, let's try to establish a TLS server connection.

Accepting a TLS server connection on the command line

Follow these steps for accepting a TLS server connection on the command line:

1. To accept a TLS server connection, we will use the s_server subcommand of the openssl tool. Its documentation can be found on its man page:

    ```
    $ man openssl-s_server
    ```

2. We will provide a port number, a server certificate, and the corresponding server keypair to openssl s_server. That's how we start a TLS server:

    ```
    $ openssl s_server \
        -port 4433 \
    ```

```
            -key server_keypair.pem \
            -cert server_cert.pem
```

3. To check that our TLS server can accept connections and send and receive data over them, we can start a TLS client in another terminal window and connect to our TLS server:

```
$ openssl s_client \
    -connect localhost:4433 \
    -verify_return_error \
    -verify_hostname localhost \
    -CAfile ca_cert.pem
```

Note that this time, we have supplied a -CAfile switch to openssl s_client so that it could find the trusted CA certificate and verify the server certificate.

4. Now, the TLS client and the TLS server running in the different terminal windows are connected and can send data to each other. Try to type something in one terminal window, press *Enter*, and you will see that your typed string will appear in another terminal window. You can finish the connection by sending EOF or by pressing *Ctrl + C*.

We have now learned how to establish TLS client and server connections on the command line and send data over them. Now, let's learn how to do it programmatically.

Understanding OpenSSL BIOs

To establish TLS connections and send data over them, we will use OpenSSL **Basic Input/Output (BIO)** objects. BIOs provide the same **Application Programming Interface (API)** for working with different types of **Input/Output (I/O)** channels, such as files, sockets, and TLS streams.

BIOs are divided into two types: **source or sink BIOs** and **filter BIOs**. A source or sink BIO represents an I/O endpoint, such as a file or a socket. A filter BIO transforms data that is being passed through the BIO. For example, a cipher BIO encrypts data when being written to and decrypts data when being read from. BIOs can be connected and form a chain of BIOs. For example, an SSL BIO can be connected to a socket BIO, providing TLS communication on a socket.

OpenSSL supports the following source or sink BIOs:

*   Accept BIO (BIO_s_accept): TCP/IP socket or Unix socket accept routines.

*   BIO BIO (BIO_s_bio): A BIO pair where whatever is written to one half of the pair can be read from another half of the pair.

*   Connect BIO (BIO_s_connect): TCP/IP socket or Unix socket connect routines.

*   FD BIO (BIO_s_fd): I/O using an integer **file descriptor (fd)**.

*   File BIO (BIO_s_file): I/O using C language FILE pointers.

- Memory BIO (`BIO_s_mem`): I/O to and from memory buffers.

- Null BIO (`BIO_s_null`): BIO that discards any data written to it and does not contain any data for reading. Works similar to a Unix `/dev/null` or a Windows NUL device.

- Socket BIO (`BIO_s_socket`): TCP/IP socket or Unix socket I/O.

OpenSSL also supports the following filter BIOs:

- Base64 BIO (`BIO_f_base64`): Base64 encoding and decoding.

- Buffering BIO (`BIO_f_buffer`): Buffering for the next BIO in the BIO chain.

- Cipher BIO (`BIO_f_cipher`): Symmetric encryption and decryption.

- Message digest BIO (`BIO_f_md`): Calculating the message digest of data written to the BIO or read through the BIO.

- Null filter BIO (`BIO_f_null`): A pass-through BIO that just passes data to the next BIO. Not to be confused with a `null` source or sink BIO.

- SSL BIO (`BIO_f_ssl`): SSL and TLS protocol routines. As a rule, it is used with a socket BIO, but can be used with other BIO types as well. Due to historical reasons, OpenSSL still has an *SSL* substring in the object and function names instead of a *TLS* substring.

- Read buffering BIO (`BIO_f_readbuffer`): A read-only BIO that uses its own buffer to add tell or seek support for a stream BIO

In order to work with BIOs, you use a BIO API consisting of functions with the `BIO_` prefix.

You can create a BIO using the `BIO_new()` function or BIO-type-specific functions, such as `BIO_new_socket()` or `BIO_new_accept()`. Some functions can even create short BIO chains. For instance, the `BIO_new_buffer_ssl_connect()` function creates a BIO chain consisting of a buffering BIO, an SSL BIO, and a connect BIO.

Reading from BIOs and writing to BIOs can be done using functions such as `BIO_read()`, `BIO_write()`, `BIO_read_ex()`, `BIO_write_ex()`, `BIO_gets()`, `BIO_get_line()`, and `BIO_puts()`.

The `BIO_puts()` function is convenient when it is needed to write a null-terminated string to a BIO. Note that unlike the `puts()` function from the standard C library, `BIO_puts()` does not add a new line to the output. Rather, `BIO_puts()` works as `fputs()` does, which also does not add an extra new line.

`BIO_gets()` reads a line from a BIO and, as with `fgets()`, preserves the new line character in the read input data. `BIO_gets()` returns the number of read bytes but has the following caveat: if the read data contains a null character, `BIO_gets()` will return the number of bytes up to the first read null character, even if more bytes were read. Therefore, it is better to use the `BIO_get_line()` function introduced in OpenSSL 3.0, which always returns the number of read bytes irrespective of the null characters encountered.

Reading and writing functions are supported by most BIOs. But some BIOs also support BIO-specific functions. For example, SSL BIOs have a `BIO_do_handshake()` function that performs the TLS handshake.

When an error happens during a BIO operation, the error is usually both signaled via a function return code and an error added to the OpenSSL error queue. Therefore, the OpenSSL error queue must be inspected, handled, and cleared after the BIO operations.

When a BIO object is not needed anymore, it must be freed by the `BIO_free()` function. When `BIO_free()` is called, it may have effects on the underlying I/O structures – for example, a file or a network connection may be closed. There is also the `BIO_free_all()` function, which frees the whole BIO chain.

More information about BIOs can be found on the relevant man pages. Here are some of them:

```
$ man bio
$ man BIO_new
$ man BIO_s_connect
$ man BIO_s_accept
$ man BIO_f_ssl
$ man BIO_read
$ man BIO_push
$ man BIO_ctrl
```

In the next section, we will put BIOs to some use. We will use a BIO to establish a TLS connection, send and receive some data over it, and properly shut it down.

Establishing a TLS client connection programmatically

We are going to develop a small `tls-client` program that will connect to an HTTPS server via TLS, make an HTTP request, and read the response from the server.

To do so, we will use an OpenSSL BIO API and SSL API. The BIO API will help us to make a TLS connection, send and receive data over the connection, and properly shut it down. The SSL API will help us with setting up server certificate verification, detecting whether the connection is still alive, and distinguishing error types on the connection. As was mentioned, due to historical reasons, OpenSSL still has the *SSL* substring instead of *TLS* in the names of objects and functions that work with TLS.

More information about the SSL API can be found on the OpenSSL man pages. Here are some relevant pages:

```
$ man ssl
$ man SSL_CTX_new
```

```
$ man SSL_CTX_free
$ man SSL_CTX_load_verify_locations
$ man SSL_CTX_use_certificate_chain_file
$ man SSL_CTX_set_verify
$ man SSL_new
$ man SSL_free
$ man SSL_set_tlsext_host_name
$ man SSL_set1_host
```

Our program will take three command-line arguments:

1. The server hostname
2. The server port
3. Optional argument: the name of the file containing one or more trusted CA certificates for server certificate verification

Our high-level implementation plan will be as follows:

1. Create an SSL context, an SSL_CTX object.
2. Load the trusted CA certificates into the SSL context.
3. Enable server certificate verification in the SSL context.
4. Create an SSL BIO from the SSL context.
5. Establish a TLS connection with the server.
6. Send an HTTP request to the server.
7. Read the server response.
8. Shut down the TLS connection.

Implementing the tls-client program

Let's implement the tls-client program according to our plan:

1. First, allocate read and write access to the buffers:

    ```
    const size_t BUF_SIZE = 16 * 1024;
    char* in_buf  = malloc(BUF_SIZE);
    char* out_buf = malloc(BUF_SIZE);
    ```

2. Next, create an SSL context:

    ```
    SSL_CTX* ctx = SSL_CTX_new(TLS_client_method());
    ```

An SSL context is an object that stores common settings and data for TLS session establishment. An example of common data is a collection of trusted CA certificates. An example of a common setting is a peer certificate verification flag. We will use both examples in our code. Many settings that can be set to an SSL context can also be set to individual TLS connections, represented by objects of the SSL type. If the same setting is set to both the SSL_CTX object and the SSL object, the setting in the SSL object takes precedence.

Note that we used TLS_client_method() as the argument to SSL_CTX_new(). This is how we specify that TLS connections created in this context will be TLS client connections.

3. The next step is to load the trusted certificates. If the third argument is provided to our program, we will load the certificates from the provided file. Otherwise, we will load certificates from the default locations, such as /etc/ssl/certs on Ubuntu Linux or the paths specified by the SSL_CERT_DIR and SSL_CERT_FILE environment variables:

```
const char* trusted_cert_fname = argv[3];
if (trusted_cert_fname)
    err = SSL_CTX_load_verify_locations(
        ctx, trusted_cert_fname, NULL);
else
    err = SSL_CTX_set_default_verify_paths(ctx);
if (err <= 0) {
    if (error_stream)
        fprintf(
            error_stream,
            "Could not load trusted certificates\n");
    goto failure;
}
```

4. Let's also set some settings in the SSL context:

```
SSL_CTX_set_verify(ctx, SSL_VERIFY_PEER, NULL);
SSL_CTX_set_mode(ctx, SSL_MODE_AUTO_RETRY);
```

Setting the SSL_VERIFY_PEER flag enables verification of the peer certificate. In our case, the peer is the TLS server, so the server certificate will be verified. If the verification fails, the TLS handshake will fail as well and the TLS connection will be aborted.

Setting the SSL_MODE_AUTO_RETRY flag simplifies TLS I/O programming. Sometimes, when we want to write some user data to a TLS connection, the TLS protocol wants to read some service data to proceed, and the writing attempt results in the SSL_ERROR_WANT_READ error. In such a case, we have to read from the connection and then retry writing. And vice versa, sometimes we want to read but the TLS protocol wants to write and then we get the

SSL_ERROR_WANT_WRITE error. When the SSL_MODE_AUTO_RETRY flag is set, OpenSSL will retry reading or writing as necessary and handling of the SSL_ERROR_WANT_READ and SSL_ERROR_WANT_WRITE errors will not be needed.

5. The next step is to create an SSL BIO using the SSL context and set the hostname and port of the remote TLS server:

```
const char* hostname = argv[1];
const char* port = argv[2];
BIO* ssl_bio = BIO_new_ssl_connect(ctx);
BIO_set_conn_hostname(ssl_bio, hostname);
BIO_set_conn_port(ssl_bio, port);
```

The SSL BIO contains an SSL object, representing a TLS connection.

6. We have to get that SSL object and set some parameters on it:

```
SSL* ssl = NULL;
BIO_get_ssl(ssl_bio, &ssl);
SSL_set_tlsext_host_name(ssl, hostname);
SSL_set1_host(ssl, hostname);
```

The SSL_set_tlsext_host_name() function sets the hostname for the SNI extension so that it is possible to connect to the correct server on shared hosting. The SSL_set1_host() function sets the hostname for the peer certificate verification. During the handshake, OpenSSL will try to match the provided hostname with the certificate **Common Name (CN)** and **Subject Alternative Names (SANs)**. In case of a hostname mismatch, the TLS handshake will fail and the TLS connection will be aborted. If SSL_set1_host() is not called, the hostname verification will not be done – only the certificate chain verification will be done.

7. The next step is to establish the TLS connection:

```
err = BIO_do_connect(ssl_bio);
if (err <= 0) {
    if (error_stream)
        fprintf(
            error_stream,
            "Could not connect to server %s on port
%s\n",
            hostname,
            port);
    goto failure;
}
```

The BIO_do_connect() call will attempt to perform both TCP and TLS handshaking. For our convenience, SSL BIO allows us to skip an explicit BIO_do_connect() call. Both TCP and TLS handshaking would also be attempted on the first read or write attempt on the SSL BIO. However, it usually makes sense to establish a TLS connection explicitly and handle possible connection errors after the call.

8. The next step is to send the HTTP request:

```
snprintf(
    out_buf,
    BUF_SIZE,
    "GET / HTTP/1.1\r\n"
    "Host: %s\r\n"
    "Connection: close\r\n"
    "User-Agent: Example TLS client\r\n"
    "\r\n",
    hostname);
int request_length = strlen(out_buf);
printf("*** Sending to the server:\n");
printf("%s", out_buf);
int nbytes_written =
    BIO_write(ssl_bio, out_buf, request_length);
if (nbytes_written != request_length) {
    if (error_stream)
        fprintf(
            error_stream,
            "Could not send all data to the server\n");
    goto failure;
}
printf("*** Sending to the server finished\n");
```

9. Next, read the server response:

```
printf("*** Receiving from the server:\n");
while ((SSL_get_shutdown(ssl) & SSL_RECEIVED_SHUTDOWN)
        != SSL_RECEIVED_SHUTDOWN) {
    int nbytes_read = BIO_read(ssl_bio, in_buf, BUF_
SIZE);
    if (nbytes_read <= 0) {
```

```
            int ssl_error = SSL_get_error(ssl, nbytes_read);
            if (ssl_error == SSL_ERROR_ZERO_RETURN)
                break;
            if (error_stream)
                fprintf(
                    error_stream,
                    "Error %i while reading data"
                    " from the server\n",
                    ssl_error);
            goto failure;
        }
        fwrite(in_buf, 1, nbytes_read, stdout);
    }
    printf("*** Receiving from the server finished\n");
```

10. We are reading from the server until the server shuts down its side of the TLS connection. Then, it is good practice to also shut down our side of the connection:

```
    BIO_ssl_shutdown(ssl_bio);
```

11. After the closed connection, we have to free the used objects and buffers:

```
    if (ssl_bio)
        BIO_free_all(ssl_bio);
    if (ctx)
        SSL_CTX_free(ctx);
    free(out_buf);
    free(in_buf);
```

12. Finally, we have to check and clear the OpenSSL error queue:

```
    if (ERR_peek_error()) {
        exit_code = 1
        if (error_stream) {
            fprintf(
                error_stream,
                "Errors from the OpenSSL error queue:\n");
            ERR_print_errors_fp(error_stream);
        }
```

```
        ERR_clear_error();
    }
```

The complete source code of our `tls-client` program can be found on GitHub as the `tls-client.c` file: `https://github.com/PacktPublishing/Demystifying-Cryptography-with-OpenSSL-3/blob/main/Chapter09/tls-client.c`.

Running the tls-client program

Let's run our program against the `example.org` website:

```
$ ./tls-client example.org 443
*** Sending to the server:
GET / HTTP/1.1
Host: example.org
Connection: close
User-Agent: Example TLS client
*** Sending to the server finished
*** Receiving from the server:
HTTP/1.1 200 OK
...
*** Receiving from the server finished
TLS communication succeeded
```

As we can observe, our `tls-client` program could successfully connect to the server, send and receive some data, and successfully close the connection.

Let's also check how error handling works in `tls-client`. To do so, let's try to run `tls-client` against a non-TLS port from the same server:

```
$ ./tls-client example.org 80
Could not connect to server example.org on port 80
Errors from the OpenSSL error queue:
C0F17C57A97F0000:error:0A00010B:SSL routines:ssl3_get_record
:wrong version number
:ssl/record/ssl3_record.c:354:
C0F17C57A97F0000:error:0A000197:SSL routines:SSL_shutdown
:shutdown while in init
:ssl/ssl_lib.c:2242:
TLS communication failed
```

As we can see, our `tls-client` program has detected errors and reported them. We can conclude that the `tls-client` program can both communicate with a TLS server and handle errors.

In the next section, we will learn how to establish TLS server connections and send data over them.

Accepting a TLS server connection programmatically

We are going to develop a small `tls-server` program that will accept TLS connections, read an HTTP request from the connected TLS client, and send an HTTP response back to the client.

Our program will take three command-line arguments:

1. The server port
2. The name of the file containing the TLS server keypair
3. The name of the file containing the TLS server certificate chain

In our case, the certificate chain file will only contain one certificate – the server certificate. But if we had intermediate CA certificates, we could include them in the file after the server certificate to help the TLS client with the server certificate verification. It does not make much sense to include the root CA certificate in the certificate chain file, because the TLS client must have the root CA certificate among the trusted certificates anyway to be able to verify the server certificate.

Our high-level implementation plan will be as follows:

1. Create an SSL context, an `SSL_CTX` object.
2. Load the TLS server keypair into the SSL context.
3. Load the TLS server certificate chain into the SSL context.
4. Check that the loaded keypair matches the loaded server certificate.
5. Create an accept BIO from the SSL context and start accepting incoming TCP connections.
6. When a TCP connection is accepted, the accept BIO will create a new socket BIO, which will represent the accepted connection. We will detach that socket BIO from the accept BIO.
7. Create a new SSL BIO and link it with the socket BIO.
8. Handle the accepted connection using the `SSL-socket` BIO chain formed. We will cover the connection handling plan shortly.
9. After the connection is handled, continue listening on the port and accepting the incoming connections.

Here is the plan on how to handle the accepted connection:

1. Perform a TLS handshake on the accepted connection.
2. Read an `HTTP` request from the TLS client.

3.   Send the server response.

4.   Shut down the TLS connection.

Implementing the tls-server program

Let's implement the `tls-server` program according to our plans:

1.   First, create an SSL context:

```
SSL_CTX* ctx = SSL_CTX_new(TLS_server_method());
```

Note that we used `TLS_server_method()` as the argument to `SSL_CTX_new()` this time. This is how we specify that TLS connections created in this context will be TLS server connections.

2.   Next, load the server keypair:

```
const char* server_keypair_fname = argv[2];
err = SSL_CTX_use_PrivateKey_file(
        ctx, server_keypair_fname, SSL_FILETYPE_PEM);
if (err <= 0) {
    if (error_stream)
        fprintf(
            error_stream,
            "Could not load server keypair from file
%s\n",
            server_keypair_fname);
    goto failure;
}
```

3.   Next, load the server certificate chain:

```
const char* server_cert_chain_fname = argv[3];
err = SSL_CTX_use_certificate_chain_file(
        ctx, server_cert_chain_fname);
if (err <= 0) {
    if (error_stream)
        fprintf(
            error_stream,
            "Could not load server certificate chain"
            " from file %s\n",
```

```
                    server_cert_chain_fname);
        goto failure;
    }
```

4. Next, check that the loaded keypair matches the server certificate, which is the first certificate in the loaded certificate chain:

```
err = SSL_CTX_check_private_key(ctx);
if (err <= 0) {
    if (error_stream)
        fprintf(
            error_stream,
            "Server keypair does not match"
            " server certificate\n");
    goto failure;
}
```

5. Next, set the same SSL_MODE_AUTO_RETRY flag as we set when developing tls-client in the previous section, *Establishing a TLS client connection programmatically*:

```
SSL_CTX_set_mode(ctx, SSL_MODE_AUTO_RETRY);
```

In the server mode, we are not going to request and check the peer (client) certificate – thus, we will not enable the SSL_VERIFY_PEER option.

6. Next, create a new accept BIO and start listening on the specified port:

```
const char* port = argv[1];
BIO* accept_bio = BIO_new_accept(port);
err = BIO_do_accept(accept_bio);
if (err <= 0) {
    if (error_stream)
        fprintf(
            error_stream,
            "Could not bind to port %s and start
listening"
            " for incoming TCP connections\n",
            port);
    goto failure;
}
```

7. Next, organize a loop that will listen for incoming TCP connections:

```
while (1) {
    printf("\n");
    printf("*** Listening on port %s\n", port);
    printf("\n");
```

8. Inside the loop, try to accept an incoming TCP connection:

```
err = BIO_do_accept(accept_bio);
if (err <= 0) {
    if (error_stream)
        fprintf(
            error_stream,
            "Error when trying to accept connection\n");
    if (ERR_peek_error()) {
        if (error_stream) {
            fprintf(
                error_stream,
                "Errors from the OpenSSL error
queue:\n");
            ERR_print_errors_fp(error_stream);
        }
        ERR_clear_error();
    }
    continue;
}
```

Note that we are calling BIO_do_accept() the second time. That's how the accept BIO works. The first BIO_do_accept() call sets up the listening socket. It is equivalent to invoking the bind() and listen() system calls. The second BIO_do_accept() call actually accepts an incoming TCP connection on the listening socket. It is equivalent to invoking the accept() system call.

When a TCP connection is successfully accepted, the accept BIO will create a new socket BIO, similar to how the accept() system call creates a new connection socket. The accept BIO will also attach to the newly created socket BIO, creating an accept-socket BIO chain. The newly created BIO represents the accepted connection, as opposed to the listening socket or BIO. We are going to detach the socket BIO, create and attach an SSL BIO in front of the socket BIO, and do the rest of the communication on the newly created SSL BIO. Let's do it step by step.

9. Detach the socket BIO from the accept BIO:

    ```
    BIO* socket_bio = BIO_pop(accept_bio);
    ```

10. Create a new SSL BIO:

    ```
    BIO* ssl_bio = BIO_new_ssl(ctx, 0);
    ```

11. Attach the SSL BIO in front of the socket BIO:

    ```
    BIO_push(ssl_bio, socket_bio);
    ```

12. We will do the rest of the communication on the SSL BIO in a separate function, called
    handle_accepted_connection():

    ```
    handle_accepted_connection(ssl_bio, error_stream);
    ```

13. Remember that we are still in the listening while() loop, so let's close it:

    ```
    } // end of while loop
    ```

    The handle_accepted_connection() function will perform TLS handshaking, receive
    and send data on the connection, shut it down, handle errors, and free both the SSL BIO and
    the socket BIO. The handle_accepted_connection() function can be run in a separate
    thread if desired. In such a case, several incoming connections can be handled simultaneously.
    The accept BIO is already detached from the socket BIO, so the accept BIO can accept the next
    connections without affecting the running connections. For simplicity and portability, we will
    run a single thread in this example.

Time to implement the handle_accepted_connection() function:

1. First, allocate the read buffer:

    ```
    const size_t BUF_SIZE = 16 * 1024;
    char* in_buf = malloc(BUF_SIZE);
    ```

2. Next, perform the TLS handshake:

    ```
    err = BIO_do_handshake(ssl_bio);
    if (err <= 0) {
        if (error_stream)
            fprintf(error_stream, "TLS handshaking error\n");
        goto failure;
    }
    ```

3. Next, read an HTTP request from the client. For simplicity, we are not going to parse the request thoroughly, but we are going to stop reading from the client when we encounter the first empty line:

```
printf("*** Receiving from the client:\n");
while ((SSL_get_shutdown(ssl) & SSL_RECEIVED_SHUTDOWN)
        != SSL_RECEIVED_SHUTDOWN) {
    int nbytes_read =
        BIO_get_line(ssl_bio, in_buf, BUF_SIZE);
    if (nbytes_read <= 0) {
        int ssl_error = SSL_get_error(ssl, nbytes_read);
        if (ssl_error == SSL_ERROR_ZERO_RETURN)
                break;
        if (error_stream)
            fprintf(
                error_stream,
                "Error %i while reading data"
                " from the client\n",
                ssl_error);
        goto failure;
    }
    fwrite(in_buf, 1, nbytes_read, stdout);
    if (!strcmp(in_buf, "\r\n") || !strcmp(in_buf, "\n"))
            break;
}
printf("*** Receiving from the client finished\n");
```

4. After the client request is read, we will send the server response:

```
const char* response =
    "HTTP/1.0 200 OK\r\n"
    "Content-type: text/plain\r\n"
    "Connection: close\r\n"
    "Server: Example TLS server\r\n"
    "\r\n"
    "Hello from the TLS server!\n";
int response_length = strlen(response);
printf("*** Sending to the client:\n");
```

```
printf("%s", response);
int nbytes_written =
    BIO_write(ssl_bio, response, response_length);
if (nbytes_written != response_length) {
    if (error_stream)
        fprintf(
            error_stream,
            "Could not send all data to the client\n");
    goto failure;
}
printf("*** Sending to the client finished\n");
```

5. After the response is sent to the client and no more data is to be sent further, it is a good practice to shut down our side of the TLS connection:

```
BIO_ssl_shutdown(ssl_bio);
```

6. After the communication is over, we have to free the used objects and buffers:

```
if (ssl_bio)
    BIO_free_all(ssl_bio);
free(in_buf);
```

7. Finally, let's inspect and clear the OpenSSL error queue. Note that we do the error queue handling per incoming connection, not per application run:

```
if (ERR_peek_error()) {
    exit_code = 1;
    if (error_stream) {
        fprintf(
            error_stream,
            "Errors from the OpenSSL error queue:\n");
        ERR_print_errors_fp(error_stream);
    }
    ERR_clear_error();
}
```

That would be the end of the handle_accepted_connection() function. After the handle_accepted_connection() function is finished, the execution returns to the while() loop that is accepting incoming connections, and a new incoming connection can be accepted and handled.

The complete source code of our `tls-server` program can be found on GitHub as the `tls-server.c` file: `https://github.com/PacktPublishing/Demystifying-Cryptography-with-OpenSSL-3/blob/main/Chapter09/tls-server.c`.

Running the tls-server program

Let's run our `tls-server` program and handle some incoming connections:

1. Open a terminal window and start the `tls-server` program:

```
$ ./tls-server 4433 server_keypair.pem server_cert.pem
*** Listening on port 4433
```

The server is now running and accepting connections.

2. Open another terminal window and run the previously developed `tls-client` program against the running `tls-server` program:

```
$ ./tls-client localhost 4433 ca_cert.pem
*** Sending to the server:
GET / HTTP/1.1
Host: localhost
Connection: close
User-Agent: Example TLS client
*** Sending to the server finished
*** Receiving from the server:
HTTP/1.0 200 OK
Content-type: text/plain
Connection: close
Server: Example TLS server
Hello from the TLS server!
*** Receiving from the server finished
TLS communication succeeded
```

As we can observe, the TLS connection has proceeded quite well from the `tls-client` point of view. Note that this time, we gave the third command-line argument to `tls-client`, namely the file containing the server CA certificate, so that `tls-client` could verify the server certificate.

3. Switch to the first terminal window and check the `tls-server` output:

```
*** Receiving from the client:
GET / HTTP/1.1
Host: localhost
```

```
Connection: close
User-Agent: Example TLS client
*** Receiving from the client finished
*** Sending to the client:
HTTP/1.0 200 OK
Content-type: text/plain
Connection: close
Server: Example TLS server
Hello from the TLS server!
*** Sending to the client finished
*** Listening on port 4433
```

As we can see, `tls-server` has successfully handled the connection from `tls-client` and continued to listen for the next incoming connections.

4. Let's try one more thing, another TLS client, the `curl` utility. Let's run the following command in the second terminal windows:

```
$ curl https://localhost:4433 --cacert ca_cert.pem
Hello from the TLS server!
```

As we can observe, `tls-server` is also compatible with `curl`! The `tls-server` output in the first terminal window confirms that our `tls-server` program has just serviced `curl`. See the `User-Agent` header in the request:

```
*** Receiving from the client:
GET / HTTP/1.1
Host: localhost:4433
User-Agent: curl/7.74.0
Accept: */*
*** Receiving from the client finished
*** Sending to the client:
HTTP/1.0 200 OK
Content-type: text/plain
Connection: close
Server: Example TLS server
Hello from the TLS server!
*** Sending to the client finished
*** Listening on port 4433
```

`tls-server` will run and accept connections until it is aborted. It can be done, for example, by pressing *Ctrl* + *C* in the terminal window where it is running.

We have come to the end of the practical part of this chapter. We have learned how to establish TLS connections and use BIOs, and wrote two excellent example programs that use those features.

Let's proceed to the summary.

Summary

In this chapter, we learned about the importance of the TLS protocol, why it is needed, and where it is used. We also learned about how the protocol works on a high level, what is included in the TLS handshake, and what happens after the handshake. We finished the theoretical part by taking a look at the TLS protocol history, learning about its development, and how old and new versions of SSL and TLS differ from each other.

In the practical part of the chapter, we learned how to establish client and server TLS connections, both on the command line and programmatically using C code. We also learned about OpenSSL BIOs.

In the next chapter, we will learn about the more advanced usage of X.509 certificates in TLS, including user-controlled certificate verification and client TLS certificates.

10

Using X.509 Certificates in TLS

In *Chapter 8, X.509 Certificates and PKI*, we learned about **X.509 certificates**, while in *Chapter 9, Establishing TLS Connections and Sending Data over Them*, we learned about the **Transport Layer Security** (**TLS**) protocol and why certificates are important for TLS. We also reviewed some straightforward yet very popular usages of certificates in TLS, such as default server certificate verification performed by OpenSSL, hostname verification, and using an X.509 certificate to accept a TLS server connection.

In this chapter, we will expand on X.509 certificate usage in TLS and cover more advanced use cases.

In this chapter, we will cover the following topics:

- Custom verification of peer certificates in C programs
- Using Certificate Revocation Lists in C programs
- Using the Online Certificate Status Protocol
- Using TLS client certificates

Technical requirements

This chapter will contain commands that you can run on a command line and C source code that you can build and run. For the command line commands, you will need the `openssl` command-line tool, along with OpenSSL dynamic libraries. To build the C code, you will need OpenSSL dynamic or static libraries, library headers, a C compiler, and a linker.

We will implement some example programs in this chapter to practice the topics at hand. The full source code for those programs can be found at `https://github.com/PacktPublishing/Demystifying-Cryptography-with-OpenSSL-3/tree/main/Chapter10`.

Custom verification of peer certificates in C programs

Every TLS connection is established between two peers: the client and the server. Each peer can request and verify the other peer's certificate. In real life, the server certificate is almost always verified during the TLS handshake. Before TLS 1.3, the TLS protocol supported anonymous ciphers, which allowed the server to operate without a certificate. In practice, those anonymous ciphers were rarely used and were forbidden by default. So, in practice, a certificate for TLS has always been required. On the contrary, TLS client certificates are seldom used. However, verifying a client certificate in an application using OpenSSL is very similar to verifying a server certificate. Therefore, it makes sense to talk about peer certificate verification instead of limiting ourselves to server certificate verification. We will verify the server certificate in most of our code examples. More information about verifying client certificates will be provided later in the *Requesting and verifying a TLS client certificate on the server side programmatically* section.

You can verify the TLS peer certificate using OpenSSL in several ways:

- By using an OpenSSL built-in certificate verification code by calling `SSL_CTX_set_verify(ctx, SSL_VERIFY_PEER, NULL)` or `SSL_set_verify(ctx, SSL_VERIFY_PEER, NULL)`, as we did in the `tls-client` program in *Chapter 9, Establishing TLS Connections and Sending Data over Them*. OpenSSL built-in verification can be adjusted by enabling optional checks such as hostname verification, by using the `SSL_set1_host()` function, or purpose verification, by using the `SSL_CTX_set_purpose()` or `SSL_set_purpose()` function.

- By combining the OpenSSL built-in verification code with your own verification callback function by calling `SSL_CTX_set_verify(ctx, SSL_VERIFY_PEER, verify_callback)` or `SSL_set_verify(ctx, SSL_VERIFY_PEER, verify_callback)`. Note that the last function argument is not NULL, but a pointer to your verification callback function.

- By using a "big" certificate verification callback function instead of the OpenSSL built-in verification code by calling `SSL_CTX_set_cert_verify_callback(ctx, cert_verify_callback, arg)`.

- By getting and checking the peer certificate after the completed handshake, which you can do using functions such as `SSL_get_peer_certificate()`, `SSL_get_peer_cert_chain()`, and `SSL_get0_verified_chain()`. It is possible to force completion of the handshake by calling `SSL_CTX_set_verify()` or `SSL_set_verify()` with the `SSL_VERIFY_NONE` flag, or by always returning the successful return code from the verification callbacks.

In this section, we will write a small `verify-callback` program to demonstrate how to use the "small" verification callback, which can be set by the `SSL_CTX_set_verify()` or `SSL_set_verify()` function.

The following are some relevant man pages for functions that we are going to use:

```
$ man SSL_CTX_set_verify
$ man SSL_get_app_data
$ man X509_STORE_CTX_get_ex_data
$ man X509_STORE_CTX_get_error
$ man X509_STORE_CTX_get_current_cert
$ man X509_get_subject_name
$ man X509_NAME_print_ex
$ man BIO_s_mem
```

As we can read on the `SSL_CTX_set_verify()` man page, a verification callback function must have the following synopsis:

```
int SSL_verify_cb(
    int preverify_ok, X509_STORE_CTX* x509_store_ctx);
```

This function takes the following parameters:

- `preverify_ok`: Error indicator
- `x509_store_ctx`: X.509 certificate verification context

The verification callback will be called at least once for every certificate in the peer certificate chain. The first call will be made for the last certificate in the chain, which will be a root CA certificate if the certificate chain can be completed. Then, OpenSSL will work toward the beginning of the chain, calling the verification callback for all intermediate certificates and finally for the peer certificate.

The OpenSSL library has a concept known as **certificate depth**. The depth of a certificate is a number that denotes how far that certificate is from the peer certificate in the certificate verification chain. The peer certificate always has a depth of 0. Its issuer certificate has a depth of 1, the issuer of the issuer has a depth of 2, and so on. There is also a concept known as **verify depth**, which specifies the depth or length of the whole certificate verification chain. It is possible to limit the maximum verify depth using the `SSL_CTX_set_verify_depth()` and `SSL_set_verify_depth()` functions.

When the certificate verification callback is called, the `x509_store_ctx` parameter will contain information about the certificate from the verification chain that's currently being checked. It is possible to get the current certificate using the `X509_STORE_CTX_get_current_cert()` function, and its depth using the `X509_STORE_CTX_get_error_depth()` function.

The `preverify_ok` parameter of the verification callback tells us whether OpenSSL found an issue with the current certificate. The `preverify_ok` parameter can have either a value of 0 or 1. If `preverify_ok` is 1, then OpenSSL has found no issues with the current certificate and will advance to the next certificate. If `preverify_ok` has a value of 0, this means that OpenSSL has detected an issue with the current certificate. In such a case, it is possible to get the error code using the X509_STORE_CTX_get_error() function and the error string representation using the X509_verify_cert_error_string() function. Also, OpenSSL will add an error to the error queue. As mentioned previously, it's important to process and clear the error queue – do not forget to do it.

Note that OpenSSL can call the verification callback with preverify_ok=0 several times for one certificate if the certificate has several errors. It is also nice to know that if the verification callback is called with preverify_ok=1, then the X509_STORE_CTX_get_error() function will not necessarily return X509_V_OK, which is an indication of success. If the verification callback was previously called with preverify_ok=0, then X509_STORE_CTX_get_error() will return the last known error. Only if there were no verification errors with the current and the previous certificates will the function return X509_V_OK.

The verification callback should return either 1, indicating success, or 0, indicating failure. If 0 is returned, the verification fails immediately, a TLS alert message with an error is sent to the peer, and the TLS handshake fails. If 1 is returned, the verification continues. If all the calls of the verification callback return 1, the verification succeeds.

It's worth mentioning that if NULL is provided as the verification callback via the SSL_CTX_set_verify() or SSL_set_verify() function, then the default verification callback is used. The default verification callback just returns preverify_ok.

Note that the verification callback function does not receive a void* argument pointing to user data, as many other callback functions do. Thus, if we want to avoid using global variables – and avoiding them is a good practice – it is not trivial to use data from the rest of the application in the verification callback. However, it is possible. Fortunately, we can get user data via the x509_store_ctx parameter, which is the verification context. It is possible to get the SSL* pointer from x509_store_ctx and then get the user data from the SSL object. The following code example will demonstrate how to do this.

Now, let's write a small verify-callback program that will demonstrate the usage of a verification callback function. The verify-callback program will connect to a TLS server, initiate a TLS handshake, print information about the peer certificate chain verification with the help of the verification callback, and disconnect. We are going to base our program on the tls-client program from *Chapter 9, Establishing TLS Connections and Sending Data over Them*. We will take the tls-client program code and develop it further.

The verify-callback program will take the same three command-line arguments as the tls-client program:

1. Server hostname

2. Server port

3. Optional argument: The name of the file containing one or more trusted CA certificates for server certificate verification

Registering the verification callback

In the code of our new `verify-callback` program, we will introduce a function with the following signature:

```
int verify_callback(
    int preverify_ok, X509_STORE_CTX* x509_store_ctx);
```

This function will be our verification callback.

In the `tls-client` program, we had the following line of code, which enabled the peer certificate verification process:

```
SSL_CTX_set_verify(ctx, SSL_VERIFY_PEER, NULL);
```

We will replace that code line with the following line, which will set the verification callback in the `SSL_CTX` object:

```
SSL_CTX_set_verify(ctx, SSL_VERIFY_PEER, verify_callback);
```

We will also set some user data for the verification callback. We will not set the user data in the `SSL_CTX` object; instead, we will set it in the `SSL` object. By doing this, it will be easier to get the user data in the `verify_callback` function code afterward. We can set any pointer as user data. In this example, our user data will be the `FILE* error_stream` pointer, which is the file handle for printing errors and diagnostic information. The following code line shows how we can set the user data:

```
SSL_set_app_data(ssl, error_stream);
```

`SSL_set_app_data()` is a macro for calling the `SSL_set_ex_data()` function, which is a member of the `*_set_ex_data()` function family. By using `*_set_ex_data()` functions, it is possible to set one or several so-called **extra data** pointers to objects of the `SSL`, `BIO`, and `X509` types, among others. You can read more about those functions on the `SSL_set_app_data` and `CRYPTO_set_ex_data` man pages. I find the `*_ex_data` API inconvenient and confusing, so I recommend using it as little as possible. If you need to set several user data elements to an `SSL` object, I recommend creating a structure, putting those data elements into the structure, and setting a pointer to that structure to an `SSL` object using the `SSL_set_app_data()` function, as we have done in this example.

In this example, we are interested in certificate verification, so we will not exchange request and response data with the server. Instead, we will shut down the connection after a successful or unsuccessful handshake. Because of that, we will remove the HTTP request-response code from the code inherited from the `tls-client` program.

Implementing the verification callback

Now, let's implement the verification callback:

1. Our verification callback will just print diagnostic information on the call parameters and the current certificate. We will print that information to the `FILE*` stream that we have set as the user data for the `SSL` object.

    We will start by implementing the verification callback from the function headline:

    ```
    int verify_callback(
        int preverify_ok, X509_STORE_CTX* x509_store_ctx) {
    ```

2. The first thing that we will do is get the user data, which is our error and diagnostic stream:

    ```
    int ssl_ex_data_idx = SSL_get_ex_data_X509_STORE_CTX_
    idx();
    SSL* ssl = X509_STORE_CTX_get_ex_data(
        x509_store_ctx, ssl_ex_data_idx);
    FILE* error_stream = SSL_get_app_data(ssl);
    ```

    To get the user data, which in this case is the `FILE*` stream, we have to get the `SSL` object. The `SSL` object is available as extra data with a particular index in the `x509_store_ctx` parameter. Hence, first, we have to get the index, then get the `SSL*` pointer, then the `FILE*` `error_stream` user data pointer.

3. Next, we will get the current certificate verification depth and the current error with the certificate, if any:

    ```
    int depth = X509_STORE_CTX_get_error_depth(x509_store_
    ctx);
    int error_code = preverify_ok ?
        X509_V_OK :
        X509_STORE_CTX_get_error(x509_store_ctx);
    const char* error_string =
        X509_verify_cert_error_string(error_code);
    ```

4. Next, we'll get the current certificate and its Subject:

    ```
    X509* current_cert =
        X509_STORE_CTX_get_current_cert(x509_store_ctx);
    X509_NAME* current_cert_subject =
        X509_get_subject_name(current_cert);
    ```

    Here, the Subject is an `X509_NAME` object.

5. Now, let's get a text representation of the obtained X509_NAME object by printing it to a memory BIO:

```
BIO* mem_bio = BIO_new(BIO_s_mem());
X509_NAME_print_ex(
    mem_bio,
    current_cert_subject,
    0,
    XN_FLAG_ONELINE & ~ASN1_STRFLGS_ESC_MSB);
```

6. Next, we will get a pointer to the text printed to the memory BIO and the text length:

```
char* bio_data = NULL;
long bio_data_len = BIO_get_mem_data(mem_bio, &bio_data);
```

Note that the printed text is not null terminated and may contain null characters, which is why knowing the text length is important.

7. Now that we have enough data to print the diagnostic information that we want, let's print it to error_stream:

```
fprintf(
    error_stream,
    "verify_callback() called with depth=%i, "
    "preverify_ok=%i, error_code=%i, error_string=%s\n",
    depth,
    preverify_ok,
    error_code,
    error_string);
fprintf(error_stream, "Certificate Subject: ");
fwrite(bio_data, 1, bio_data_len, error_stream);
fprintf(error_stream, "\n");
```

We could have printed the X509_NAME object containing the certificate Subject directly to error_stream using the X509_NAME_print_ex_fp() function. We haven't done this here because I wanted to demonstrate how to use memory BIO and get the text representation of an X509_NAME object. In real-world programs, we often need to get text into memory and process it further than just print it to a FILE* stream.

8. Our `verify_callback` function is almost finished. Now, we have to free some of the memory structures that we used:

```
BIO_free(mem_bio);
X509_free(current_cert);
```

Note that we have not freed the X509_NAME object containing the certificate subject. This is because the X509_NAME object is owned by the X509 object containing the certificate; the X509_NAME object will be freed when the X509 object is freed. Generally, it is hard to predict which OpenSSL objects you must free and which you must not. Usually, you can find that information in the OpenSSL documentation, but not always. If you cannot find it in the documentation, you have to find the answer in another way, such as by checking the OpenSSL source code, experimenting, or asking your local OpenSSL expert.

9. After freeing the used data structures, we have to return the exit code from our verification callback. The easiest choice is to just return `preverify_ok`:

```
return preverify_ok;
}
```

With that, you've learned how to make and use a certificate verification callback.

The complete source code for our `verify-callback` program can be found in this book's GitHub repository in the `verify-callback.c` file: `https://github.com/PacktPublishing/Demystifying-Cryptography-with-OpenSSL-3/blob/main/Chapter10/verify-callback.c`.

Running the program

Let's run our program and see how it works. We will run it against the `www.example.org` server that we used previously. Before running it, please make sure that your current installation of OpenSSL will be able to find the trusted CA certificates. Please refer to *Chapter 9, Establishing TLS Connections and Sending Data over Them*, for instructions on how to provide trusted CA certificates to OpenSSL.

Here is how we run the program:

```
$ ./verify-callback www.example.org 443
verify_callback() called with depth=2, preverify_ok=1, error_
code=0, error_string=ok
Certificate Subject: C = US, O = DigiCert Inc, OU = www.
digicert.com, CN = DigiCert Global Root CA
verify_callback() called with depth=1, preverify_ok=1, error_
code=0, error_string=ok
Certificate Subject: C = US, O = DigiCert Inc, CN = DigiCert
TLS RSA SHA256 2020 CA1
```

```
verify_callback() called with depth=0, preverify_ok=1, error_
code=0, error_string=ok
Certificate Subject: C = US, ST = California, L = Los Angeles,
O = Internet Corporation for Assigned Names and Numbers, CN =
www.example.org
TLS communication succeeded
```

As we can see, OpenSSL has built a certificate verification chain for the peer certificate and verified it, starting from the root CA certificate and ending with the server certificate. Here, our `verify-callback` program printed what we expected for a successful case. But what about a failing case?

For the failing case, we will run our `verify-callback` program against a server under the special `badssl.com` domain. This domain contains servers that have been configured to test TLS handshake failures. You can find a list of different test servers and failure reasons at `https://badssl.com/`. In the following example, we will use the `incomplete-chain.badssl.com` server. We are expecting that OpenSSL will not be able to build a verification chain for the peer certificate because it will not be able to find an issuer certificate for the certificate in the chain. Let's check whether our expectation is correct:

```
$ ./verify-callback incomplete-chain.badssl.com 443
verify_callback() called with depth=0, preverify_ok=0, error_
code=20, error_string=unable to get local issuer certificate
Certificate Subject: C = US, ST = California, L = Walnut Creek,
O = Lucas Garron Torres, CN = *.badssl.com
Could not connect to server incomplete-chain.badssl.com on port
443
Errors from the OpenSSL error queue:
C0C158FD5D7F0000:error:0A000086:SSL routines:tls_post_process_
server_certificate:certificate verify failed:ssl/statem/statem_
clnt.c:1882:
C0C158FD5D7F0000:error:0A000197:SSL routines:SSL_
shutdown:shutdown while in init:ssl/ssl_lib.c:2242:
TLS communication failed
```

As we can see, our expectation was correct. We have got the following data in the verification callback:

```
depth=0, preverify_ok=0, error_code=20,
error_string=unable to get local issuer certificate
```

We have an issue (`preverify_ok=0`) with the server certificate (`depth=0`). Here, the issue is that OpenSSL could not find the issuer certificate (`error_code=20`, `error_string=unable to get local issuer certificate`).

From this, we can conclude that our `verify-callback` program works in both successful and failing cases and can diagnose TLS handshake issues with the help of the certificate verification callback.

Errors in the certificate chain are not the only reason for possible TLS handshake failures. Sometimes, the certificate's private key becomes compromised, and the certificate is revoked because of that. The certificate revocation status can be checked via **Certificate Revocation Lists** (**CRLs**) or the **Online Certificate Status Protocol** (**OCSP**). In the next section, we will learn about CRLs.

Using Certificate Revocation Lists in C programs

A CRL is a data structure that lists revoked certificates. A certificate can be revoked for several reasons, such as private key compromise, private key loss, an error in the certificate, cessation of operations by the certificate owner, the certificate being superseded by another certificate, and so on.

CRLs can often be downloaded from the **Certificate Authority** (**CA**) web servers. Those downloadable CRLs are often represented in **Distinguished Encoding Rules** (**DER**) format. For instance, a CRL for the `www.example.org` site certificate can be downloaded from `http://crl3.digicert.com/DigiCertTLSRSASHA2562020CA1-4.crl`.

Once downloaded to a file, a CRL can be viewed with the `openssl` command-line tool using the `openssl crl` subcommand:

```
$ openssl crl \
    -in DigiCertTLSRSASHA2562020CA1-4.crl \
    -inform DER \
    -noout \
    -text \
    | less
```

We will get the following output:

```
Certificate Revocation List (CRL):
        Version 2 (0x1)
        Signature Algorithm: sha256WithRSAEncryption
        Issuer: C = US, O = DigiCert Inc,
                CN = DigiCert TLS RSA SHA256 2020 CA1
        Last Update: May 22 07:00:10 2022 GMT
        Next Update: May 29 07:00:10 2022 GMT
        CRL extensions:
            X509v3 Authority Key Identifier:
                … hex bytes …
```

```
          X509v3 CRL Number:
              238
          X509v3 Issuing Distribution Point: critical
              Full Name:
                  URI:http://crl3.digicert.com/
  DigiCertTLSRSASHA2562020CA1-4.crl
  Revoked Certificates:
      Serial Number: 048A6B01889FA7BEF34AC92DAAC36079
          Revocation Date: Jun 22 00:31:11 2021 GMT
          CRL entry extensions:
              X509v3 CRL Reason Code:
                  Key Compromise
      Serial Number: 098AB8A98137F3432A18DE8C1B7F6D2F
          Revocation Date: Jul  3 05:58:20 2021 GMT
          CRL entry extensions:
              X509v3 CRL Reason Code:
                  Key Compromise
      … more certificates …
  Signature Algorithm: sha256WithRSAEncryption
      … hex bytes …
```

As we can see, a CRL contains the following information:

- CRL format version
- The algorithm used to sign the CRL
- The CRL issuer in **Distinguished Name (DN)** format
- Last update timestamp
- Next update timestamp
- Optional CRL extensions
- List of revoked certificates
- Signature

A CRL must be signed by the issuer's private key. The issuer of the CRL is the same entity as the issuer of the certificate, which can be checked for revocation by the CRL. Only the certificate issuer has the authority to revoke the certificate by putting in a CRL.

Revoked certificates are identified by the certificate serial numbers. A revoked certificate entry in a CRL may contain a revocation reason, but it is not mandatory.

When it comes to checking a certificate against CRL programmatically, two approaches can be used:

- A CRL can be supplied to an X509_STORE object using the X509_STORE_add_crl() function. This is a good method if you already have a CRL for the target certificate. It is a good idea to cache CRLs as they may be quite large – up to tens of megabytes in size for large CAs.

- A CRL for a particular certificate can be looked up by a callback supplied by the X509_STORE_set_lookup_crls() function. This is a nice method if the checked certificate is not known in advance, which is a common situation for server certificates in TLS connections. We will use this method in the following code example.

Now, let's write a small crl-check program that will demonstrate how to use a CRL lookup callback function.

A CRL lookup callback function must have the following synopsis:

```
STACK_OF(X509_CRL)* X509_STORE_CTX_lookup_crls_fn(
    const X509_STORE_CTX* x509_store_ctx,
    const X509_NAME* x509_name);
```

This function takes the following parameters:

- x509_store_ctx: The X.509 certificate verification context
- x509_name: The subject of the certificate, whose revocation status should be checked using CRL

The function returns a stack of X509_CRL objects, which represent CRLs. OpenSSL often uses stacks as lists. As we can see, the callback function can return several CRLs if needed.

We are going to base our crl-check program on the verify-callback program, as described in the *Custom verification of peer certificates in C programs* section. We will take the verify-callback program code and develop it further.

Our crl-check program will take the same three command-line arguments as the verify-callback program:

1. Server hostname
2. Server port
3. Optional argument: Name of the file containing one or more trusted CA certificates for server certificate verification

We are going to use some OpenSSL functions that we have not used before. Here are the relevant man pages, along with the documentation for them:

```
$ man SSL_CTX_get_cert_store
$ man X509_STORE_set_lookup_crls
$ man X509_STORE_set_flags
$ man X509_NAME_print_ex_fp
$ man X509_get_ext_d2i
$ man ASN1_STRING_get0_data
$ man OSSL_HTTP_get
$ man d2i_X509_CRL_bio
```

Let's start the crl-check program implementation. First, we will register the CRL lookup callback.

Registering the CRL lookup callback

Here is how we register the CRL lookup callback:

1. In the code of our new crl-check program, we will introduce a function with the following signature:

   ```
   STACK_OF(X509_CRL)* lookup_crls(
       const X509_STORE_CTX* x509_store_ctx,
       const X509_NAME* x509_name);
   ```

   This function will be our CRL lookup callback function.

2. To ensure that our callback function will be called, we need to set it to the X509_STORE object using the X509_STORE_set_lookup_crls() function and enable CRL checking by setting the X509_V_FLAG_CRL_CHECK flag to the same X509_STORE object. The X509_STORE object is the certificate store of the SSL_CTX object. The X509_STORE object can store trusted certificates, untrusted certificates, CRLs, verification parameters, and extra application-specific data. We can get a pointer to the X509_STORE object from the SSL_CTX object.

   To set the callback function and enable the CRL check, we need to add the following code to our run_tls_client() function:

   ```
   X509_STORE* x509_store = SSL_CTX_get_cert_store(ctx);
   X509_STORE_set_lookup_crls(x509_store, lookup_crls);
   X509_STORE_set_flags(x509_store, X509_V_FLAG_CRL_CHECK);
   ```

The next step is to implement the CRL lookup callback.

Implementing the CRL lookup callback

Let's implement the CRL lookup callback function, `lookup_crls()`:

1. As we can see from the function signature, the callback function gets an X509_NAME object with the certificate Subject as the second parameter. If we had some CRL cache that could help us get the needed CRL based on the certificate Subject, that parameter would help us. But in this example, we don't have one. Instead, we are going to get the current certificate from the X509_STORE_CTX object, which was supplied as the first callback function parameter, get the CRL distribution points from the certificate, and download the relevant CRL from one of the distribution points.

    First, let's get the error stream in the same way as we did in the verify_callback() function:

    ```
    int ssl_ex_data_idx = SSL_get_ex_data_X509_STORE_CTX_
    idx();
    SSL* ssl = X509_STORE_CTX_get_ex_data(
        x509_store_ctx, ssl_ex_data_idx);
    FILE* error_stream = SSL_get_app_data(ssl);
    ```

2. Now, let's get the current certificate that needs to be checked for revocation:

    ```
    X509* current_cert =
        X509_STORE_CTX_get_current_cert(x509_store_ctx);
    ```

3. Next, let's get and print some useful information about the certificate:

    ```
    int depth = X509_STORE_CTX_get_error_depth(x509_store_
    ctx);
    X509_NAME* current_cert_subject =
        X509_get_subject_name(current_cert);
    fprintf(
        error_stream,
        "lookup_crls() called with depth=%i\n",
        depth);
    fprintf(error_stream, "Looking up CRL for certificate:
    ");
    X509_NAME_print_ex_fp(
        error_stream,
        current_cert_subject,
        0,
        XN_FLAG_ONELINE & ~ASN1_STRFLGS_ESC_MSB);
    fprintf(error_stream, "\n");
    ```

Note that this time, we used the X509_NAME_print_ex_fp() function instead of printing the certificate Subject to a BIO, as we did in the verify_callback() function.

4. The next step is to get the CRL distribution points from the certificate. Not every certificate defines CRL distribution points. Fortunately, the certificate from www.example.org that we are going to test defines them, so we can download the CRL from them. Here is how we get the CRL distribution points:

```
CRL_DIST_POINTS* crl_dist_points =
    (CRL_DIST_POINTS*) X509_get_ext_d2i(
        current_cert,
        NID_crl_distribution_points,
        NULL,
        NULL);
```

CRL_DIST_POINTS is a typedef for STACK_OF(DIST_POINT), where DIST_POINT is a structure that defines a CRL distribution point.

5. Next, we must go through the distribution points, try to download the CRL from one of them, and return the downloaded CRL:

```
int crl_dist_point_count =
    sk_DIST_POINT_num(crl_dist_points);
for (int i = 0; i < crl_dist_point_count; i++) {
    DIST_POINT* dist_point =
        sk_DIST_POINT_value(crl_dist_points, i);
    X509_CRL* crl =
        download_crl_from_dist_point(
            dist_point, error_stream);
    if (!crl)
        continue;
    STACK_OF(X509_CRL)* crls = sk_X509_CRL_new_null();
    sk_X509_CRL_push(crls, crl);
    return crls;
}
return NULL;
```

That concludes the lookup_crls() function. As we can see, the lookup_crls() function will return NULL if the CRL could not be downloaded.

You have probably noticed that we call the download_crl_from_dist_point() function to download the CRL. We have to implement that function as well.

Implementing the function for downloading a CRL from a distribution point

Let's go through the function code for downloading the CRL:

1. The `download_crl_from_dist_point()` function has the following signature:

```
X509_CRL* download_crl_from_dist_point(
    const DIST_POINT* dist_point, FILE* error_stream);
```

2. The distribution point structure can contain several strings, called general names. Let's get them:

```
const DIST_POINT_NAME* dist_point_name =
    dist_point->distpoint;
if (!dist_point_name || dist_point_name->type != 0)
    return NULL;
const GENERAL_NAMES* general_names =
    dist_point_name->name.fullname;
if (!general_names)
    return NULL;
```

3. Then, we have to loop through the general names:

```
int general_name_count = sk_GENERAL_NAME_num(general_
names);
for (int i = 0; i < general_name_count; i++) {
    const GENERAL_NAME* general_name =
        sk_GENERAL_NAME_value(general_names, i);
    ...
}
```

4. The following code represents the code inside the loop. First, we will look for a URL among general names:

```
int general_name_type = 0;
const ASN1_STRING* general_name_asn1_string =
    (const ASN1_STRING*) GENERAL_NAME_get0_value(
        general_name, &general_name_type);
if (general_name_type != GEN_URI)
    continue;
```

5. If we find a general name with a URL, we will get its text representation:

```
const char* url =
    (const char*) ASN1_STRING_get0_data(
        general_name_asn1_string);
```

6. In this example, we only support HTTP URLs, so we will skip non-HTTP URLs. This is fine since CRL distribution points are usually HTTP URLs:

```
const char* http_url_prefix = "http://";
size_t http_url_prefix_len = strlen(http_url_prefix);
if (strncmp(url, http_url_prefix, http_url_prefix_len))
    continue;
```

7. At this point, we have found an HTTP URL that points to a CRL. Let's try to download it:

```
fprintf(error_stream, "Found CRL URL: %s\n", url);
X509_CRL* crl = download_crl_from_http_url(url);
```

8. If the downloading attempt has failed, we can try another general name:

```
if (!crl) {
    fprintf(
        error_stream,
        "Failed to download CRL from %s\n", url);
    continue;
}
```

9. If we have successfully downloaded the CRL, we will return it:

```
fprintf(error_stream, "Downloaded CRL from %s\n", url);
return crl;
```

    That concludes the code inside the `for` loop.

If the `for` loop completes, this means that we could not download the CRL from the current CRL distribution point. In such a case, we will return NULL:

```
return NULL;
```

If the `download_crl_from_dist_point()` function returns NULL, the calling `lookup_crls()` function will try the next distribution point.

The `download_crl_from_dist_point()` function calls the `download_crl_from_http_url()` function to download the CRL from the found URL. Let's look at its code.

Implementing the function for downloading a CRL from an HTTP URL

The `download_crl_from_http_url()` function is relatively short:

```
X509_CRL* download_crl_from_http_url(const char* url) {
    BIO* bio = OSSL_HTTP_get(
        url,
        NULL /* proxy */,
        NULL /* no_proxy */,
        NULL /* wbio */,
        NULL /* rbio */,
        NULL /* bio_update_fn */,
        NULL /* arg */,
        65536 /* buf_size */,
        NULL /* headers */,
        NULL /* expected_content_type */,
        1 /* expect_asn1 */,
        50 * 1024 * 1024 /* max resp len */,
        60 /* timeout */);
    X509_CRL* crl = d2i_X509_CRL_bio(bio, NULL);
    BIO_free(bio);
    return crl;
}
```

In the `download_crl_from_http_url()` function, we have used two functions that we have not used before: `OSSL_HTTP_get()` and `d2i_X509_CRL_bio()`. `OSSL_HTTP_get()` is one of the functions of the OpenSSL HTTP client, a new functionality that has been introduced in OpenSSL 3.0. `d2i_X509_CRL_bio()` is a function that reads a DER-encoded CRL encoded from a BIO and converts it into an `X509_CRL` object. OpenSSL has many similar conversion functions, such as `i2d_X509()`, `d2i_RSAPublicKey_fp()`, and many others. The names of those functions consist of the following components:

- `d2i` or `i2d`, which specifies the direction of the conversion. `i` means "internal," an internal C structure in memory. `d` means "DER." Hence, `d2i` means "DER to internal" and `i2d` means "internal to DER."

- Object type – for example, `X509_CRL`.

- An optional suffix that denotes the input or output channel for reading or writing the DER-encoded object. The `bio` suffix means BIO, while the `fp` suffix means file pointer. If there is no suffix, the DER-encoded object will be read from or written to memory.

As mentioned previously, not all certificates define CRL distribution points. Even if the distribution points are defined, a CRL download may fail. What happens in such a case? If the X509_V_FLAG_CRL_CHECK flag is set and OpenSSL could not find a CRL, the certificate verification will fail with an X509_V_ERR_UNABLE_TO_GET_CRL error. Often, such a failure is unwanted because a very small share of the issued certificates is revoked. If the revocation check has failed, it's a much higher probability that the certificate has not been revoked. How can we avoid certificate verification failure if OpenSSL could not get the CRL? No flag instructs OpenSSL to ignore the X509_V_ERR_UNABLE_TO_GET_CRL error if the X509_V_FLAG_CRL_CHECK flag is set. However, all verification errors are processed by the verification callback, so it is possible to instruct OpenSSL to ignore that error by returning 1 from the verification callback. To do it, we just have to add the following lines to the verify_callback() function:

```
if (error_code == X509_V_ERR_UNABLE_TO_GET_CRL)
    return 1;
```

Those were the last few lines that we have to add to the crl-check program to make it complete.

The complete source code for our crl-check program can be found in this book's GitHub repository in the crl-check.c file: https://github.com/PacktPublishing/Demystifying-Cryptography-with-OpenSSL-3/blob/main/Chapter10/crl-check.c.

Running the program

Let's run our program and see how it works. We will run it against the www.example.org server, which we also used for the previous example:

```
$ ./crl-check example.org 443
* lookup_crls() called with depth=0
  Looking up CRL for certificate: C = US, ST = California, L =
Los Angeles, O = Internet Corporation for Assigned Names and
Numbers, CN = www.example.org
  Found CRL URL: http://crl3.digicert.com/
DigiCertTLSRSASHA2562020CA1-4.crl
  Downloaded CRL from http://crl3.digicert.com/
DigiCertTLSRSASHA2562020CA1-4.crl
* verify_callback() called with depth=2, preverify_ok=1, error_
code=0, error_string=ok
  Certificate Subject: C = US, O = DigiCert Inc, OU = www.
digicert.com, CN = DigiCert Global Root CA
* verify_callback() called with depth=1, preverify_ok=1, error_
code=0, error_string=ok
  Certificate Subject: C = US, O = DigiCert Inc, CN = DigiCert
```

```
TLS RSA SHA256 2020 CA1
* verify_callback() called with depth=0, preverify_ok=1, error_
code=0, error_string=ok
  Certificate Subject: C = US, ST = California, L = Los
Angeles, O = Internet Corporation for Assigned Names and
Numbers, CN = www.example.org
TLS communication succeeded
```

As we can see, our crl-check program successfully found and downloaded the CRL so that OpenSSL could check certificate revocation against the downloaded CRL.

Let's also check a negative case – that is, when a certificate is revoked. We can find a revoked certificate by going to the revoked.badssl.com server:

```
$ ./crl-check revoked.badssl.com 443
* lookup_crls() called with depth=0
  Looking up CRL for certificate: CN = revoked.badssl.com
  Found CRL URL: http://crl3.digicert.com/
RapidSSLTLSDVRSAMixedSHA2562020CA-1.crl
  Downloaded CRL from http://crl3.digicert.com/
RapidSSLTLSDVRSAMixedSHA2562020CA-1.crl
* verify_callback() called with depth=0, preverify_ok=0, error_
code=23, error_string=certificate revoked
  Certificate Subject: CN = revoked.badssl.com
Could not connect to server revoked.badssl.com on port 443
Errors from the OpenSSL error queue:
C081A6A4617F0000:error:0A000086:SSL routines:tls_post_process_
server_certificate:certificate verify failed:ssl/statem/statem_
clnt.c:1882:
C081A6A4617F0000:error:0A000197:SSL routines:SSL_
shutdown:shutdown while in init:ssl/ssl_lib.c:2242:
TLS communication failed
```

As we can see, the server certificate verification failed because the certificate was revoked. We can see this in the error_code=23, error_string=certificate revoked error message.

The tests we've conducted confirm that our crl-check program works as expected and can detect revoked certificates.

With that, we have learned how to check certificate revocation using CRL. But checking CRL is not the only method of checking certificate revocation. There is also another revocation checking method, known as OCSP. We are going to review it in the next section.

Using the Online Certificate Status Protocol

In this section, we will learn about OCSP. First, we will learn what it is and how it works. Then, we will learn how to use OCSP on the command line and in C programs.

Understanding the Online Certificate Status Protocol

OCSP is a more modern method of certificate revocation checking that uses much less network traffic than CRL. When using OCSP, you don't need to download large CRL files. Instead, it is possible to query an OCSP server, also known as an **OCSP responder**, about the status of a particular certificate. Similar to how CRLs are published by the issuer of a particular certificate, OCSP servers are also maintained by the certificate issuer.

When querying an OCSP responder, an OCSP client sends an ASN.1-encoded OCSP request, containing a list of certificates to check for revocation. The OCSP server responds with an ASN.1-encoded OCSP response, which contains the queried certificate statuses, the validity period of the response, some other information, and the response signature that was produced using the certificate issuer's private key.

As OCSP responses are signed, OCSP responders usually operate via unencrypted HTTP. Choosing HTTP instead of HTTPS for OCSP checks also avoids circular OCSP requests when you're verifying the HTTPS server certificate of the OCSP responder.

OCSP is sometimes criticized for privacy issues. If a TLS client, such as a web browser, checks every TLS server certificate via OCSP, then OCSP responders know which websites the browser user visited. Each OCSP responder only knows about those websites that use certificates issued by the same issuer that owns the OCSP responder. However, if someone eavesdrops on the TLS client's internet line, they can read all the OCSP requests and responses that have been sent via unencrypted HTTP. On the other hand, the eavesdropper already knows the IP addresses of the servers that the user contacts. Hence, the eavesdropper is already in the position of knowing popular websites, such as Google or Facebook, just by knowing the server IP addresses. The additional information that the eavesdropper gains includes small websites hosted on shared web hostings, where the same IP can be used by several websites, and some blogging platforms where each blog has a subdomain.

Regardless of whether privacy issues are big or small, they can be mitigated via **OCSP stapling**. OCSP stapling means that the OCSP response about the server certificate is sent to the TLS client by the TLS server during the TLS handshake so that the TLS client does not need to contact the OCSP responder. In such cases, the OCSP response is stapled to the TLS handshake. Hence, this mechanism is called OCSP stapling. OCSP stapling is implemented using the **Certificate Status Request** TLS extension. The TLS client has to request the certificate status during the handshake to get it from the TLS server. The server, on the other hand, has to periodically poll the OCSP responder for the status of its certificate, to always have a fresh OCSP response and supply it to the clients.

OpenSSL supports OCSP querying both via the command line and programmatically. First, let's learn how to check certificates for revocation on the command line.

Using OCSP on the command line

OCSP querying on the command line can be performed using the `openssl ocsp` subcommand of the `openssl` tool. Let's try this functionality:

1. First, we will need the server certificate and its issuer certificate. We can get them using the `openssl s_client` subcommand:

```
$ echo | openssl s_client \
    -connect www.example.org:443 \
    -showcerts
```

Note the `-showcerts` switch. This instructs the `openssl` tool to print certificates sent by the server to the terminal. The command will produce a long output that contains the certificates:

```
Certificate chain
 0 s:C = US, ST = California, L = Los Angeles, O =
Internet\C2\A0Corporation\C2\A0for\C2\A0Assigned\C2\
A0Names\C2\A0and\C2\A0Numbers, CN = www.example.org
   i:C = US, O = DigiCert Inc, CN = DigiCert TLS RSA
SHA256 2020 CA1
-----BEGIN CERTIFICATE-----
… base64 characters …
-----END CERTIFICATE-----
 1 s:C = US, O = DigiCert Inc, CN = DigiCert TLS RSA
SHA256 2020 CA1
   i:C = US, O = DigiCert Inc, OU = www.digicert.com, CN
= DigiCert Global Root CA
-----BEGIN CERTIFICATE-----
… base64 characters …
-----END CERTIFICATE-----
```

2. Now, we can copy and paste the first PEM-encoded certificates from the terminal to some files. Let's save the first printed certificate, with CN = `www.example.org`, to a file named `www.example.org.cert.pem` and the second certificate, with CN = `DigiCert TLS RSA SHA256 2020 CA1`, to a file named `DigiCert_Intermediate_CA1.pem`.

3. We have got the certificates – but how are we going to find out the OCSP responder URL? Fortunately, certificates often contain information about the OCSP responder URL in the **Authority Information Access** X509v3 extension. The certificate of the `www.example.org` website also contains that extension and the OCSP responder URL. We can extract this URL using the `-ocsp_uri` switch of the `openssl x509` subcommand:

```
$ openssl x509 \
    -in www.example.org.cert.pem \
```

```
    -noout \
    -ocsp_uri
http://ocsp.digicert.com
```

4. Then, we can perform a revocation check via OCSP using the following command:

```
$ openssl ocsp \
    -issuer DigiCert_Intermediate_CA1.pem \
    -cert www.example.org.cert.pem \
    -url http://ocsp.digicert.com
WARNING: no nonce in response
Response verify OK
www.example.org.cert.pem: good
        This Update: Jun 12 05:09:01 2022 GMT
        Next Update: Jun 19 04:24:01 2022 GMT
```

As we can see, the certificate is still good, which means it's not been revoked. The `Response verify OK` message means that the OCSP response has been verified successfully: it has been signed correctly by the expected issuer and is not outdated.

5. If we add the `-text` and `-resp_text` switches to the command line, we will be able to see the text representation of the OCSP request and response. Run the following command:

```
$ openssl ocsp \
    -issuer DigiCert_Intermediate_CA1.pem \
    -cert www.example.org.cert.pem \
    -url http://ocsp.digicert.com \
    -text \
    -resp_text
```

Running the preceding command will give you the following output. The first part of the output shows the OCSP request:

```
OCSP Request Data:
    Version: 1 (0x0)
    Requestor List:
        Certificate ID:
            Hash Algorithm: sha1
            Issuer Name Hash:
                E4E395A229D3D4C1C31FF0980C0B4EC0098AABD8
            Issuer Key Hash:
                B76BA2EAA8AA848C79EAB4DA0F98B2C59576B9F4
            Serial Number:
```

```
                    0FAA63109307BC3D414892640CCD4D9A
        Request Extensions:
            OCSP Nonce:
                0410C5D14D224CCCEA68EEEC1478533D0DF8
```

The second part of the output shows the OCSP response and verification status of the response and the certificate:

```
OCSP Response Data:
    OCSP Response Status: successful (0x0)
    Response Type: Basic OCSP Response
    Version: 1 (0x0)
    Responder Id: B76BA2EAA8AA848C79EAB4DA0F98B2C59576B9F4
    Produced At: Jun 12 05:25:33 2022 GMT
    Responses:
    Certificate ID:
      Hash Algorithm: sha1
      Issuer Name Hash:
        E4E395A229D3D4C1C31FF0980C0B4EC0098AABD8
      Issuer Key Hash:
        B76BA2EAA8AA848C79EAB4DA0F98B2C59576B9F4
      Serial Number:
        0FAA63109307BC3D414892640CCD4D9A
    Cert Status: good
    This Update: Jun 12 05:09:01 2022 GMT
    Next Update: Jun 19 04:24:01 2022 GMT
    Signature Algorithm: sha256WithRSAEncryption
        … hex bytes …
WARNING: no nonce in response
Response verify OK
www.example.org.cert.pem: good
        This Update: Jun 12 05:09:01 2022 GMT
        Next Update: Jun 19 04:24:01 2022 GMT
```

As we can see, both OCSP requests and OCSP responses are rather simple. Both contain a compound certificate ID and an optional nonce. The response contains important additional data, such as certificate status, validity timestamps, and the signature.

Now that we've checked the revocation status of a good certificate via OCSP, let's take a look at a revoked certificate:

1. We already know that we can find a revoked certificate at `revoked.badssl.com`. As in the previous example, let's make a connection to the server and get the server certificate chain without the root CA certificate:

```
$ echo | openssl s_client \
    -connect revoked.badssl.com:443 \
    -showcerts
```

Let's save the certificates from the command output to the terminal, the server certificate to the `revoked.badssl.com.cert.pem` file, and its issuer certificate to the `RapidSSL_Intermediate_CA1.pem` file.

2. Next, let's get the OCSP responder URL:

```
$ openssl x509 \
    -in revoked.badssl.com.cert.pem \
    -noout \
    -ocsp_uri
http://ocsp.digicert.com
```

3. Finally, let's check the server certificate revocation status:

```
$ openssl ocsp \
    -issuer RapidSSL_Intermediate_CA1.pem \
    -cert revoked.badssl.com.cert.pem \
    -url http://ocsp.digicert.com
WARNING: no nonce in response
Response verify OK
revoked.badssl.com.cert.pem: revoked
        This Update: Jun 12 01:09:02 2022 GMT
        Next Update: Jun 19 00:24:02 2022 GMT
        Revocation Time: Oct 27 21:38:48 2021 GMT
```

As we can see, this time, the certificate status is reported as `revoked`. Our observations confirm that the `openssl ocsp` subcommand can get the revocation statuses of both good and revoked certificates.

With that, we have learned how to use OCSP on the command line. Now, let's learn how to use OCSP programmatically.

Using OCSP in C programs

We can check the certificate revocation status programmatically in the following ways:

- Sending explicit OCSP requests to the OCSP responder. This method depends on the possibility to obtain the OCSP responder URL, such as via the **Authority Information Access** X509v3 extension in the server certificate.

- Using OCSP stapling and an OCSP stapling callback. This method depends on whether the TLS server has OCSP stapling support. We are going to use this method in the following example program.

Now, let's write a small `ocsp-check` program that demonstrates how to use an OCSP stapling callback function.

An OCSP stapling callback function must have the following synopsis:

```
int ocsp_callback(SSL* ssl, void* arg);
```

This function takes the following parameters:

- `ssl`: TLS connection object
- `arg`: User data pointer

The callback function should return one of the following values:

- A positive value if the stapled OCSP response is good
- 0 if the stapled OCSP response is bad
- A negative value if an error has occurred in the callback

To use the OCSP stapling callback, the Certificate Status Request TLS extension must be activated using the `SSL_CTX_set_tlsext_status_type()` function. The callback is set to the `SSL_CTX` object using the `SSL_CTX_set_tlsext_status_cb()` function. The user data pointer that will be passed to the callback function can be set using the `SSL_CTX_set_tlsext_status_arg()` function.

We are going to base our `ocsp-check` program on the `verify-callback` program, as described in the *Custom verification of peer certificates in C programs* section. We will take the `verify-callback` program code and develop it further.

Our `ocsp-check` program will take the same three command-line arguments as the `verify-callback` program:

1. Server hostname
2. Server port
3. Optional argument: Name of the file containing one or more trusted CA certificates for server certificate verification

We are going to use some OpenSSL functions that we have not used before. Here are the relevant man pages, along with the documentation for them:

```
$ man SSL_CTX_set_tlsext_status_type
$ man OCSP_response_status
$ man SSL_get0_verified_chain
$ man SSL_get_SSL_CTX
$ man SSL_CTX_get_cert_store
$ man OCSP_basic_verify
$ man OCSP_cert_to_id
```

Let's begin by implementing the ocsp-check program with the OCSP callback registration.

Registering the OCSP callback

Here is how we register the OCSP callback:

1. First, we will declare the following function. This will be our OCSP stapling callback:

    ```
    int ocsp_callback(SSL* ssl, void* arg);
    ```

2. In the run_tls_client() function, we have to activate the Certificate Status Request TLS extension and supply the OCSP stapling callback:

    ```
    SSL_CTX_set_tlsext_status_type(ctx, TLSEXT_STATUSTYPE_
    ocsp);
    SSL_CTX_set_tlsext_status_cb(ctx, ocsp_callback);
    ```

    Here, we could also supply a user data void pointer using the SSL_CTX_set_tlsext_status_arg() function, but we don't need it in this example. We already supply user data using the SSL_set_app_data() function.

    Those were the only code changes that we needed to supply and activate the OCSP stapling callback. Now, let's implement the callback itself.

Implementing the OCSP callback

Here is how we implement the OCSP callback:

1. We will start the callback's implementation by defining the default exit code for the function:

    ```
    int ocsp_callback(SSL* ssl, void* arg) {
        int exit_code = 1;
    ```

In this example, I want to give the maximum benefit of the doubt to the server certificate. This means that we will only consider the certificate to be revoked if it can be proven by the OCSP response. If something is wrong with the OCSP response – for example, it is unparseable or outdated – we will ignore the OCSP response and consider the server certificate as still valid. We're doing this because it is much more probable that some error occurred when the TLS server fetched the OCSP response from the OCSP responder than that the certificate has been revoked.

2.   The first parameter that we receive in the OCSP stapling callback is the pointer to the SSL object, which stores information about the current TLS connection. This means that we don't have to get the SSL object in a sophisticated way as in the verify_callback() function. The SSL object is immediately available to us, and we can easily get our user data from it:

```
FILE* error_stream = SSL_get_app_data(ssl);
```

3.   The next step is quite important – that is, getting the OCSP response:

```
const unsigned char* resp = NULL;
long resp_len = SSL_get_tlsext_status_ocsp_resp(ssl,
&resp);
if (resp_len <= 0 || !resp) {
    if (error_stream)
        fprintf(
            error_stream,
            "* ocsp_callback() called "
            "without OCSP response\n");
    goto cleanup;
}
```

The preceding code will get the OCSP response as DER-encoded data.

4.   The next step is to decode that data into an OCSP_RESPONSE object:

```
OCSP_RESPONSE* ocsp_response =
    d2i_OCSP_RESPONSE(NULL, &resp, resp_len);
if (!ocsp_response) {
    if (error_stream)
        fprintf(
            error_stream,
            "* ocsp_callback() could not decode "
            "OCSP response\n");
    goto cleanup;
}
```

5. The next thing we can do is print the decoded OCSP response. As of OpenSSL 3.0, the OpenSSL library does not have a function that can print an OCSP response to a FILE stream. There is only the OCSP_RESPONSE_print() function, which prints the response to a BIO. Therefore, we will have to use the FILE pointer BIO:

```
if (error_stream) {
    BIO* bio = BIO_new_fp(error_stream, BIO_NOCLOSE);
    assert(bio);
    fprintf(
        error_stream,
        "* ocsp_callback() called "
        "with the following OCSP response:\n");
    fprintf(error_stream, "  -----\n  ");
    OCSP_RESPONSE_print(bio, ocsp_response, 0);
    fprintf(error_stream, "  -----\n");
    BIO_free(bio);
}
```

Note that we used the BIO_NOCLOSE flag when creating the BIO. This was quite important. Because of that flag, the later call to BIO_free() will not attempt to close the underlying FILE stream when we free the BIO.

6. The next step is to check the general status of the whole OCSP response:

```
int res = OCSP_response_status(ocsp_response);
if (res != OCSP_RESPONSE_STATUS_SUCCESSFUL) {
    if (error_stream)
        fprintf(
            error_stream,
            "OCSP response status is not successful\n");
    goto cleanup;
}
```

The OCSP response status tells us whether the OCSP responder could successfully process the OCSP request and form the OCSP response.

7. The next step is to verify the OCSP response signature:

```
OCSP_BASICRESP* ocsp_basicresp =
    OCSP_response_get1_basic(ocsp_response);
STACK_OF(X509)* verified_chain =
    SSL_get0_verified_chain(ssl);
```

```
SSL_CTX* ctx = SSL_get_SSL_CTX(ssl);
X509_STORE* x509_store = SSL_CTX_get_cert_store(ctx);
res = OCSP_basic_verify(
    ocsp_basicresp, verified_chain, x509_store, 0);
if (res != 1) {
    if (error_stream)
        fprintf(
            error_stream,
            "OCSP response verification failed\n");
    goto cleanup;
}
```

Note the SSL_get0_verified_chain() function call. This function should only be called after the verification chain of the server certificate has been built; otherwise, the function may return a partial or incorrect chain. Fortunately, the OCSP callback is called after the server certificate has been verified, so we can safely call SSL_get0_verified_chain().

8. The next thing that we have to do is find the status of the TLS server certificate in the OCSP response. An OCSP response can contain revocation information about several certificates, so we have to search for the status of the necessary certificate in the response:

```
X509* server_cert = sk_X509_value(verified_chain, 0);
X509* issuer_cert = sk_X509_value(verified_chain, 1);
OCSP_CERTID* server_cert_id =
    OCSP_cert_to_id(NULL, server_cert, issuer_cert);
ASN1_GENERALIZEDTIME* revocation_time  = NULL;
ASN1_GENERALIZEDTIME* this_update_time = NULL;
ASN1_GENERALIZEDTIME* next_update_time = NULL;
int revocation_status = V_OCSP_CERTSTATUS_UNKNOWN;
int revocation_reason = OCSP_REVOKED_STATUS_NOSTATUS;
res = OCSP_resp_find_status(
    ocsp_basicresp,
    server_cert_id,
    &revocation_status,
    &revocation_reason,
    &revocation_time,
    &this_update_time,
    &next_update_time);
if (res != 1) {
```

```
    if (error_stream)
        fprintf(
            error_stream,
            "Server certificate status is not found "
            " in the OCSP response\n");
    goto cleanup;
}
```

The `OCSP_resp_find_status()` call that we've just made provided us with information about the revocation status of the certificate, the time when the OCSP response was produced, and when the next OCSP response for the same certificate must be fetched.

9. Let's check whether the response is still valid:

```
res = OCSP_check_validity(
    this_update_time, next_update_time, 300, -1);
if (res != 1) {
    if (error_stream)
        fprintf(
            error_stream,
            "OCSP response is outdated\n");
    goto cleanup;
}
```

10. Now that we've validated the OCSP response, let's check the certificate revocation status and change the `exit_code` variable if the certificate has been revoked:

```
switch (revocation_status) {
    case V_OCSP_CERTSTATUS_REVOKED:
        if (error_stream)
            fprintf(
                error_stream,
                "Server certificate is revoked\n");
        exit_code = 0;
        break;
    case V_OCSP_CERTSTATUS_GOOD:
        if (error_stream)
            fprintf(
                error_stream,
                "Server certificate is not revoked\n");
```

```
            break;
        default:
            if (error_stream)
                fprintf(
                    error_stream,
                    "Server certificate revocation status "
                    "is unknown\n");
    }
```

11. We will finish the OCSP stapling callback function by freeing the objects that are not needed anymore and returning the exit code:

```
cleanup:
    if (server_cert_id)
        OCSP_CERTID_free(server_cert_id);
    if (ocsp_basicresp)
        OCSP_BASICRESP_free(ocsp_basicresp);
    if (ocsp_response)
        OCSP_RESPONSE_free(ocsp_response);
    return exit_code;
}
```

The complete source code for our `ocsp-check` program can be found in this book's GitHub repository in the `ocsp-check.c` file: `https://github.com/PacktPublishing/Demystifying-Cryptography-with-OpenSSL-3/blob/main/Chapter10/ocsp-check.c`.

Now that we've finished implementing the `ocsp-check` program, let's run it.

Running the program

We can run our `ocsp-check` program like so:

```
$ ./ocsp-check www.example.org 443
* verify_callback() called with depth=2, preverify_ok=1, error_
code=0, error_string=ok
  Certificate Subject: C = US, O = DigiCert Inc, OU = www.
digicert.com, CN = DigiCert Global Root CA
* verify_callback() called with depth=1, preverify_ok=1, error_
code=0, error_string=ok
  Certificate Subject: C = US, O = DigiCert Inc, CN = DigiCert
TLS RSA SHA256 2020 CA1
```

```
* verify_callback() called with depth=0, preverify_ok=1, error_
code=0, error_string=ok
   Certificate Subject: C = US, ST = California, L = Los
Angeles, O = Internet Corporation for Assigned Names and
Numbers, CN = www.example.org
* ocsp_callback() called with the following OCSP response:
   -----
   OCSP Response Data:
     ...
     Cert Status: good
     ...
   -----
   Server certificate is not revoked
TLS communication succeeded
```

As we can see, our `ocsp-check` program can successfully check the server certificate revocation status via OCSP.

In the previous sections, we learned how to extensively verify a TLS server certificate by using a custom verification callback, CRL, and OCSP. Those were important aspects of using X.509 certificates in the TLS protocol. In the next section, we will learn about another important aspect of using certificates in TLS: TLS client certificates.

Using TLS client certificates

In this section, we will learn how to use TLS client certificates: generate them, package them into **Public Key Cryptography Standards #12 (PKCS #12)** containers, request them from TLS servers, and supply them to TLS clients.

Generating TLS client certificates

Apart from a TLS server, a TLS client can also provide a certificate on a TLS connection. However, according to the TLS protocol, the TLS client does not send its certificate by default, even if the client has it. The TLS client only sends its certificate if the TLS server requests it.

Another peculiarity of TLS client certificates is that a client certificate is often stored together with its certificate private key (or rather a key pair) in the PKCS #12 format. PKCS #12 is a file format that can store several cryptographic objects, such as X.509 certificates and key pairs. These stored objects can be encrypted using a symmetric cipher and authenticated using a **Hash-based Message Authentication Code (HMAC)**. A typical PKCS #12 file with a TLS client certificate is protected by a password and contains the client certificate, its key pair, and the CA certificates that form the client certificate verification chain. Even though a typical PKCS #12 file contains more than a client certificate, it is usually called a client certificate file.

The filename extensions for PKCS #12 files are `.p12` and `.pfx`. If you want to use a TLS client certificate in a popular web browser, such as Mozilla Firefox or Google Chrome, you will need to supply the client certificate to the browser in the PKCS #12 container file, preferably with the `.p12` or `.pfx` extension. We are going to read a client certificate from a PKCS #12 file in an upcoming code example.

Let's learn how to generate a client certificate and package it into the PKCS #12 container.

We will generate a client certificate very similar to how we generated a server certificate in *Chapter 9, Establishing TLS Connections and Sending Data over Them*. We will also reuse the root CA certificate and its key pair from the previous chapter:

```
$ openssl req \
    -newkey ED448 \
    -subj "/CN=Client certificate" \
    -addext "basicConstraints=critical,CA:FALSE" \
    -noenc \
    -keyout client_keypair.pem \
    -out client_csr.pem
$ openssl x509 \
    -req \
    -in client_csr.pem \
    -copy_extensions copyall \
    -CA ca_cert.pem \
    -CAkey ca_keypair.pem \
    -days 3650 \
    -out client_cert.pem
```

After running the specified commands, we will have a client certificate and its key pair saved to the PEM files. In the next section, we will learn how to package them into a PKCS #12 container.

Packaging client certificates into PKCS #12 container files

To package the generated client certificate, its key pair, and the CA certificate into a PKCS #12 container, we can use the `openssl pkcs12` subcommand of the `openssl` command-line tool. The documentation for this subcommand is available on the `openssl-pkcs12` man page:

```
$ man openssl-pkcs12
```

Here's how we package our key pair and certificates into a PKCS #12 container:

```
$ openssl pkcs12 \
    -export \
```

```
-inkey client_keypair.pem \
-in client_cert.pem \
-certfile ca_cert.pem \
-passout 'pass:SuperPa$$w0rd' \
-out client_cert.p12
```

Note that we supplied a password for the PKCS #12 container – that is, `SuperPa$$w0rd`. It is not very secure to supply a password on the command line because the command may be saved in the command's history and may be visible in the process list. In this example, we just did this for simplicity. Note that the `openssl` tool supports more secure ways to supply a password, such as reading a password from a file or stdin. You can read more about supplying a password to the `openssl` tool on the following man page:

```
$ man openssl-passphrase-options
```

With that, we have successfully created the PKCS #12 container file. Now, we can check what's inside:

```
$ openssl pkcs12 \
    -in client_cert.p12 \
    -passin 'pass:SuperPa$$w0rd' \
    -noenc \
    -info
MAC: sha256, Iteration 2048
MAC length: 32, salt length: 8
PKCS7 Encrypted data: PBES2, PBKDF2, AES-256-CBC, Iteration
2048, PRF hmacWithSHA256
Certificate bag
Bag Attributes
    localKeyID: 63 8B 00 96 4A 4D B7 E9 AF BD C2 09 A5 4A B8 3D
A2 FB 40 85
subject=CN = Client certificate
issuer=CN = Root CA
-----BEGIN CERTIFICATE-----
… base64-encoded data …
-----END CERTIFICATE-----
Certificate bag
Bag Attributes: <No Attributes>
subject=CN = Root CA
issuer=CN = Root CA
```

```
-----BEGIN CERTIFICATE-----
… base64-encoded data …
-----END CERTIFICATE-----
PKCS7 Data
Shrouded Keybag: PBES2, PBKDF2, AES-256-CBC, Iteration 2048,
PRF hmacWithSHA256
Bag Attributes
    localKeyID: 63 8B 00 96 4A 4D B7 E9 AF BD C2 09 A5 4A B8 3D
A2 FB 40 85
Key Attributes: <No Attributes>
-----BEGIN PRIVATE KEY-----
… base64-encoded data …
-----END PRIVATE KEY-----
```

As we can see, the produced PKCS #12 container file contains the client certificate, the CA certificate, and the client certificate key pair. The container's contents are encrypted with AES-256-CBC and authenticated with HMAC-SHA256.

Now that we have prepared the client certificate, let's implement a small TLS server program that will request and verify it.

Requesting and verifying a TLS client certificate on the server side programmatically

In this section, we are going to write a small TLS server program that requests and verifies a TLS client certificate. We are going to base it on the `tls-server` program from *Chapter 9, Establishing TLS Connections and Sending Data over Them*. We will take the code of the `tls-server` program and develop it further. Our new program will be called `tls-server2`.

Our `tls-server2` program will take the following command-line parameters:

1. Server port
2. The name of the file containing the TLS server key pair
3. The name of the file containing the TLS server certificate chain
4. The name of the file containing a trusted CA certificate that can verify the client certificate

To be able to verify a client certificate, we have to load the corresponding trusted CA certificate and enable peer certificate verification.

Verifying the TLS client certificate

Here is how we verify the client certificate:

1. First, we have to load the needed trusted CA certificate. We have to capture the fourth command-line argument and send it to the run_tls_server() function. Let's add the following line to the main() function:

    ```
    const char* trusted_cert_fname = argv[4];
    ```

2. We must also pass the trusted_cert_fname parameter to the run_tls_server() function and add the following code inside the run_tls_server() function after the code that loads and checks the private key:

    ```
    err = SSL_CTX_load_verify_locations(
        ctx, trusted_cert_fname, NULL);
    if (err <= 0) {
        if (error_stream)
            fprintf(
                error_stream,
                "Could not load trusted certificates\n");
        goto failure;
    }
    ```

3. We also have to change the following code to request the client certificate and enable its verification:

    ```
    SSL_CTX_set_verify(ctx, SSL_VERIFY_PEER, NULL);
    ```

    The SSL_VERIFY_PEER flag instructs OpenSSL to request the client certificate. Note that if the client did not supply a certificate, the absence of the certificate will not be considered an error on the server side. This behavior can be changed by setting the SSL_VERIFY_FAIL_IF_NO_PEER_CERT flag together with the SSL_VERIFY_PEER flag, like this:

    ```
    SSL_CTX_set_verify(
        ctx,
        SSL_VERIFY_PEER | SSL_VERIFY_FAIL_IF_NO_PEER_CERT,
        NULL);
    ```

    If both the SSL_VERIFY_PEER and SSL_VERIFY_FAIL_IF_NO_PEER_CERT flags are set, and the client did not supply a certificate, then the TLS handshake will fail.

This code is enough to request the client certificate and verify it. However, it would also be nice to print the client certificate Subject, to make sure that the TLS client has sent its certificate and the TLS server has verified it. To do this, we will introduce a `construct_response()` function, which will construct a server response that will contain information about the client certificate. In `tls-server2`, we will use a response created by that function instead of the static response that we used in the original `tls-server` program.

Implementing the response generation function

The function will have the following signature:

```
BIO* construct_response(SSL* ssl);
```

The `ssl` parameter is needed to get the client certificate. The function will return a memory BIO that will contain the server response.

Let's implement the `construct_response()` function:

1. We will start by creating a memory BIO and printing the server response headers there:

    ```
    BIO* mem_bio = BIO_new(BIO_s_mem());
    const char* response_headers =
        "HTTP/1.0 200 OK\r\n"
        "Content-type: text/plain\r\n"
        "Connection: close\r\n"
        "Server: Example TLS server\r\n"
        "\r\n";
    BIO_puts(mem_bio, response_headers);
    ```

2. The next step is to get the client certificate:

    ```
    X509* peer_cert = SSL_get_peer_certificate(ssl);
    ```

    Note that in our example, we are not using the `SSL_VERIFY_FAIL_IF_NO_PEER_CERT` flag, which is why the TLS client can choose not to supply a certificate. In such a case, the `peer_cert` pointer will be NULL. We have to take this into account later.

3. The next step is to print information about the client certificate or its absence to the memory BIO:

    ```
    if (peer_cert) {
        X509_NAME* peer_cert_subject =
            X509_get_subject_name(peer_cert);
        BIO_puts(
            mem_bio,
    ```

```
        "The TLS client certificate subject:\n");
    X509_NAME_print_ex(
        mem_bio,
        peer_cert_subject,
        0,
        XN_FLAG_ONELINE & ~ASN1_STRFLGS_ESC_MSB);
    BIO_puts(mem_bio, "\n");
    X509_free(peer_cert);
} else {
    BIO_puts(
        mem_bio,
        "The TLS client has not provided a
certificate\n");
}
```

4. We finish the construct_response() function by returning the memory BIO:

    ```
    return mem_bio;
    ```

    Very nice – we have implemented the construct_response() function! We will call that function from the handle_accepted_connection() function, instead of the code that constructed the static response and calculated its length.

5. The following code is from the original tls-server program:

    ```
    const char* response =
        "HTTP/1.0 200 OK\r\n"
        "Content-type: text/plain\r\n"
        "Connection: close\r\n"
        "Server: Example TLS server\r\n"
        "\r\n"
        "Hello from the TLS server!\n";
    int response_length = strlen(response);
    ```

    We must replace it with the following code:

    ```
    BIO* mem_bio = construct_response(ssl);
    char* response = NULL;
    long response_length = BIO_get_mem_data(mem_bio,
    &response);
    ```

6. Don't forget to free the memory BIO that we have introduced in our new code! To free it, we must add the following code at the end of the `handle_accepted_connection()` function:

```
if (mem_bio)
    BIO_free(mem_bio);
```

Those were all the changes that we needed to make to the TLS server code.

The complete source code for our `tls-server2` program can be found in this book's GitHub repository in the `tls-server2.c` file: `https://github.com/PacktPublishing/Demystifying-Cryptography-with-OpenSSL-3/blob/main/Chapter10/tls-server2.c`.

Running the program

Let's run our `tls-server2` program and see how it works:

1. We have not written a TLS client program that supplies a client certificate yet. However, we can use the `openssl s_client` subcommand or the `curl` utility for testing. We will need two terminal windows – one for the TLS server and another for the TLS client. Let's start our `tls-server2` program in the first terminal window:

```
$ ./tls-server2 \
    4433 \
    server_keypair.pem \
    server_cert.pem \
    ca_cert.pem
*** Listening on port 4433
```

2. Let's launch the `openssl` tool as a TLS client with a client certificate in the second terminal window:

```
$ openssl s_client \
    -connect localhost:4433 \
    -CAfile ca_cert.pem \
    -key client_keypair.pem \
    -cert client_cert.pem
```

3. When `openssl` is launched, it will connect to `tls-server2` and output a lot of information. Just press the *Enter* key after. The `openssl` tool will output the following:

```
HTTP/1.0 200 OK
Content-type: text/plain
Connection: close
```

```
Server: Example TLS server
The TLS client certificate subject:
CN = Client certificate
```

4. Let's examine the first terminal window where `tls-server2` is running. We will see the following output:

```
*** Receiving from the client:
*** Receiving from the client finished
*** Sending to the client:
HTTP/1.0 200 OK
Content-type: text/plain
Connection: close
Server: Example TLS server
The TLS client certificate subject:
CN = Client certificate
*** Sending to the client finished
```

As we can see, our `tls-server2` program has requested, received, and successfully verified the client certificate, as well as reported the client certificate's Subject.

5. We can perform the same test using the `curl` utility. Let's run it in the second terminal window:

```
$ curl \
    https://localhost:4433 \
    --cacert ca_cert.pem \
    --cert 'client_cert.p12:SuperPa$$w0rd' \
    --cert-type P12
The TLS client certificate subject:
CN = Client certificate
```

Note that we have supplied the client certificate to `curl` in PKCS #12 format.

As we can see, our `tls-server2` program can provide a nice report about the client certificate if the TLS client supplies it. But what will happen if the TLS client does not supply a certificate?

6. Let's check this using the `openssl` tool. Let's launch `openssl s_client` without the certificate:

```
$ openssl s_client \
    -connect localhost:4433 \
    -CAfile ca_cert.pem
```

7. After connecting and pressing *Enter*, we will get the following report:

```
HTTP/1.0 200 OK
Content-type: text/plain
Connection: close
Server: Example TLS server
The TLS client has not provided a certificate
```

8. We will get a similar report using `curl`:

```
$ curl https://localhost:4433 --cacert ca_cert.pem
The TLS client has not provided a certificate
```

From this, we can conclude that our `tls-server2` program works as expected. It can request, verify, and report information about the TLS client certificate, as well as gracefully handle the absence of the client certificate.

The `tls-server2` program will run and accept connections until it is aborted. You can abort it by pressing *Ctrl + C* in the terminal window where it is running.

With that, we have learned how to request a client certificate from the server side and verify it. In the next section, we will learn how to load a TLS client certificate onto the client side and use it for the TLS connection.

Establishing a TLS client connection with a client certificate programmatically

In this section, we are going to write a small TLS client program that uses a TLS client certificate. We are going to base it on the `tls-client` program from *Chapter 9, Establishing TLS Connections and Sending Data over Them*. Here, we will take the code of the `tls-client` program and develop it further. Our new program will be called `tls-client2`.

Our `tls-client2` program will take the following command-line parameters:

1. Server hostname
2. Server port
3. Name of the file containing the trusted CA certificate for server certificate verification
4. Name of the PKCS #12 file containing the client certificate and its key pair
5. Password for the PKCS #12 file, along with the client certificate

Compared to the original `tls-client` program, `tls-client2` takes two more parameters. All five parameters are now mandatory.

We are going to load the client certificate from a PKCS #12 container file. It is also possible to load the client certificate and its key pair from PEM files using the SSL_CTX_use_certificate_chain_ file() and SSL_CTX_use_PrivateKey_file() functions, as we do in the tls-server and tls-server2 programs. However, I want to demonstrate loading from a PKCS #12 file because client certificates are often distributed in PKCS #12 files.

We are going to use some OpenSSL functions that we have not used before. Here are the relevant man pages, along with the documentation for them:

```
$ man BIO_new_file
$ man d2i_PKCS12_bio
$ man PKCS12_parse
$ man SSL_CTX_use_cert_and_key
$ man PKCS12_free
```

Now, let's start implementing the tls-client2 program with the changes to the code that we inherited from the tls-client program.

Changing the code inherited from the tls-client program

Here is what we need to change:

1. As we have two more command-line parameters, we should capture them in the named variables in the main() function:

    ```
    const char* client_cert_fname    = argv[4];
    const char* client_cert_password = argv[5];
    ```

2. We also have to pass the two new parameters to the run_tls_client() function. Hence, the run_tls_client() function will look like this:

    ```
    int run_tls_client(
        const char* hostname,
        const char* port,
        const char* trusted_cert_fname,
        const char* client_cert_fname,
        const char* client_cert_password,
        FILE* error_stream);
    ```

    The run_tls_client() call in the main() function will look like this:

    ```
    run_tls_client(
        hostname,
    ```

```
                    port,
                    trusted_cert_fname,
                    client_cert_fname,
                    client_cert_password,
                    stderr);
```

3. Inside the `run_tls_client()` function, after loading the trusted certificates, we must add a call to the `load_client_certificate()` function that loads the client certificate into the `SSL_CTX` object:

    ```
    int load_exit_code = load_client_certificate(
        client_cert_fname,
        client_cert_password,
        ctx,
        error_stream);
    if (load_exit_code != 0)
        goto failure;
    ```

Now, we have to implement the `load_client_certificate` function.

Loading the TLS client certificate

The `load_client_certificate` function will have the following signature:

```
int load_client_certificate(
    const char* client_cert_fname,
    const char* client_cert_password,
    SSL_CTX* ctx,
    FILE* error_stream);
```

The function will return 0 on success and a non-zero exit code on failure.

Let's proceed with the function's implementation:

1. First, we must define the function exit code, which can be changed if a failure occurs:

    ```
    int exit_code = 0;
    ```

2. Then, we must create a file BIO and open the client certificate file for reading:

    ```
    BIO* client_cert_bio = BIO_new_file(client_cert_fname,
    "rb");
    if (!client_cert_bio) {
    ```

```
    if (error_stream)
        fprintf(
            error_stream,
            "Could not open client certificate file
%s\n",
            client_cert_fname);
    goto failure;
}
```

3. The next step is to load the client certificate file into the PKCS12 object:

```
PKCS12* pkcs12 = d2i_PKCS12_bio(client_cert_bio, NULL);
if (!pkcs12) {
    if (error_stream)
        fprintf(
            error_stream,
            "Could not load client certificate "
            "from file %s\n",
            client_cert_fname);
    goto failure;
}
```

Note that we could open the client certificate file using `fopen()` and load it using `d2i_PKCS12_fp()`. However, I wanted to demonstrate the usage of yet another BIO type – the `file` BIO.

4. The `d2i_PKCS12_bio()` function has loaded the PKCS #12 container but did not decrypt or parse it. The next step is to verify the password so that we can decrypt the PKCS #12 container. This step is optional, but it can be useful for troubleshooting:

```
int res = PKCS12_verify_mac(
    pkcs12,
    client_cert_password,
    strlen(client_cert_password));
if (res != 1) {
    if (error_stream)
        fprintf(
            error_stream,
            "Invalid password was provided "
            "for client certificate file %s\n",
```

```
                        client_cert_fname);
            goto failure;
    }
```

5. After we have verified the PKCS #12 container password, we must try to decrypt it, and then parse and get the client certificate, its key pair, and CA certificates for the verification chain:

```
res = PKCS12_parse(
    pkcs12,
    client_cert_password,
    &pkey,
    &cert,
    &cert_chain);
if (res != 1) {
    if (error_stream)
        fprintf(
            error_stream,
            "Could not decode client certificate "
            "loaded from file %s\n",
            client_cert_fname);
    goto failure;
}
```

6. If the PKCS #12 container has been parsed successfully, we can set the client certificate, its key pair, and the CA certificates to the SSL_CTX object:

```
res = SSL_CTX_use_cert_and_key(
    ctx,
    cert,
    pkey,
    cert_chain,
    1);
if (res != 1) {
    if (error_stream)
        fprintf(
            error_stream,
            "Could not use client certificate "
            "loaded from file %s\n",
```

```
                            client_cert_fname);
            goto failure;
    }
```

Note that the SSL_CTX_use_cert_and_key() function will increase the reference count on the cert, pkey, and cert_chain objects. Thus, we will have to free them at the end of the function. As the SSL_CTX object will still hold references for them, the mentioned objects will not be deallocated on that freeing at the end of the function. Instead, they will be deallocated when the SSL_CTX object itself is deallocated.

7. When it comes to potential troubleshooting, it's a good idea to check that the loaded client certificate key pair matches the client certificate:

```
res = SSL_CTX_check_private_key(ctx);
if (res != 1) {
    if (error_stream)
        fprintf(
        error_stream,
        "Client keypair does not match "
        "client certificate\n");
    goto failure;
}
```

At this point, we have successfully loaded the client certificate, its key pair, and the CA certificate, and set it to the SSL_CTX object.

8. Now, let's finish up the load_client_certificate() function code by freeing the used objects and returning the exit code:

```
        goto cleanup;
failure:
    exit_code = 1;
cleanup:
    if (cert_chain)
        sk_X509_pop_free(cert_chain, X509_free);
    if (cert)
        X509_free(cert);
    if (pkey)
        EVP_PKEY_free(pkey);
    if (pkcs12)
        PKCS12_free(pkcs12);
```

```
    if (client_cert_bio)
        BIO_free(client_cert_bio);
    return exit_code;
}
```

Note that the BIO_free(client_cert_bio) call will close the underlying file before deallocating the file BIO.

With that, we have finished implementing the load_client_certificate() function and the whole tls-client2 program. The complete source code for our tls-client2 program can be found in this book's GitHub repository in the tls-client2.c file: https://github.com/PacktPublishing/Demystifying-Cryptography-with-OpenSSL-3/blob/main/Chapter10/tls-client2.c.

Running the program

Now, let's try to run the tls-client2 program and check how it works:

1. As in the previous example, we will need two terminal windows. In the first window, we will run the tls-server2 program:

    ```
    $ ./tls-server2 \
        4433 \
        server_keypair.pem \
        server_cert.pem \
        ca_cert.pem
    *** Listening on port 4433
    ```

2. In the second terminal window, we will run our tls-client2 program:

    ```
    $ ./run-tls-client2.sh
    *** Sending to the server:
    GET / HTTP/1.1
    Host: localhost
    Connection: close
    User-Agent: Example TLS client
    *** Sending to the server finished
    *** Receiving from the server:
    HTTP/1.0 200 OK
    Content-type: text/plain
    Connection: close
    Server: Example TLS server
    ```

```
The TLS client certificate subject:
CN = Client certificate
*** Receiving from the server finished
TLS communication succeeded
```

As we can see, our `tls-client2` could load the client certificate and use it in the TLS connection. The `tls-server2` program has reported that it has got the client certificate on the server side. From this, we can conclude that the `tls-client2` program works as expected.

With that, we have learned how to use TLS client certificates. Now, let's summarize this chapter.

Summary

This chapter was different from the previous ones. In the previous chapters, we covered one big topic per chapter. In this chapter, however, we covered several small topics and wrote more example programs.

In this chapter, we learned about how to verify the peer certificate during a TLS handshake. We also learned about the CRL and OCSP methods. Then, we learned about TLS client certificates and PKCS #12 containers. After that, we learned how to request and verify a TLS client certificate on the server side and how to load and use client certificates on the client side. We finished this chapter by connecting our TLS server and TLS client programs, both of which support TLS client certificates, to each other.

The knowledge you've gained from this chapter will help you perform advanced client and server certificate processing on TLS connections in your TLS-enabled programs.

In the next chapter, we will learn about more advanced and special uses of TLS.

11

Special Usages of TLS

In *Chapter 9, Establishing TLS Connections and Sending Data over Them*, we learned about the **Transport Layer Security** (**TLS**) protocol and how to establish TLS connections straightforwardly. In this chapter, we will learn about the advanced usage of TLS and special use cases.

We are going to cover the following topics in this chapter:

- Understanding TLS certificate pinning
- Using TLS certificate pinning
- Understanding blocking and non-blocking sockets
- Using TLS on non-blocking sockets
- Understanding TLS on non-standard sockets
- Using TLS on non-standard sockets

Technical requirements

This chapter will contain commands that you can run on a command line and C source code that you can build and run. For the command- line commands, you will need the `openssl` command-line tool with OpenSSL dynamic libraries. To build the C code, you will need OpenSSL dynamic or static libraries, library headers, a C compiler, and a linker.

The source code for this chapter can be found here: `https://github.com/PacktPublishing/Demystifying-Cryptography-with-OpenSSL-3/tree/main/Chapter11`

Understanding TLS certificate pinning

Sometimes certificate verification is not done using traditional **Public Key Infrastructure (PKI)** rules with a certificate store, trusted certificates, and certificate verification chains. One of the non-standard certificate verification methods is TLS certificate pinning. The TLS client *pins* a particular certificate to a server, meaning that it expects the server to have that exact certificate. There are variations of certificate pinning, such as pinning a few possible certificates instead of just one, pinning a certificate public key instead of the certificate itself, or pinning a particular issuer certificate. It is possible to use TLS certificate pinning both as an addition to the standard certificate verification and as a replacement for it.

Certificate pinning is not a very popular certificate verification method for HTTPS servers on the public internet. However, while you might have never thought about it, public key pinning is actually the main public key verification method in the SSH protocol. An SSH server public key is pinned on the clients in the `known_hosts` file, either in advance or on the first connection. SSH user public keys are pinned on the server in the `authorized_keys` file.

When it comes to the TLS protocol, certificate pinning is used in some applications that communicate over the internet with only one server. It is especially popular in mobile banking applications.

Why do people choose certificate pinning? To understand that, let us examine the current situation with the PKI model based on certificate chains, trusted certificates, and the certificate store used in most TLS-capable software.

The default PKI model used for TLS allows any **Certificate Authority (CA)** from the trusted certificate store to sign a certificate for any server. A typical **Operating System (OS)** or browser certificate store contains more than 100 trusted CA certificates. This means that we are relying on the assumption that none of those CAs will issue a rogue certificate that can be used for a **Man in the Middle (MITM)** attack. But sometimes CAs issue rogue certificates because sometimes CAs are hacked, as happened with the DigiNotar, GlobalSign, and Comodo CAs. Equally, sometimes, CAs issue intermediate certificates for MITM boxes used by law enforcement agencies. These kinds of MITM boxes are placed at the ISP of a suspected criminal. The suspect's TLS connections are routed through the MITM box. The MITM box mounts a MITM attack against the suspect by issuing certificates in real time for any server that is accessed through the MITM box. This kind of MITM attack allows the MITM box to intercept and decrypt the TLS connections of the suspect.

There is also another kind of MITM box – commercial MITM boxes. They are installed in organizations by system administrators of those organizations to inspect TLS traffic for viruses and trojans. In such a case, the CA certificate in the MITM box is not issued by a publicly known CA – it is issued by a CA of that organization instead. Then, the organization makes sure that the root CA certificate of the organization's CA is installed as a trusted certificate into the certificate stores on all employee machines.

Yet another way to attack the default PKI model is to install a rogue root CA certificate in the user's certificate store. This can be done by hacking into the user's machine or using social engineering methods.

Do the three described scenarios pose an acceptable risk? Everyone decides for themselves. But many banks decided to use TLS certificate pinning in their applications to mitigate the risk of MITM attacks.

In addition to increased security, TLS certificate pinning may also save some costs. Instead of buying a server certificate from a commercial CA, you can generate the certificate yourself. You can even use a self-signed certificate to reduce maintenance. When checking the pinned server certificate in a TLS client, you can drop many checks on the certificate that are usually done during certificate verification. If you have pinned a certificate, that means that it is pre-verified and is known to be good.

There are also some drawbacks associated with TLS certificate pinning. The usual way to pin certificates is to supply the certificates or their digests to the client application. If you trust just one pinned certificate supplied to the application, you can only update the pinned certificate through the application update. Also, in such cases, you have to synchronize the update of the certificate on the server with the update of the application. This is not very practical, but there are several solutions to the issue. One is to pin several allowed certificates to the server in the application – for example, the current and the planned next certificate. If the lifetime of a server certificate is a year or longer, it is reasonable to ask the users to update the application often in order to also update the certificate. Another solution is to implement your own automatic update mechanism in the application that will fetch the next certificate through the connection protected by the current certificate. Yet another solution is to pin the issuer (CA) certificate instead of or in addition to the server certificate. This solution provides less security than pinning the server certificate, but still more security than no pinning. But then we get the same issue with updating the pinned issuer certificate. We have to either update it through the application update or implement an update mechanism within the application.

Another drawback of using TLS certificate pinning as a replacement for the default PKI is that you have to implement revocation yourself. Implementing it is not impossible though. Also, it is worth remembering that when a MITM attack against the default PKI model is performed, the attacker can very easily block the TLS client's connections to **Certificate Revocation List (CRL)** distribution servers and **Online Certificate Status Protocol (OCSP)** servers, as well as omitting **OCSP stapling** on the client-facing side. Hence, the argument for revocation is not very strong.

To summarize, TLS certificate pinning, when used instead of the default PKI model, has the following pros and cons:

Pros:

- Increased security – lower risk of a MITM attack.

- It's possible to use a home-generated certificate instead of buying a certificate from a commercial CA.

- Reduced maintenance because you don't need to make a **Certificate Signing Request (CSR)** and communicate with a CA. You can even use a self-signed certificate.

Cons:

- Increased maintenance because you have to organize pinning updates yourself.

- Increased maintenance because you have to organize revocation yourself.

In the next section, we will learn how to implement simple TLS certificate pinning on the client side programmatically.

Using TLS certificate pinning

To learn how to use TLS certificate pinning in C code, we are going to write a small `tls-cert-pinning` program. We are going to use a simple variant of TLS certificate pinning: we will pin just one server certificate and will use TLS certificate pinning instead of the default PKI model, not in addition to it.

We are going to use the "big" certificate verification callback set with the `SSL_CTX_set_cert_verify_callback()` function, as opposed to the "small" callback set with the `SSL_CTX_set_verify()` function, in order to learn another type of callback.

The `SSL_CTX_set_cert_verify_callback()` function sets a callback function that is supposed to perform the whole certificate verification procedure. The default OpenSSL implementation of that function builds the certificate verification chain, verifies certificate signatures, and the validity dates, and, among other things, calls the callback function set by the `SSL_CTX_set_verify()` function, if there is one. It's important to understand that setting a callback using the `SSL_CTX_set_cert_verify_callback()` function overrides this whole default verification process. Therefore, the `SSL_CTX_set_cert_verify_callback()` function must be used with great care. The wrong implementation of the "big" callback may have terrible consequences. If you are unsure, better set a "small" verification callback by the `SSL_CTX_set_verify()` function, which we reviewed in *Chapter 10, Using X.509 Certificates in TLS.*

We consider our pinned certificate to already be verified. Thus, we don't even need to build the certificate verification chain when checking the server certificate; our callback function will just check that the server certificate matches the pinned certificate.

As with many other OpenSSL functions, the `SSL_CTX_set_cert_verify_callback()` function has a man page:

```
$ man SSL_CTX_set_cert_verify_callback
```

Our `tls-cert-pinning` program will be based on the `tls-client` program from *Chapter 9, Establishing TLS Connections and Sending Data over Them.* We are going to take the `tls-client` program source code and add TLS certificate pinning functionality.

The `tls-cert-pinning` program will take the following command-line arguments:

1. Server hostname

2. Server port

3. Pinned server certificate

Unlike in the `tls-client` program, in our `tls-cert-pinning` program, the third command-line argument is mandatory.

Let's start the `tls-client` program implementation.

Changing the run_tls_client() function

In this section, we will add the certificate verification callback declaration and make changes to the `run_tls_client` function:

1. First, we have to declare our certificate verification callback:

   ```
   int cert_verify_callback(
       X509_STORE_CTX* x509_store_ctx, void* arg);
   ```

   As we can see, it takes two arguments:

   - `x509_store_ctx` – X.509 certificate verification context

   - `arg` – An arbitrary void pointer with user data

   The certificate verification context is created by OpenSSL. The user data argument is set by the `SSL_CTX_set_cert_verify_callback()` function at the same time that the certificate verification callback is set. The callback function must return either 1 to indicate certificate verification success or 0 to indicate verification failure.

2. Our next implementation step is to load the pinned certificate from the file supplied as the third command-line argument. To do that, we have to replace some code from the `tls-client` program. We will replace the following code:

   ```
   const char* trusted_cert_fname = argv[3];
   if (trusted_cert_fname)
       err = SSL_CTX_load_verify_locations(
           ctx, trusted_cert_fname, NULL);
   else
       err = SSL_CTX_set_default_verify_paths(ctx);
   if (err <= 0) {
       if (error_stream)
           fprintf(
   ```

```
                    error_stream,
                    "Could not load trusted certificates\n");
            goto failure;
        }
```

The following is what we will replace it with:

```
const char* pinned_server_cert_fname = argv[3];
FILE* pinned_server_cert_file = NULL;
X509* pinned_server_cert = NULL;
pinned_server_cert_file = fopen(
    pinned_server_cert_fname, "rb");
if (pinned_server_cert_file)
    pinned_server_cert = PEM_read_X509(
        pinned_server_cert_file, NULL, NULL, NULL);
if (!pinned_server_cert) {
    if (error_stream)
        fprintf(
            error_stream,
            "Could not load pinned server
certificate\n");
    goto failure;
}
```

3. The next step is to set the certificate verification callback:

```
SSL_CTX_set_cert_verify_callback(
    ctx, cert_verify_callback, pinned_server_cert);
```

Note that we have set `pinned_server_cert` as the user data for the callback.

4. In the callback function, we will also need another pointer, `error_stream`. We could combine `pinned_server_cert` and `error_stream` into a C structure, make an object out of that structure, and set it as the user data argument for the `SSL_CTX_set_cert_verify_callback()` function. But we can pass the `error_stream` pointer to the callback more easily, in the same way as we did in *Chapter 10, Using X.509 Certificates in TLS*, with the help of the `SSL_set_app_data()` function:

```
SSL_set_app_data(ssl, error_stream);
```

That's almost everything that we have to do in the `run_tls_client()` function of our program.

5. We also have to free some newly used objects at the end of the `run_tls_client()` function:

```
if (pinned_server_cert)
    X509_free(pinned_server_cert);
if (pinned_server_cert_file)
    fclose(pinned_server_cert_file);
```

With that, we are done with making changes to the `run_tls_client()` function.

Implementing the cert_verify_callback() function

Now, let's implement the `cert_verify_callback()` function:

1. We will start the implementation of the `cert_verify_callback()` function by getting the `error_stream` and `pinned_server_cert` pointers that we sent to the callback function from the `run_tls_client()` function:

```
int ssl_ex_data_idx = SSL_get_ex_data_X509_STORE_CTX_
idx();
SSL* ssl = X509_STORE_CTX_get_ex_data(
    x509_store_ctx, ssl_ex_data_idx);
FILE* error_stream = SSL_get_app_data(ssl);
X509* pinned_server_cert = arg;
```

2. Our next step is to get the actual server certificate:

```
X509* actual_server_cert =
    X509_STORE_CTX_get0_cert(x509_store_ctx);
```

Note that the `X509_STORE_CTX_get_current_cert()` function would not give you the server certificate this time. When the "big" certificate verification callback function is called, very few data elements in the `x509_store_ctx` object are set. The current certificate is not set. It is actually the job of the "big" callback to set the current certificate, its depth, and its verification status.

3. After we get the server certificate, let's print some diagnostic information:

```
if (error_stream) {
    X509_NAME* pinned_cert_subject =
        X509_get_subject_name(pinned_server_cert);
    X509_NAME* actual_cert_subject =
        X509_get_subject_name(actual_server_cert);
    fprintf(
```

```
        error_stream,
        "cert_verify_callback() called with the following
"
        "pinned certificate:\n");
    X509_NAME_print_ex_fp(
        error_stream,
        pinned_cert_subject,
        2,
        XN_FLAG_ONELINE & ~ASN1_STRFLGS_ESC_MSB);
    fprintf(error_stream, "\n");
    fprintf(
        error_stream,
        "The server presented the following
certificate:\n");
    X509_NAME_print_ex_fp(
        error_stream,
        actual_cert_subject,
        2,
        XN_FLAG_ONELINE & ~ASN1_STRFLGS_ESC_MSB);
    fprintf(error_stream, "\n");
}
```

4.   The next step is to compare the pinned and the actual certificates:

```
int cmp = X509_cmp(pinned_server_cert, actual_server_
cert);
```

5.   Before checking the comparison result and returning from the function, let us also set the current certificate and its depth to the verification context:

```
X509_STORE_CTX_set_current_cert(
    x509_store_ctx, actual_server_cert);
X509_STORE_CTX_set_depth(x509_store_ctx, 0);
```

6.   Finally, let's check the certificate comparison result, set the correct verification error code, and return the correct result from the callback function:

```
if (cmp == 0) {
    if (error_stream)
        fprintf(
```

```
            error_stream,
            "The certificates match. "
            "Proceeding with the TLS connection.\n");
        X509_STORE_CTX_set_error(x509_store_ctx, X509_V_OK);
        return 1;
    } else {
        if (error_stream)
            fprintf(
                error_stream,
                "The certificates do not match. "
                "Aborting the TLS connection.\n");
        X509_STORE_CTX_set_error(
            x509_store_ctx, X509_V_ERR_APPLICATION_
VERIFICATION);
        return 0;
    }
```

That's the end of the `cert_verify_callback()` function and the end of the program implementation.

The complete source code for our `tls-cert-pinning` program can be found on GitHub as the `tls-cert-pinning.c` file: `https://github.com/PacktPublishing/Demystifying-Cryptography-with-OpenSSL-3/blob/main/Chapter11/tls-cert-pinning.c`.

Running the tls-cert-pinning program

Let's run our `tls-cert-pinning` program and see how it works. We will need the `tls-server` program from *Chapter 9, Establishing TLS Connections and Sending Data over Them*. We will also need the server certificate file as the pinned certificate for our `tls-cert-pinning` program.

This is how we will test that our `tls-cert-pinning` program works:

1. Let's open two terminal windows.
2. In the first window, we will start the `tls-server` program:

    ```
    $ ./tls-server 4433 server_keypair.pem server_cert.pem
    *** Listening on port 4433
    ```

3. In the second window, we will run our `tls-cert-pinning` program:

    ```
    $ ./tls-cert-pinning localhost 4433 server_cert.pem
    * cert_verify_callback() called with the following pinned
    ```

```
certificate:
  CN = localhost
  The server presented the following certificate:
  CN = localhost
  The certificates match. Proceeding with the TLS
connection.
*** Sending to the server:
GET / HTTP/1.1
Host: localhost
Connection: close
User-Agent: Example TLS client
*** Sending to the server finished
*** Receiving from the server:
HTTP/1.0 200 OK
Content-type: text/plain
Connection: close
Server: Example TLS server
Hello from the TLS server!
*** Receiving from the server finished
TLS communication succeeded
```

As we can observe, the server certificate matched the pinned certificate, and the TLS communication has succeeded.

4. Next, let us also check what happens if the certificates do not match:

```
$ ./tls-cert-pinning www.example.org 443 server_cert.pem
* cert_verify_callback() called with the following pinned
certificate:
  CN = localhost
  The server presented the following certificate:
  C = US, ST = California, L = Los Angeles, O = Internet
Corporation for Assigned Names and Numbers, CN = www.
example.org
  The certificates do not match. Aborting the TLS
connection.
Could not connect to server www.example.org on port 443
Errors from the OpenSSL error queue:
4017BA4F1B7F0000:error:0A000086
```

```
:SSL routines:tls_post_process_server_certificate
:certificate verify failed
:../ssl/statem/statem_clnt.c:1883:
4017BA4F1B7F0000:error:0A000197
:SSL routines:SSL_shutdown
:shutdown while In init
:../ssl/ssl_lib.c:2244:
TLS communication failed
```

As we can see, this time, the server certificate did not match the pinned certificate – therefore, the TLS connection was aborted. From our observations, we can conclude that our simple implementation of TLS certificate pinning works correctly.

We have now learned how to use TLS certificate pinning, which is one of the advanced TLS use cases. In the next two sections, we will learn about another advanced TLS use case: using TLS connections on non-blocking sockets. Non-blocking sockets can help your application become more responsive or handle more connections simultaneously.

Understanding blocking and non-blocking sockets

Network connections can be established on **blocking sockets** or **non-blocking sockets**. The default mode depends on the OS, but for most OSes, it is blocking mode.

In blocking mode, if a program requests an **Input/Output (I/O)** operation on a socket, the operation must be performed, at least partially, or an error must occur, before the control returns to the program. How can an operation be performed partially? For example, if a program tries to read 100 bytes from a blocking socket, the reading function (for instance, `recv()`) will only return when it is possible to read at least one byte from the socket – otherwise, an error occurs. If no data is coming from the network, the execution of the current thread of the program will be blocked, meaning that the current thread will wait until some data comes. In some cases, a thread may wait on a blocking socket indefinitely. When attempting to send data, the current thread may block if the OS network sending buffers is full. In this case, the sending function (for instance, `send()`) will wait until the OS sends the buffered data to the network, free its sending buffers, and copy the data that the program wants to send to the network to those buffers. The `send()` function will only return if the program data was fully or partially (depending on the OS) copied to the OS buffers, or if an error occurred.

Unlike blocking sockets, non-blocking sockets do not block the program execution. If an I/O operation cannot be performed, the corresponding I/O function, such as `send()` or `recv()`, will return immediately with the `would block` error. The program is then supposed to retry the I/O operation after some time. In the meantime, the program can do other things on the same thread – for example, process some data, send or receive data on another network connection, update progress indicators, or react to the program's **User Interface (UI)**. The program can also check whether the socket is ready to send or receive data or wait for socket readiness. Most OSes provide functions that can wait with a timeout for I/O readiness on several sockets simultaneously. Examples of such functions are `select()` and `poll()`. OpenSSL provides its own functions for the same purpose, such as `BIO_wait()` and `BIO_socket_wait()`, but those functions are limited to one **Basic Input/Output** (**BIO**) object. However, if simultaneous waiting on several BIOs is needed, it is possible to get socket descriptors from the needed BIOs using the `BIO_get_fd()` function and supply a collection of those socket descriptors to `select()`, `poll()`, `epoll_wait()`, `kevent()`, `WSAEventSelect()`, `WSAPoll()`, or whichever function your OS provides.

Using non-blocking sockets, a program can retain a responsive UI even on slow network connections without detaching networking into separate threads. Another popular usage of non-blocking sockets is on the server side. A server can serve several network connections on one thread without being blocked by slow connections. This kind of strategy uses fewer system resources than serving each connection on a separate thread or in a separate process.

All our previous code examples used blocking sockets. In the next section, we will learn how to programmatically use TLS on a non-blocking socket.

Using TLS on non-blocking sockets

In order to learn how to use TLS on a non-blocking socket, we are going to write a small `tls-client-non-blocking` program.

We are going to use some OpenSSL functions that we have not used before. Here are their man pages:

```
$ man BIO_set_nbio
$ man BIO_should_retry
$ man BIO_wait
```

Our `tls-client-non-blocking` program will be based on the `tls-client` program from *Chapter 9, Establishing TLS Connections and Sending Data over Them*. We are going to take the `tls-client` program source code and change it to use a non-blocking socket instead of a blocking socket. Or, rather, a non-blocking BIO instead of a blocking BIO.

We will only need to change the `run_tls_client()` function to accomplish this.

Changing the run_tls_client() function

Here is what we are going to change:

1. The first thing that we are going to do is to switch the BIO to the non-blocking mode. To accomplish this, we need to add the following lines:

```
BIO_set_nbio(ssl_bio, 1);
if (err <= 0) {
```

```
    if (error_stream)
        fprintf(
            error_stream,
            "Could not enable non-blocking mode\n");
    goto failure;
}
```

It's important to switch the BIO to the non-blocking mode before the connection attempt – otherwise, the switching will fail, and the BIO will remain in the blocking mode. In our case, it means that BIO_set_nbio() must be called before BIO_do_connect().

2. The next thing that we need to do is to define timeout variables that will later be used in BIO_wait() calls:

```
const time_t TIMEOUT_SECONDS = 10;
const unsigned int NAP_MILLISECONDS = 100;
time_t deadline = time(NULL) + TIMEOUT_SECONDS;
```

In our example program, for simplicity, we will use a 10-second timeout for the whole TLS connection. This should be okay because the whole program usually takes less than 1 second to run.

3. The next step is to update the connection-establishing code to be non-blocking-aware. The original connection-establishing code from the tls-client program looks as follows:

```
err = BIO_do_connect(ssl_bio);
if (err <= 0) {
    if (error_stream)
        fprintf(
            error_stream,
            "Could not connect to server %s on port
%s\n",
            hostname,
            port);
    goto failure;
}
```

We will need to add a retrying loop and change the connection-establishing code to the following:

```
err = BIO_do_connect(ssl_bio);
while (err <= 0 && BIO_should_retry(ssl_bio)) {
    int wait_err = BIO_wait(
        ssl_bio,
```

```
                    deadline,
                    NAP_MILLISECONDS);
          if (wait_err != 1)
                    break;
          err = BIO_do_connect(ssl_bio);
     }
     if (err <= 0) {
          if (error_stream)
                    fprintf(
                              error_stream,
                              "Could not connect to server %s on port
%s\n",
                              hostname,
                              port);
          goto failure;
     }
```

In the retrying loop, we are calling the BIO_should_retry() function to check whether the last I/O error was would block and we should retry the connection attempt. If we should retry, then we wait for activity on the BIO using the BIO_wait() function and retry it.

As you can see, we are supplying the deadline and NAP_MILLISECONDS arguments to the BIO_wait() function. The deadline argument is the maximum time point until which the BIO_wait() function will wait. The NAP_MILLISECONDS argument will only be used if OpenSSL was compiled without socket support. Compilation of OpenSSL without socket support is needed if the OS does not support standard Berkeley sockets and uses its own non-standard sockets instead. Those kinds of OSs can usually be found on embedded devices. If OpenSSL is compiled without socket support, BIO_wait() will not be able to check network activity on a socket and will just sleep at NAP_MILLISECONDS and return. If the current OS supports standard sockets, which is the most common case, the NAP_MILLISECONDS argument will be ignored and BIO_wait() will return when either the socket is available to retry the I/O operation, the deadline time point has been reached, or an error has occurred.

BIO_wait() is a convenient function because it takes a BIO (not a socket) as a parameter, has a simple signature, and abstracts the complexity of low-level OS functions away from a developer. However, it is important to be aware that BIO_wait() is much less flexible compared to low-level OS functions, such as select() and poll:

- As already mentioned, BIO_wait() can wait for only one BIO, whereas the low-level OS functions can wait for many sockets simultaneously.

- The deadline time given to `BIO_wait()` is measured in whole seconds, which is not very granular. Low-level OS functions take timeouts with milliseconds of precision at least.

- `BIO_wait()` can only wait for the resolution of the previous I/O error on a BIO. Low-level OS functions can wait for different types of events on any socket passed to them. However, `BIO_wait()` automatically resolves which type of event to wait for, and that is an advantage.

If you need more flexibility than `BIO_wait()` can offer, you can extract the BIO's underlying file descriptor using the `BIO_get_fd()` function and use the low-level OS functions on it.

When your program exchanges data via TLS, the TLS protocol may want to read from the network when your program wants to write to the network, and vice versa, the TLS protocol may want to write when your program wants to read. For example, any side of the TLS connection during the communication may decide to refresh the session keys at any time. In our `tls-client-non-blocking` program, these situations are handled automatically using the `BIO_should_retry()` and `BIO_wait()` functions. In another program, a developer may use OS sockets directly and wait on them using a low-level OS function, such as `select()` or `poll()`, instead of `BIO_wait()`. In such a case, the developer has to know what to wait for, whether reading or writing. It can be determined by such functions as `BIO_should_read()`, `BIO_should_write()`, `BIO_should_io_special()`, and `BIO_retry_type()`. It is also possible to use the `SSL_get_error()` function and analyze its returned error code, which can be `SSL_ERROR_WANT_READ` or `SSL_ERROR_WANT_WRITE`. Let's suppose that our program wants to read, using the `BIO_read()` function, but the TLS protocol wants to write, and we have determined it by receiving `true` from the `BIO_should_write()` function. What do we do? Do we need to write something to the TLS connection using the `BIO_write()` function? But what do we write if we have nothing to write – call `BIO_write()` for writing zero bytes? No. We don't need to write anything. Instead, we have to wait on the OS socket until it is *possible to write* to that socket. After that, we have to retry the *reading* operation that we wanted to perform in the first place, such as `BIO_read()`. It may sound counter-intuitive, but yes, we should retry reading even though the TLS protocol wants to write. The OpenSSL library will take care of the needed reading and writing operations to satisfy the TLS protocol. OpenSSL will read and write the service data as needed and will then read the application data from the TLS connection and provide it to us.

Now, let's continue with changing the `run_tls_client()` function:

4.　Our next step is to update the data-sending code for the non-blocking mode. The original code from the `tls-client` program looks as follows:

```
int nbytes_written = BIO_write(
    ssl_bio, out_buf, request_length);
if (nbytes_written != request_length) {
    if (error_stream)
        fprintf(
            error_stream,
```

```
                              "Could not send all data to the server\n");
        goto failure;
    }
```

Note that the preceding code is a bit simplified, even for the blocking mode, for the sake of showing simpler example code. The code suggests that `BIO_write()` in a successful case will only return after sending the whole request. In most cases, this will be true, because our request is rather small, and we have not filled the OS network buffers with the previous data sent. But it would be more robust if there was a sending loop that would check whether the request was only partially sent, and the sending must be resumed from the correct offset. In our sending code for the non-blocking mode, we will introduce such a loop. We will also use the `BIO_should_retry()` and `BIO_wait()` functions to determine when the BIO is ready for writing. Here is how the sending code for the non-blocking mode will look:

```
int nbytes_written_total = 0;
while (nbytes_written_total < request_length) {
    int nbytes_written = BIO_write(
        ssl_bio,
        out_buf + nbytes_written_total,
        request_length - nbytes_written_total);
    if (nbytes_written > 0) {
        nbytes_written_total += nbytes_written;
        continue;
    }
    if (BIO_should_retry(ssl_bio)) {
        BIO_wait(
            ssl_bio,
            deadline,
            NAP_MILLISECONDS);
        continue;
    }
    if (error_stream)
        fprintf(
            error_stream,
            "Could not send all data to the server\n");
    goto failure;
}
```

5. The next step is to update the data-receiving code from the `tls-client` program for the non-blocking mode. This is how it looks:

```
while ((SSL_get_shutdown(ssl) & SSL_RECEIVED_SHUTDOWN)
        != SSL_RECEIVED_SHUTDOWN) {
    int nbytes_read = BIO_read(ssl_bio, in_buf, BUF_
SIZE);
    if (nbytes_read <= 0) {
        int ssl_error = SSL_get_error(ssl, nbytes_read);
        if (ssl_error == SSL_ERROR_ZERO_RETURN)
            break;
        if (error_stream)
            fprintf(
                error_stream,
                "Error %i while reading data "
                "from the server\n",
                ssl_error);
        goto failure;
    }
    fwrite(in_buf, 1, nbytes_read, stdout);
}
```

As we can see, the original code already has a receiving loop. We will add the retry code for the non-blocking mode and will update the receiving code as follows:

```
while ((SSL_get_shutdown(ssl) & SSL_RECEIVED_SHUTDOWN)
        != SSL_RECEIVED_SHUTDOWN) {
    int nbytes_read = BIO_read(ssl_bio, in_buf, BUF_
SIZE);
    if (nbytes_read > 0) {
        fwrite(in_buf, 1, nbytes_read, stdout);
        continue;
    }
    if (BIO_should_retry(ssl_bio)) {
        err = BIO_wait(
            ssl_bio,
            deadline,
            NAP_MILLISECONDS);
        continue;
```

```
        }
        int ssl_error = SSL_get_error(ssl, nbytes_read);
        if (ssl_error == SSL_ERROR_ZERO_RETURN)
            break;
        if (error_stream)
            fprintf(
                error_stream,
                "Error %i while reading data "
                "from the server\n",
                ssl_error);
        goto failure;
    }
```

Those were all the changes that we had to make in order to use TLS on a non-blocking socket.

The complete source code of our tls-client-non-blocking program can be found on GitHub in the tls-client-non-blocking.c file: https://github.com/PacktPublishing/Demystifying-Cryptography-with-OpenSSL-3/blob/main/Chapter11/tls-client-non-blocking.c

Running the tls-client-non-blocking program

Let's run our tls-client-non-blocking program and see how it works. As with the previous example, we will need the tls-server program from *Chapter 9, Establishing TLS Connections and Sending Data over Them*. We will also need the ca_cert.pem CA certificate file to verify the server certificate by the tls-client-non-blocking program.

This's how we will test that our tls-client-non-blocking program works:

1. Let's open two terminal windows.

2. In the first window, we will start the tls-server program:

    ```
    $ ./tls-server 4433 server_keypair.pem server_cert.pem
    *** Listening on port 4433
    ```

3. In the second window, we will run our tls-client-non-blocking program:

    ```
    $ ./tls-client-non-blocking localhost 4433 ca_cert.pem
    *** Sending to the server:
    GET / HTTP/1.1
    Host: localhost
    ```

```
Connection: close
User-Agent: Example TLS client
*** Sending to the server finished
*** Receiving from the server:
HTTP/1.0 200 OK
Content-type: text/plain
Connection: close
Server: Example TLS server
Hello from the TLS server!
*** Receiving from the server finished
TLS communication succeeded
```

As we can observe, TLS communication with `localhost` on a non-blocking socket has succeeded, and we could both send and receive data from the server. But will it work over the internet?

4. We can try communicating with the `www.example.org` server and find out:

```
$ ./tls-client-non-blocking www.example.org 443
*** Sending to the server:
GET / HTTP/1.1
Host: localhost
Connection: close
User-Agent: Example TLS client
*** Sending to the server finished
*** Receiving from the server:
… much text …
*** Receiving from the server finished
TLS communication succeeded
```

As we can see, communication with www.example.org also works flawlessly. We can conclude that our non-blocking code works as expected.

Using TLS on non-blocking sockets is quite an important use case. In the next two sections, we will learn about another advanced TLS use case: using TLS connections on non-standard sockets using memory BIOs. You may need it if your target OS does not support standard sockets.

Understanding TLS on non-standard sockets

Standard Berkeley network sockets are supported by most OSes. But there are some OSes, especially embedded ones, that only support their own non-standard sockets or connection handlers. How can we use OpenSSL on these kinds of OSes? It is possible with the help of OpenSSL memory BIOs. OpenSSL can establish TLS connections purely in memory.

The following diagram shows how the data flows to and from the non-standard socket via memory BIOs:

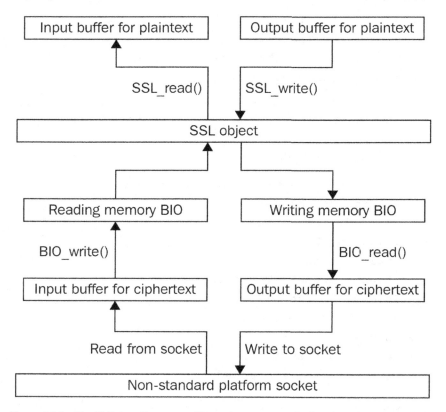

Figure 11.1 – The TLS data flow to and from the non-standard socket via memory BIOs

This way, when a program wants to receive plaintext from the TLS connection, the following happens:

1. The program receives some ciphertext from the non-standard socket to the ciphertext input buffer.

2. The program writes the ciphertext into the reading memory BIO.

3. OpenSSL decrypts the ciphertext from the reading memory BIO and puts the resulting plaintext into the plaintext input buffer.

4. The program gets the plaintext received on the TLS connection from the plaintext input buffer.

When a program wants to send plaintext on the TLS connection, the data is processed in the opposite direction:

1. The program puts the plaintext to be sent on the TLS connection into the plaintext output buffer.

2. OpenSSL encrypts the plaintext according to the TLS protocol and puts the resulting ciphertext into the writing memory BIO.

3. The program reads the ciphertext from the writing memory BIO into the ciphertext output buffer.

4. The program sends the ciphertext to the non-standard platform socket.

In the next section, we will learn how to accomplish TLS on non-standard sockets programmatically.

Using TLS on non-standard sockets

To learn how to use TLS on a non-standard socket, we are going to write a small `tls-client-memory-bio` program.

Our `tls-client-memory-bio` program will be based on the `tls-client` program from *Chapter 9, Establishing TLS Connections and Sending Data over Them*. We are going to take the `tls-client` program source code and change it to work via memory BIOs.

We are going to change quite a lot in the `tls-client` source code. For instance, we are not going to use an SSL BIO this time. An SSL BIO is a wrapper around an SSL object. In the previous example programs, it was convenient to use an SSL BIO, which was automatically chained with a connect BIO. This time, we are not going to automatically chain with a connect BIO. Instead, we will use I/O directly on an SSL object, using functions such as `SSL_read()` and `SSL_write()` instead of `BIO_read()` and `BIO_write()`. Using I/O directly on the SSL object will not only simplify the code but will also demonstrate the usage of some new functions.

As we are going to use new OpenSSL functions, it makes sense to read their man pages:

```
$ man SSL_new
$ man SSL_set_bio
$ man SSL_connect
$ man SSL_want_read
$ man SSL_read
$ man SSL_write
$ man SSL_shutdown
$ man SSL_free
$ man BIO_new_connect
$ man BIO_set_mem_eof_return
$ man BIO_pending
```

We will need to attach two underlying memory BIOs to the SSL object. One memory BIO will be used for reading ciphertext and another one for writing ciphertext. The SSL object will read and write ciphertext to those BIOs automatically. There will be no BIOs for plaintext attached to the SSL object. Instead, the SSL_read() and SSL_write() functions will be used for reading and writing plaintext.

A non-standard network socket will be represented by an OpenSSL connect BIO. A connect BIO is not really a non-standard socket, but it will be good enough to demonstrate how to transfer data between memory BIOs and the network connection. Also, unlike real non-standard sockets, connect BIOs work on a usual PC, which is where we are going to run our example program.

Let's start the tls-client-memory-bio program implementation.

Implementing the service_bios() function

First, we are going to implement a function for transferring data between memory BIOs that the SSL object uses and the network socket, represented by a connect BIO:

1. The function will be called before SSL_read() or after other SSL_*() I/O functions. As the function services three BIOs, we will call it service_bios():

    ```
    int service_bios(
        BIO* mem_rbio,
        BIO* mem_wbio,
        BIO* tcp_bio,
        int want_read);
    ```

The function takes the following parameters:

- mem_rbio – The memory BIO from which the SSL object reads ciphertext.

- mem_wbio – The memory BIO to which the SSL object writes ciphertext.

- tcp_bio – The connect BIO that reads and writes to the network.

- want_read – The Boolean flag. If true, then the service_bios() function is requested not only to write pending data to the network but also to read from the network. If false, then the service_bios() function will only write to the network.

The service_bios() function returns 1 on success or -1 on failure.

The function starts with the definition of the default return code and allocates some buffers:

```
int err = 1;
const size_t BUF_SIZE = 16 * 1024;
char* in_buf  = malloc(BUF_SIZE);
char* out_buf = malloc(BUF_SIZE);
```

2. The next thing is to write the pending data to the network:

```
while (BIO_pending(mem_wbio)) {
    int nbytes_read =
        BIO_read(mem_wbio, out_buf, BUF_SIZE);
    int nbytes_written_total = 0;
    while (nbytes_written_total < nbytes_read) {
        int nbytes_written =
            BIO_write(tcp_bio, out_buf, nbytes_read);
        if (nbytes_written > 0) {
            nbytes_written_total += nbytes_written;
            continue;
        } else {
            goto failure;
        }
    }
}
```

As you can see, we are just reading data from mem_wbio and writing it to tcp_bio.

3. The next step is to read data from the network if it was requested:

```
if (want_read) {
    int nbytes_read =
        BIO_read(tcp_bio, in_buf, BUF_SIZE);
    if (nbytes_read > 0) {
        BIO_write(mem_rbio, in_buf, nbytes_read);
    } else {
        goto failure;
    }
}
```

This time, we are reading data from tcp_bio and writing it to mem_rbio for further consumption by the SSL object.

4. The function is finished by cleaning up and returning the error code:

```
    goto cleanup;
failure:
    err = -1;
cleanup:
```

```
    free(out_buf);
    free(in_buf);
    return err;
```

That's all for the service_bios() function.

Reimplementing the run_tls_client() function

Now let's reimplement the run_tls_client() function that contains most of the code:

1. The run_tls_client() function starts by defining variables and allocating buffers:

```
int exit_code = 0;
int err = 1;
SSL_CTX* ctx = NULL;
BIO* tcp_bio = NULL;
BIO* mem_rbio = NULL;
BIO* mem_wbio = NULL;
SSL* ssl = NULL;
const size_t BUF_SIZE = 16 * 1024;
char* in_buf  = malloc(BUF_SIZE);
char* out_buf = malloc(BUF_SIZE);
```

2. The next step is creating the SSL_CTX object, loading trusted certificates, and enabling peer certificate verification. It is the same code as in the original tls-client program:

```
ERR_clear_error();
ctx = SSL_CTX_new(TLS_client_method());
if (trusted_cert_fname)
    err = SSL_CTX_load_verify_locations(
        ctx, trusted_cert_fname, NULL);
else
    err = SSL_CTX_set_default_verify_paths(ctx);
if (err <= 0) {
    if (error_stream)
        fprintf(
            error_stream,
            "Could not load trusted certificates\n");
```

```
        goto failure;
    }
    SSL_CTX_set_verify(ctx, SSL_VERIFY_PEER, NULL);
```

3. The next step is establishing a *TCP* (not a TLS) connection to the server. We will establish a TLS connection in a later step. As mentioned, a connect BIO is used to emulate a non-standard socket:

```
    tcp_bio = BIO_new_connect(hostname);
    BIO_set_conn_port(tcp_bio, port);
    err = BIO_do_connect(tcp_bio);
    if (err <= 0) {
        if (error_stream)
            fprintf(
                error_stream,
                "Could not connect to server %s on port
    %s\n",
                hostname,
                port);
        goto failure;
    }
```

4. The next step is to create and set up reading and writing memory BIOs for the SSL object:

```
    mem_rbio = BIO_new(BIO_s_mem());
    BIO_set_mem_eof_return(mem_rbio, -1);
    mem_wbio = BIO_new(BIO_s_mem());
    BIO_set_mem_eof_return(mem_wbio, -1);
```

The BIO_set_mem_eof_return() call is needed to avoid an end-of-file error if the BIO is empty.

5. Next, create the SSL object representing the TLS connection, and attach the newly created reading and writing memory BIOs to it:

```
    ssl = SSL_new(ctx);
    SSL_set_bio(ssl, mem_rbio, mem_wbio);
```

Note that after the SSL_set_bio() call, the SSL object owns the attached BIOs. When the SSL object is freed with the SSL_free() function, the BIOs will be deallocated with the BIO_free_all() function.

6. The next step is setting the hostname for the **Server Name Indication (SNI)** TLS extension and the certificate hostname verification. It is the same code as in the `tls-client` program:

```
SSL_set_tlsext_host_name(ssl, hostname);
SSL_set1_host(ssl, hostname);
```

7. The next step is the TLS handshake:

```
while (1) {
    err = SSL_connect(ssl);
    int ssl_error = SSL_get_error(ssl, err);
    if (ssl_error == SSL_ERROR_WANT_READ
        || ssl_error == SSL_ERROR_WANT_WRITE
        || BIO_pending(mem_wbio)) {
        int service_bios_err = service_bios(
            mem_rbio, mem_wbio, tcp_bio, SSL_want_
read(ssl));
        if (service_bios_err != 1) {
            if (error_stream)
                fprintf(
                    error_stream,
                    "Socket error during TLS
handshake\n");
            goto failure;
        }
        continue;
    }
    break;
}
if (err <= 0) {
    if (error_stream)
        fprintf(
            error_stream,
            "TLS error %i during TLS handshake\n",
            SSL_get_error(ssl, err));
    goto failure;
}
```

Note that we are repeatedly calling `SSL_connect()` and `service_bios()` until the TLS handshake is finished. Here, during the handshake, and later during writing and reading, we are checking for both `SSL_ERROR_WANT_READ` and `SSL_ERROR_WANT_WRITE`. We do so because, as explained before, the TLS protocol may want to read or write its service data at any time. A TLS handshake, depending on the TLS version and whether any cached session data from the previous connections exists, requires up to two network data round trips. Therefore, we may need to both read and write on the OS socket in the `service_bios()` function a couple of times during the handshake.

8. Next, create the HTTP request that will be sent to the server. It is the same code as in the `tls-client` program:

```
snprintf(
    out_buf,
    BUF_SIZE,
    "GET / HTTP/1.1\r\n"
    "Host: %s\r\n"
    "Connection: close\r\n"
    "User-Agent: Example TLS client\r\n"
    "\r\n",
    hostname);
int request_length = strlen(out_buf);
```

9. The next step is sending the newly created request to the server:

```
printf("*** Sending to the server:\n");
printf("%s", out_buf);
int nbytes_written_total = 0;
while (nbytes_written_total < request_length) {
    int nbytes_written = SSL_write(
        ssl,
        out_buf + nbytes_written_total,
        request_length - nbytes_written_total);
    if (nbytes_written > 0) {
        nbytes_written_total += nbytes_written;
        continue;
    }
    int ssl_error = SSL_get_error(ssl, err);
    if (ssl_error == SSL_ERROR_WANT_READ
        || ssl_error == SSL_ERROR_WANT_WRITE
```

```
                    || BIO_pending(mem_wbio)) {
                int service_bios_err = service_bios(
                    mem_rbio, mem_wbio, tcp_bio, SSL_want_
    read(ssl));
                if (service_bios_err != 1) {
                    if (error_stream)
                        fprintf(
                            error_stream,
                            "Socket error while sending data "
                            "to the server\n");
                    goto failure;
                }
                continue;
            }
            if (error_stream)
                fprintf(
                    error_stream,
                    "TLS error %i while reading data "
                    "to the server\n",
                    ssl_error);
            goto failure;
        }
        printf("*** Sending to the server finished\n");
```

Similar to the previous code, we are repeatedly calling `SSL_write()` and `service_bios()` until the whole request is sent. Even though we are only writing the request to the TLS connection, we are checking for both `SSL_ERROR_WANT_READ` and `SSL_ERROR_WANT_WRITE`, because the TLS protocol may want to both read and write the protocol service data, and we have to satisfy those reading and writing requests in the `service_bios()` function.

10. After the request is sent, we should read the server response:

```
        printf("*** Receiving from the server:\n");
        while ((SSL_get_shutdown(ssl) & SSL_RECEIVED_SHUTDOWN)
                != SSL_RECEIVED_SHUTDOWN) {
            int service_bios_err = 1;
            if (!BIO_pending(mem_rbio))
                service_bios_err = service_bios(
                    mem_rbio, mem_wbio, tcp_bio, 1);
```

```
        if (service_bios_err != 1) {
            if (error_stream)
                fprintf(
                    error_stream,
                    "Socket error while reading data "
                    "from the server\n");
            goto failure;
        }
        int nbytes_read = SSL_read(ssl, in_buf, BUF_SIZE);
        if (nbytes_read > 0) {
            fwrite(in_buf, 1, nbytes_read, stdout);
            continue;
        }
        int ssl_error = SSL_get_error(ssl, err);
        if (ssl_error == SSL_ERROR_NONE
            || ssl_error == SSL_ERROR_WANT_READ
            || ssl_error == SSL_ERROR_WANT_WRITE
            || BIO_pending(mem_wbio))
            continue;
        if (ssl_error == SSL_ERROR_ZERO_RETURN)
            break;
        if (error_stream)
            fprintf(
                error_stream,
                "TLS error %i while reading data "
                "from the server\n",
                ssl_error);
        goto failure;
    }
    printf("*** Receiving from the server finished\n");
```

Similar to the previous code, we are repeatedly calling SSL_read() and service_bios()
until we get the whole server response. But note that we are calling service_bios() before
the SSL I/O function this time. We also check whether any pending data already exists in the
reading BIO, mem_rbio. This kind of function call order makes sense because, first, we have
to read from the network, and only after that can we process the received ciphertext using the
SSL_read() function. As before, we have to process both the SSL_ERROR_WANT_READ
and SSL_ERROR_WANT_WRITE errors, even though we are only reading the application data.

11. After the server response is read, we can shut down the TLS connection:

```
while (1) {
    err = SSL_shutdown(ssl);
    int ssl_error = SSL_get_error(ssl, err);
    if (ssl_error == SSL_ERROR_WANT_READ
            || ssl_error == SSL_ERROR_WANT_WRITE
            || BIO_pending(mem_wbio)) {
        int service_bios_err = service_bios(
                mem_rbio, mem_wbio, tcp_bio, SSL_want_
read(ssl));
        if (service_bios_err != 1) {
            if (error_stream)
                fprintf(
                    error_stream,
                    "Socket error during TLS
shutdown\n");
            goto failure;
        }
        continue;
    }
    break;
}
if (err != 1) {
    if (error_stream)
        fprintf(
            error_stream,
            "TLS error during TLS shutdown\n");
    goto failure;
}
```

12. We finish the `run_tls_client()` function with cleanups, error reporting, and by returning the `exit` code:

```
failure:
    exit_code = 1;
cleanup:
    if (ssl)
```

```
        SSL_free(ssl);
    if (tcp_bio)
        BIO_free_all(tcp_bio);
    if (ctx)
        SSL_CTX_free(ctx);
    free(out_buf);
    free(in_buf);
    if (ERR_peek_error()) {
        exit_code = 1;
        if (error_stream) {
            fprintf(
                error_stream,
                "Errors from the OpenSSL error
queue:\n");
            ERR_print_errors_fp(error_stream);
        }
        ERR_clear_error();
    }
    return exit_code;
```

The complete source code of our tls-client-memory-bio program can be found on GitHub as the tls-client-memory-bio.c file: https://github.com/PacktPublishing/Demystifying-Cryptography-with-OpenSSL-3/blob/main/Chapter11/tls-client-memory-bio.c

Running the tls-client-memory-bio program

Let's run our tls-client-memory-bio program and see how it works.

As with the previous example, we will need the tls-server program from *Chapter 9, Establishing TLS Connections and Sending Data over Them*. We will also need the CA certificate file ca_cert.pem to verify the server certificate.

This is how we will test that our tls-client-memory-bio program works:

1. Let's open two terminal windows.

   I.   In the first window, we will start the tls-server program:

   ```
   $ ./tls-server 4433 server_keypair.pem server_cert.pem
   *** Listening on port 4433
   ```

II.   In the second window, we will run our `tls-client-memory-bio` program:

```
$ ./tls-client-memory-bio localhost 4433 ca_cert.pem
*** Sending to the server:
GET / HTTP/1.1
Host: localhost
Connection: close
User-Agent: Example TLS client
*** Sending to the server finished
*** Receiving from the server:
HTTP/1.0 200 OK
Content-type: text/plain
Connection: close
Server: Example TLS server
Hello from the TLS server!
*** Receiving from the server finished
TLS communication succeeded
```

As we can observe, TLS communication with `localhost` via memory BIOs and non-standard socket emulation has succeeded.

2. We can also try communicating with the `www.example.org` server to test that our `tls-client-memory-bio` program also works with internet servers:

```
$ ./tls-client-memory-bio www.example.org 443
*** Sending to the server:
GET / HTTP/1.1
Host: localhost
Connection: close
User-Agent: Example TLS client
*** Sending to the server finished
*** Receiving from the server:
… much text …
*** Receiving from the server finished
TLS communication succeeded
```

As we can see, communication with `www.example.org` also works very well. We can conclude that our `tls-client-memory-bio` program works as expected.

This brings us to the end of this chapter. Now, we'll summarize everything we learned here.

Summary

In this chapter, we learned about what TLS certificate pinning is and in which situations it can be helpful. We also learned how to implement TLS certificate pinning with the help of a certificate verification callback. Then, we learned about the differences between blocking and non-blocking sockets and how to use non-blocking network connections. After that, we learned how to use OpenSSL memory BIOs to establish TLS connections over non-standard sockets. This knowledge can help you to write more secure, responsive, and performant applications, as well as to adapt your programs to embedded OSes.

In the next chapter, we will learn how to run a mini-CA that can issue certificates for internal usage within an organization.

Part 5:
Running a Mini-CA

In this part, we will learn how to use OpenSSL command-line utilities to run a mini-**Certificate Authority** (**CA**) that can issue certificates for internal usage in an organization. A mini-CA can be useful in organizations for establishing internal Public Key Infrastructure, gaining control of internally used certificates, and saving costs on ordering certificates from commercial CAs. The usage of a mini-CA will be illustrated using configuration files and command-line examples.

This part contains the following chapter:

- *Chapter 12, Running a Mini-CA*

12

Running a Mini-CA

In *Chapter 8, X.509 Certificates and PKI*, we learned about **Public Key Infrastructure (PKI)** based on X.509 certificates. In this chapter, we will learn how to use the `openssl ca` subcommand to run a mini-**Certificate Authority (CA)** that can issue certificates for internal usage in an organization. A mini-CA can be useful in organizations for establishing internal PKI, gaining control of internally used certificates, and saving costs on ordering certificates from commercial CAs. The usage of a mini-CA will be illustrated by command-line examples.

We are going to cover the following topics in this chapter:

- Understanding the `openssl ca` subcommand
- Generating a root CA certificate
- Generating an intermediate CA certificate
- Generating a certificate for a web server
- Generating a certificate for a web and email client
- Revoking certificates and generating CRLs
- Providing certificate revocation status via OCSP

Technical requirements

This chapter will contain commands that you can run on a command line. You will need the `openssl` command-line tool and the OpenSSL dynamic libraries.

We will use many configuration files and commands in this chapter. Those configuration files and commands, saved as Shell scripts, can be found here: `https://github.com/PacktPublishing/Demystifying-Cryptography-with-OpenSSL-3/tree/main/Chapter12`.

Understanding the openssl ca subcommand

The openssl ca subcommand can be useful for running a mini-CA inside an organization. This kind of CA can, for instance, issue certificates for internal servers. Using an internal CA saves costs compared to using an external commercial CA. But it is not the only advantage. Many internal servers should not be exposed to access from the internet. This limitation hinders automatic server checks from the external CAs, which are needed to issue cheap or free certificates. Also, in some cases, it is undesirable to expose knowledge about the existence or name of the internal servers. When ordering a certificate from an external CA, you have to expose the internal server's name to the CA. Furthermore, the CA may publish the certificate information to a **Certificate Transparency (CT)** log, leading to even more unwanted information exposure about the company's internal servers.

Another reason to have an internal CA is to issue client certificates. Using a certificate issued by an internal CA on a public internet web server is not very convenient because every user of that web server has to install the internal CA certificate to their browser's trusted store. But a client certificate issued by an internal CA does not have this disadvantage because such a certificate is usually only used to authenticate against a few servers.

In some organizations, using an internal CA for internal purposes can give some degree of freedom, compared to using an external CA. For example, you may need approval from a security team to get an external certificate or from an accounting manager to get a paid certificate. With an internal CA, you can freely issue certificates for your internal needs without any approvals.

The openssl ca subcommand can take parameters for its work from the command line and the OpenSSL config file. The OpenSSL config file can store various options for the OpenSSL library and utilities. The default OpenSSL config file is supplied in the OpenSSL distribution as the apps/openssl.cnf file. During OpenSSL installation, the default config file will be installed into the ssl directory – for instance, as /opt/openssl-3.0.0/ssl/openssl.cnf or /etc/ssl/openssl.cnf. For openssl ca operations, it is usual to create a custom config file representing a particular CA, such as a root CA or an intermediate CA, instead of using the default OpenSSL config file.

It is preferable to specify most parameters for the openssl ca subcommand in the config file in order to avoid repeating them on the command line when issuing different certificates. Besides, some parameters can only be specified in the config file. If the same parameters are provided in both the config file and on the command line, the command line parameters take precedence.

Documentation about openssl ca parameters and config files can be found on the following man pages:

```
$ man openssl-ca
$ man 5ssl config
$ man x509v3_config
```

Along with the config file, openssl ca also uses other mandatory or optional files, such as certificate index files, serial number files, random seed files, and CRL number files.

The `openssl ca` subcommand can issue certificates, revoke certificates, and generate **Certificate Revocation Lists (CRLs)**. When issuing or revoking a certificate, `openssl ca` updates the certificate index file, also known as the certificate database.

`openssl ca` can issue certificates with sequential or random serial numbers. If sequential serial numbers are used, the next serial number is stored and automatically updated in the serial number file. However, for security reasons, it is better to issue certificates with random serial numbers.

A CRL can be generated with or without a **CRL number**. A CRL number is basically a CRL version. It is a positive integer number that is incremented by one each time a CA issues its next full CRL. It is better to include a CRL number in a CRL because it helps to check CRL issuance continuity and makes it possible to generate **delta CRLs**. A delta CRL is a CRL that only contains changes since a particular release of an ordinary full CRL. The full CRL that the delta CRL is based on is called a **base CRL**. However, delta CRLs are not supported by `openssl ca` yet – you will need to use another tool if you want to generate them. If you generate a CRL with a CRL number, that number will be stored in the CRL number file and updated automatically by `openssl ca`.

Let's learn how to use the `openssl ca` subcommand. We will start by generating a root CA certificate.

Generating a root CA certificate

We will create some needed directories and files and then proceed with generating the root CA certificate:

1. First, we will make the `mini-ca` directory where we will put all our CA-related files:

    ```
    $ mkdir mini-ca
    $ cd mini-ca
    ```

2. Inside the `mini-ca` directory, we will create the `root` directory for the files related to the root CA:

    ```
    $ mkdir root
    $ cd root
    ```

3. Inside the `root` directory, we will create a directory for issued certificates, a certificate index file, and a CRL number file:

    ```
    $ mkdir issued
    $ echo -n >index.txt
    $ echo 01 >crlnumber.txt
    ```

4. Now, we have to make a config file for our root CA; we will name this file `root.cnf`. We will start the config file with some mandatory parameters:

```
[ca]
default_ca = CA_default
[CA_default]
database                    = index.txt
new_certs_dir               = issued
certificate                 = root_cert.pem
private_key                 = private/root_keypair.pem
```

The `database` parameter specifies the certificate index file, also known as the certificate database. It is a text file where each line has information about one certificate. The `new_certs_dir` parameter specifies a directory where newly issued certificates will be written. The `certificate` and `private_key` parameters specify the certificate and the corresponding private key of the current CA – in our case, the root CA.

5. Next, we will define some optional parameters. Our root CA will issue only intermediate CA certificates; hence, we can set the default issued certificate validity to 10 years:

```
default_days                = 3650
```

6. The following parameter sets the message digest algorithm to use for signing certificates issued by our root CA. There is a special `default` value for the `default_md` parameter. It means that the same message digest algorithm that was used in a signing certificate will be used in the signed certificate. For instance, if a signing certificate is signed using the SHA-256 hash function itself, the issued certificate will also use the SHA-256 hash function for its signature. In our case, this parameter will not make any difference because ED448 certificates always use the SHAKE256 message digest algorithm when signing other certificates. We will include this parameter here just to demonstrate the capabilities of the `openssl ca` subcommand:

```
default_md                  = default
```

7. The next parameter instructs `openssl ca` to issue certificates with random serial numbers, as opposed to sequential serial numbers:

```
rand_serial                 = yes
```

8. The subsequent parameter allows us to issue several certificates with the same Subject. It can be useful for replacing expired certificates:

```
unique_subject              = no
```

9. The next parameters control how certificate details are shown before signing. The OpenSSL documentation recommends setting these parameters – otherwise, an old broken display format will be used:

    ```
    name_opt                    = ca_default
    cert_opt                    = ca_default
    ```

10. The following parameter is mandatory and specifies the config section that defines the default issued certificate's Subject policy. We will review it more closely when we come to the section itself:

    ```
    policy                      = policy_intermediate_cert
    ```

11. The next parameter specifies the default X509v3 extensions section:

    ```
    x509_extensions             = v3_intermediate_cert
    ```

12. This next parameter instructs OpenSSL to copy the X509v3 extensions from the **Certificate Signing Request** (**CSR**) that are not added by the CA to the issued certificate. Selective copying allows a CSR to supply useful X509v3 extensions, such as *subjectAltName*, but forbids overriding important extensions set by the CA, such as *basicConstraints* or *keyUsage*:

    ```
    copy_extensions             = copy
    ```

13. The next parameters are CRL-related. They set the default config section with CRL extensions, CRL number files, and the default validity of an issued CRL:

    ```
    crl_extensions              = crl_extensions_root_ca
    crlnumber                   = crlnumber.txt
    default_crl_days            = 30
    ```

14. The following parameters define the default Subject and X509v3 extensions for a CSR when the CSR is made with this config file. The only CSR made with this config file should be the CSR for the root CA certificate. Therefore, it is convenient to define the root CA certificate's Subject and X509v3 extensions in the config file, both for generating the CSR and, subsequently, the root CA certificate. Having certificate data in the config file is also helpful as a reminder about which CA certificate is used with it:

    ```
    [req]
    prompt                      = no
    distinguished_name          = distinguished_name_root_cert
    x509_extensions             = v3_root_cert
    [distinguished_name_root_cert]
    countryName                 = NO
    stateOrProvinceName         = Oslo
    ```

```
localityName            = Oslo
organizationName        = TLS Experts
commonName              = Root CA
```

15. The next config section defines the default issued certificate's Subject policy:

```
[policy_intermediate_cert]
countryName             = match
stateOrProvinceName     = match
localityName            = match
organizationName        = match
organizationalUnitName  = optional
commonName              = supplied
emailAddress            = optional
```

As per the defined policy, we require the issued intermediate CA certificate's Subject to have the same geographical location and organization as the root CA certificate's Subject. It makes sense because we are running a mini-CA inside one organization.

16. The next config sections define the X509v3 extensions for the root CA certificate and the issued `intermediate` CA certificate. The required section can be selected using the `-extensions` command-line switch:

```
[v3_root_cert]
subjectKeyIdentifier = hash
authorityKeyIdentifier = keyid:always, issuer
basicConstraints = critical, CA:TRUE
keyUsage = critical, digitalSignature, cRLSign,
keyCertSign
crlDistributionPoints = URI:http://crl.tls-experts.no/
root_crl.der
[v3_intermediate_cert]
subjectKeyIdentifier = hash
authorityKeyIdentifier = keyid:always, issuer
basicConstraints = critical, CA:TRUE, pathlen:0
keyUsage = critical, digitalSignature, cRLSign,
keyCertSign
crlDistributionPoints = URI:http://crl.tls-experts.no/
root_crl.der
```

17. The last config section defines the CRL extensions that will be added to issued CRLs:

```
[crl_extensions_root_ca]
authorityKeyIdentifier = keyid:always, issuer
crlDistributionPoints = URI:http://crl.tls-experts.no/
root_crl.der
```

The full root CA config file can be found on GitHub as the root.cnf file: https://github.com/PacktPublishing/Demystifying-Cryptography-with-OpenSSL-3/blob/main/Chapter12/mini-ca/root/root.cnf.

18. Our root CA config file is ready. Let's proceed to the next step, which is the generation of the root CA keypair:

```
$ mkdir private
$ chmod 0700 private
$ openssl genpkey \
    -algorithm ED448 \
    -out private/root_keypair.pem
```

19. The next step is generating the root CA CSR:

```
$ openssl req \
    -config root.cnf \
    -new \
    -key private/root_keypair.pem \
    -out root_csr.pem \
    -text
```

Note that we have not supplied the root certificate's Subject on the command line. The openssl req subcommand will figure out the Subject from the root.cnf config file, namely from the req and distinguished_name_root_cert sections.

20. After the CSR is ready, we can issue the root CA certificate:

```
$ openssl ca \
    -config root.cnf \
    -extensions v3_root_cert \
    -selfsign \
    -in root_csr.pem \
    -out root_cert.pem
Using configuration from root.cnf
Check that the request matches the signature
```

```
Signature ok
Certificate Details:
        Serial Number:
            ... (long hex number) ...
        Validity
            Not Before: Jul 18 18:54:11 2022 GMT
            Not After : Jul 15 18:54:11 2032 GMT
        Subject:
            countryName              = NO
            stateOrProvinceName      = Oslo
            localityName             = Oslo
            organizationName         = TLS Experts
            commonName               = Root CA
        X509v3 extensions:
        X509v3 Subject Key Identifier:
            ... (long hex number) ...
        X509v3 Authority Key Identifier:
            ... (long hex number) ...
        X509v3 Basic Constraints: critical
            CA:TRUE
        X509v3 Key Usage: critical
            Digital Signature, Certificate Sign, CRL
Sign
        X509v3 CRL Distribution Points:
            Full Name:
                URI:http://crl.tls-experts.no/root_crl.
der
Certificate is to be certified until Jul 15 18:54:11 2032
GMT (3650 days)
Sign the certificate? [y/n]:y
1 out of 1 certificate requests certified, commit? [y/n]y
Write out database with 1 new entries
Data Base Updated
```

Note that we have used the `openssl ca` subcommand instead of `openssl x509` in order to issue the certificate. Also, note that we have supplied most of the parameters in the config file instead of on the command line. We have not supplied the private key, duration, or X509v3 extensions on the command line – they all have been taken from the config file. We have used the `-selfsigned` switch to instruct `openssl ca` to issue a self-signed root CA certificate. We will not use that switch when issuing other certificates.

After issuing the certificate, `openssl ca` saves a copy of the issued certificate in the `issued` directory (specified by the `new_certs_dir` parameter in the configuration) and updates the certificate index file (specified by the `database` parameter in the configuration).

We have successfully generated the root CA certificate. In the next section, we will find out how to generate an intermediate CA certificate.

Generating an intermediate CA certificate

Generating an intermediate CA certificate will be similar to generating a root CA certificate. We will use another directory for our intermediate CA; let's call the directory `intermediate` and place it at the same level as the `root` directory inside the `mini-ca` directory:

1. Let's create the `intermediate` directory and initialize it with the needed files and subdirectory:

    ```
    $ cd mini-ca
    $ mkdir intermediate
    $ cd intermediate
    $ mkdir issued
    $ echo -n >index.txt
    $ echo 01 >crlnumber.txt
    ```

2. Now, we have to make a config file for our intermediate CA; we will name this file `intermediate.cnf`. The config file for the intermediate CA will be similar to that of the root CA. We will start the config file with the same parameters as in the root CA configuration:

    ```
    [ca]
    default_ca = CA_default
    [CA_default]
    database                = index.txt
    new_certs_dir           = issued
    certificate             = intermediate_cert.pem
    private_key             = private/intermediate_keypair.
    pem
    default_days            = 365
    ```

```
default_md                    = default
rand_serial                   = yes
unique_subject                = no
name_opt                      = ca_default
cert_opt                      = ca_default
policy                        = policy_server_cert
x509_extensions               = v3_server_cert
copy_extensions               = copy
crl_extensions                = crl_extensions_intermediate_ca
crlnumber                     = crlnumber.txt
default_crl_days              = 30
```

Note that the `default_days` parameter in this config file is lower than the same parameter in the root CA config file. It is because our intermediate CA will issue leaf certificates that usually have a shorter lifetime than root or intermediate CA certificates.

3. We will continue the config file with the parameters that will help to build the Subject of our intermediate CA certificate:

```
[req]
prompt                        = no
distinguished_name            = distinguished_name_
intermediate_cert
[distinguished_name_intermediate_cert]
countryName                   = NO
stateOrProvinceName           = Oslo
localityName                  = Oslo
organizationName              = TLS Experts
commonName                    = Intermediate CA
```

4. Our intermediate CA is going to issue both server and client certificates. Hence, we need to define the Subject policies for those categories of certificates:

```
[policy_server_cert]
countryName                   = optional
stateOrProvinceName           = optional
localityName                  = optional
organizationName              = optional
organizationalUnitName        = optional
commonName                    = supplied
```

```
emailAddress                  = optional
[policy_client_cert]
countryName                   = optional
stateOrProvinceName           = optional
localityName                  = optional
organizationName              = optional
organizationalUnitName        = optional
commonName                    = supplied
emailAddress                  = supplied
```

As you can observe, the policies defined in the intermediate CA configuration are more relaxed than those in the root CA configuration. This is because we may potentially want to issue a certificate to an entity outside of our organization – for instance, to a customer or a partner – and because it is nice to have some variations in our demos.

5. The next sections in the intermediate CA configuration define X509v3 extensions that will be added to different kinds of issued certificates, such as server certificates, client certificates, and certificates for **Online Certificate Status Protocol (OCSP)** responders:

```
[v3_server_cert]
subjectKeyIdentifier = hash
authorityKeyIdentifier = keyid:always, issuer
basicConstraints = critical, CA:FALSE
nsCertType = server
keyUsage = critical, digitalSignature, keyEncipherment
extendedKeyUsage = serverAuth
crlDistributionPoints = URI:http://crl.tls-experts.no/
intermediate_crl.der
authorityInfoAccess = OCSP;URI:http://ocsp.tls-experts.
no/
[v3_client_cert]
subjectKeyIdentifier = hash
authorityKeyIdentifier = keyid:always, issuer
basicConstraints = critical, CA:FALSE
nsCertType = client, email
keyUsage = critical, nonRepudiation, digitalSignature,
keyEncipherment
extendedKeyUsage = clientAuth, emailProtection
crlDistributionPoints = URI:http://crl.tls-experts.no/
intermediate_crl.der
```

```
authorityInfoAccess = OCSP;URI:http://ocsp.tls-experts.
no/
[v3_ocsp_cert]
subjectKeyIdentifier = hash
authorityKeyIdentifier = keyid:always, issuer
basicConstraints = critical, CA:FALSE
keyUsage = critical, digitalSignature
extendedKeyUsage = critical, OCSPSigning
crlDistributionPoints = URI:http://crl.tls-experts.no/
intermediate_crl.der
authorityInfoAccess = OCSP;URI:http://ocsp.tls-experts.
no/
```

6. The last section in the config file defines extensions that will be added to the issued CRLs:

```
[crl_extensions_intermediate_ca]
authorityKeyIdentifier = keyid:always, issuer
crlDistributionPoints = URI:http://crl.tls-experts.no/
intermediate_crl.der
authorityInfoAccess = OCSP;URI:http://ocsp.tls-experts.
no/
```

The full intermediate CA config file can be found on GitHub as the intermediate.cnf file: https://github.com/PacktPublishing/Demystifying-Cryptography-with-OpenSSL-3/blob/main/Chapter12/mini-ca/intermediate/intermediate.cnf.

7. Our intermediate CA config file is ready. Now, let's generate the intermediate CA keypair and CSR:

```
$ mkdir private
$ chmod 0700 private
$ openssl genpkey \
    -algorithm ED448 \
    -out private/intermediate_keypair.pem
```

8. Next, generate the intermediate CA CSR:

```
$ openssl req \
    -config intermediate.cnf \
    -new \
    -key private/intermediate_keypair.pem \
    -out intermediate_csr.pem \
    -text
```

9. As with the root CA certificate, we have supplied the certificate Subject components from the config file instead of the command line.

10. The next step is to issue the intermediate CA certificate, but it must be issued by the root CA. Therefore, we will issue it from the `root` directory:

```
$ cd ../root/
$ openssl ca \
    -config root.cnf \
    -extensions v3_intermediate_cert \
    -in  ../intermediate/intermediate_csr.pem \
    -out ../intermediate/intermediate_cert.pem
Using configuration from root.cnf
Check that the request matches the signature
Signature ok
Certificate Details:

    ...

Certificate is to be certified until Jul 15 18:55:11 2032
GMT (3650 days)
Sign the certificate? [y/n]:y
1 out of 1 certificate requests certified, commit? [y/n]y
Write out database with 1 new entries
Data Base Updated
```

Note that this time we have used X509v3 extensions from the `v3_intermediate_cert` section of the `root.cnf` file, unlike the previous time, when we used the `v3_root_cert` section for the root CA certificate.

We have now generated the intermediate CA certificate. In the next section, we will use it to issue a leaf certificate.

Generating a certificate for a web server

The next certificate that we will generate is a certificate for a web server. As for the previous certificates, we will make a separate directory and a config file for this certificate:

1. However, as we are going to issue a leaf certificate, we will not need to create CA-related files in its directory. We will just need to create the directory and change our current directory there:

    ```
    $ cd mini-ca
    $ mkdir server
    $ cd server
    ```

    The server certificate config file will be much shorter than the previously made CA certificate config files:

    ```
    [req]
    prompt                    = no
    distinguished_name        = distinguished_name_server_cert
    req_extensions            = v3_server_cert
    [distinguished_name_server_cert]
    countryName               = NO
    stateOrProvinceName       = Oslo
    localityName              = Oslo
    organizationName          = TLS Experts
    commonName                = internal.tls-experts.no
    [v3_server_cert]
    subjectAltName = DNS:mirror1.tls-experts.no, DNS:mirror2.
    tls-experts.no
    ```

    As you can observe, this time, we have defined an X509v3 extension, subjectAltNames, which is going to be added to the CSR. We have supplied several values for the extension and separated them using commas. There is also another method of supplying several values – by making a separate config section with each value on a separate line. We will review that method later when we create a client certificate. The mentioned extension is not present in the intermediate CA configuration, and the intermediate CA configuration contains the copy_extensions = copy option. Hence, the X509v3 extension from the CSR will be copied to the resulting certificate together with other extensions that are defined in the intermediate CA config file. Of course, when issuing the certificate, we will be able to review the certificate details and see all the included X509v3 extensions.

2. The next step is to generate a keypair and a CSR for our server certificate:

```
$ mkdir private
$ chmod 0700 private
$ openssl genpkey \
    -algorithm ED448 \
    -out private/server_keypair.pem
$ openssl req \
    -config server.cnf \
    -new \
    -key private/server_keypair.pem \
    -out server_csr.pem \
    -text
```

Note that we don't have to supply the `-reqexts v3_server_cert` option on the command line, because `v3_server_cert` is the default extensions section, specified by the `req_extensions = v3_server_cert` option in the config file.

3. Now, it's time to generate our server certificate. As it will be issued by the intermediate CA, we will run the `openssl ca` subcommand from the `intermediate` directory:

```
$ cd ../intermediate/
$ openssl ca \
    -config intermediate.cnf \
    -in ../server/server_csr.pem \
    -out ../server/server_cert.pem
Using configuration from intermediate.cnf
Check that the request matches the signature
Signature ok
Certificate Details:
       ...
Certificate is to be certified until Jul 19 15:36:44 2023
GMT (365 days)
Sign the certificate? [y/n]:y
1 out of 1 certificate requests certified, commit? [y/n]y
Write out database with 1 new entries
Data Base Updated
```

Look how easy the certificate-issuing command was! Just three arguments. All the other parameters were taken from the configuration, including the default policy and the X509v3 extensions. Having configured everything in the config file, we can use such a simple command and issue server certificates with ease.

Issuing a client certificate is a little bit different, but also not very difficult. We will learn how to do so in the next section.

Generating a certificate for a web and email client

Generating a client certificate is similar to generating a server certificate:

1. As usual, we will make a separate directory for this certificate and change our current directory there:

```
$ cd mini-ca
$ mkdir client
$ cd client
```

2. We will use the following configuration saved in the `client.cnf` file for generating the client certificate:

```
[req]
prompt                      = no
distinguished_name          = distinguished_name_client_cert
req_extensions              = v3_client_cert
[distinguished_name_client_cert]
countryName                 = NO
stateOrProvinceName         = Oslo
localityName                = Oslo
organizationName            = TLS Experts
commonName                  = Thor Odinson
emailAddress                = thor@tls-experts.no
[v3_client_cert]
subjectAltName = @subject_alt_names
[subject_alt_names]
email.1 = postmaster@tls-experts.no
email.2 = hostmaster@tls-experts.no
```

As last time, we use the `subjectAltName` extension with multiple values, but now we supply several values using a separate config section.

3. Let's generate the certificate keypair and the CSR:

```
$ mkdir private
$ chmod 0700 private
$ openssl genpkey \
    -algorithm ED448 \
    -out private/client_keypair.pem
$ openssl req \
    -config client.cnf \
    -new \
    -key private/client_keypair.pem \
    -out client_csr.pem \
    -text
```

4. The next step is to issue the client certificate:

```
$ cd ../intermediate/
$ openssl ca \
    -config intermediate.cnf \
    -policy policy_client_cert \
    -extensions v3_client_cert \
    -in  ../client/client_csr.pem \
    -out ../client/client_cert.pem
Using configuration from intermediate.cnf
Check that the request matches the signature
Signature ok
Certificate Details:
        ...
Certificate is to be certified until Jul 19 15:37:44 2023
GMT (365 days)
Sign the certificate? [y/n]:y
1 out of 1 certificate requests certified, commit? [y/n]y
Write out database with 1 new entries
Data Base Updated
```

For the client certificate, the issuing command is slightly longer than for the server certificate because we have to supply the -policy and -extensions switches. The default policy and extension sections are reserved for server certificates because they are issued more often than client certificates. However, if it is not the case in your organization, you can very well use client policy and extension sections as defaults.

5. One more thing that can be useful when making a client certificate is packaging the certificate, its private key, and its verification chain into a **Public Key Cryptography Standards #12 (PKCS #12)** container:

```
$ cd ../client/
$ cat \
    ../intermediate/intermediate_cert.pem \
    ../root/root_cert.pem \
    >certfile.pem
$ openssl pkcs12 \
    -export \
    -inkey private/client_keypair.pem \
    -in client_cert.pem \
    -certfile certfile.pem \
    -passout 'pass:SuperPa$$w0rd' \
    -out client_cert.p12
```

As we see, issuing certificates with `openssl ca` is rather easy. But how do we revoke certificates and generate CRLs? Let's find out in the next section.

Revoking certificates and generating CRLs

Before revoking a certificate, we must issue it first. Let's issue a sample certificate, similar to how we did so before:

1. As usual, the first step is to make a directory for the certificate files:

```
$ cd mini-ca
$ mkdir server2
$ cd server2
```

2. Next, make the following certificate configuration and save it to the `server2.cnf` file:

```
[req]
prompt                       = no
distinguished_name           = distinguished_name_server_cert
[distinguished_name_server_cert]
countryName                  = NO
stateOrProvinceName          = Oslo
localityName                 = Oslo
```

```
organizationName          = TLS Experts
commonName                = server2.tls-experts.no
```

3. Next, make the keypair, the CSR, and issue the certificate:

```
$ mkdir private
$ chmod 0700 private
$ openssl genpkey \
    -algorithm ED448 \
    -out private/server2_keypair.pem
$ openssl req \
    -config server2.cnf \
    -new \
    -key private/server2_keypair.pem \
    -out server2_csr.pem \
    -text
$ cd ../intermediate/
$ openssl ca \
    -config intermediate.cnf \
    -in   ../server2/server2_csr.pem \
    -out  ../server2/server2_cert.pem
Using configuration from intermediate.cnf
Check that the request matches the signature
Signature ok
Certificate Details:
        ...
Certificate is to be certified until Jul 19 15:38:44 2023
GMT (365 days)
Sign the certificate? [y/n]:y
1 out of 1 certificate requests certified, commit? [y/n]y
Write out database with 1 new entries
Data Base Updated
```

We have just generated a new certificate. We are still in the intermediate directory. Let's generate a CRL when the server2 certificate is not revoked yet first.

4. This is how we generate a CRL for our intermediate CA:

```
$ openssl ca \
    -config intermediate.cnf \
    -gencrl \
    -out intermediate_crl.pem
```

5. Let's view the generated CRL as text:

```
$ openssl crl \
    -in intermediate_crl.pem \
    -noout \
    -text
Certificate Revocation List (CRL):
        Version 2 (0x1)
        Signature Algorithm: ED448
        Issuer: C = NO, ST = Oslo, L = Oslo, O = TLS
Experts, CN = Intermediate CA
        Last Update: Jul 19 16:56:47 2022 GMT
        Next Update: Aug 18 16:56:47 2022 GMT
        CRL extensions:
            X509v3 Authority Key Identifier:
                ... (hex values) ...
            X509v3 CRL Distribution Points:
                Full Name:
                  URI:http://crl.tls-experts.no/
intermediate_crl.der
            Authority Information Access:
                OCSP - URI:http://ocsp.tls-experts.no/
            X509v3 CRL Number:
                1
No Revoked Certificates.
    Signature Algorithm: ED448
    Signature Value:
        ... (hex values) ...
```

We have just generated our first CRL with an X509v3 CRL Number value of 1. This number has been taken from the crlnumber.txt file, which is configured by the crlnumber = crlnumber.txt line in the intermediate CA config file. That file contains the next CRL number in hex. After a CRL is issued, openssl ca increments the number in that file by one.

6. As we can see, the CRL states that no certificates are revoked. Let's revoke the server2 certificate and regenerate the CRL.

That is how we revoke a certificate:

```
$ openssl ca \
    -config intermediate.cnf \
    -revoke ../server2/server2_cert.pem \
    -crl_reason keyCompromise
Using configuration from intermediate.cnf
Revoking Certificate
1651F3139172DEE541B914DFCB371D8E11BA209F.
Data Base Updated
```

The revocation information is saved in the certificate index file, index.txt. The certificate status in that file is changed from V (valid) to R (revoked).

7. After the certificate is revoked, we have to regenerate the CRL:

```
$ openssl ca \
    -config intermediate.cnf \
    -gencrl \
    -out intermediate_crl.pem
```

8. Let's inspect the updated CRL:

```
$ openssl crl \
    -in intermediate_crl.pem \
    -noout \
    -text
Certificate Revocation List (CRL):
        Version 2 (0x1)
        Signature Algorithm: ED448
        Issuer: C = NO, ST = Oslo, L = Oslo, O = TLS
Experts, CN = Intermediate CA
        Last Update: Jul 19 17:43:49 2022 GMT
        Next Update: Aug 18 17:43:49 2022 GMT
        CRL extensions:
```

```
        X509v3 Authority Key Identifier:
            ... (hex values) ...
        X509v3 CRL Distribution Points:
            Full Name:
                URI:http://crl.tls-experts.no/
intermediate_crl.der
            Authority Information Access:
                OCSP - URI:http://ocsp.tls-experts.no/
        X509v3 CRL Number:
            2
Revoked Certificates:
    Serial Number:
1651F3139172DEE541B914DFCB371D8E11BA209F
        Revocation Date: Jul 19 17:41:39 2022 GMT
        CRL entry extensions:
            X509v3 CRL Reason Code:
                Key Compromise
    Signature Algorithm: ED448
    Signature Value:
        ... (hex values) ...
```

As we can observe, now the X509v3 CRL Number value is 2 and the CRL contains one revoked certificate. We can conclude that the revocation of certificates and the generation of CRLs work as expected.

9. Another thing that is useful to do is to convert the issued CRL from the **Privacy-Enhanced Mail (PEM)** format to the **Distinguished Encoding Rules (DER)** format because CRL distribution points usually serve CRLs in the DER format:

```
$ openssl crl \
    -in intermediate_crl.pem \
    -out intermediate_crl.der \
    -outform DER
```

We have now learned how to revoke certificates and generate CRLs. As we know, serving CRLs is not the only method of serving information about certificate revocation. Another method is OCSP. Let's learn a little bit more about OCSP in the next section.

Providing certificate revocation status via OCSP

To serve OCSP responses, we have to sign them. An OCSP response for a certificate can be signed by its issuer certificate. The same issuer can also issue another certificate for signing OCSP requests. That certificate must have OCSPSigning included in the X509v3 extendedKeyUsage extension.

When we created the intermediate CA config file, we included the following X509v3 extensions section:

```
[v3_ocsp_cert]
subjectKeyIdentifier = hash
authorityKeyIdentifier = keyid:always, issuer
basicConstraints = critical, CA:FALSE
keyUsage = critical, digitalSignature
extendedKeyUsage = critical, OCSPSigning
crlDistributionPoints = URI:http://crl.tls-experts.no/
intermediate_crl.der
authorityInfoAccess = OCSP;URI:http://ocsp.tls-experts.no/
```

That X509v3 extensions section will help us to generate a certificate for an OCSP responder. Let's make this certificate:

1. As usual, we will start by preparing the directory:

   ```
   $ cd mini-ca
   $ mkdir ocsp
   $ cd ocsp
   ```

2. Then, we will make a configuration for the OCSP responder certificate and save it to the ocsp. cnf file:

   ```
   [req]
   prompt                   = no
   distinguished_name       = distinguished_name_ocsp_cert
   [distinguished_name_ocsp_cert]
   countryName              = NO
   stateOrProvinceName      = Oslo
   localityName             = Oslo
   organizationName         = TLS Experts
   commonName               = OCSP Responder
   ```

3. Using the saved configuration, we will create the OCSP responder certificate:

```
$ mkdir private
$ chmod 0700 private
$ openssl genpkey \
    -algorithm ED448 \
    -out private/ocsp_keypair.pem
$ openssl req \
    -config ocsp.cnf \
    -new \
    -key private/ocsp_keypair.pem \
    -out ocsp_csr.pem \
    -text
$ cd ../intermediate/
$ openssl ca \
    -config intermediate.cnf \
    -in  ../ocsp/ocsp_csr.pem \
    -out ../ocsp/ocsp_cert.pem
Using configuration from intermediate.cnf
Check that the request matches the signature
Signature ok
Certificate Details:
    …
Certificate is to be certified until Jul 19 17:45:44 2023
GMT (365 days)
Sign the certificate? [y/n]:y
1 out of 1 certificate requests certified, commit? [y/n]y
Write out database with 1 new entries
Data Base Updated
```

The generated certificate can be used by an OCSP responder. Let us test it. The openssl utility includes the openssl ocsp subcommand, which can act as a simple OCSP server. We can use such an OCSP server for our testing. That OCSP server takes certificate validity data right from the certificate index file, index.txt. Very practical for testing, if you ask me.

4. You can read the openssl ocsp documentation on its man page:

```
$ man openssl-ocsp
```

5. We will start our test OCSP server from the `ocsp` directory:

```
$ cd ../ocsp/
$ openssl ocsp \
      -port 4480 \
      -index ../intermediate/index.txt \
      -CA ../intermediate/intermediate_cert.pem \
      -rkey private/ocsp_keypair.pem \
      -rsigner ocsp_cert.pem
ACCEPT 0.0.0.0:4480 PID=124271
ocsp: waiting for OCSP client connections...
```

We have provided our OCSP responder certificate and its private key to `openssl ocsp` for signing the OCSP responses.

6. But the `openssl ocsp` subcommand is so nice that it can act not only as an OCSP server but also as an OCSP client. Let's use it in client mode and check the validity of the `server` certificate that we recently issued. To do so, we need to open another terminal window, change to the `mini-ca/ocsp` directory, and run the following command:

```
openssl ocsp \
      -url http://localhost:4480 \
      -sha256 \
      -CAfile ../root/root_cert.pem \
      -issuer ../intermediate/intermediate_cert.pem \
      -cert ../server/server_cert.pem
Response verify OK
../server/server_cert.pem: good
        This Update: Jul 19 19:59:06 2022 GMT
```

As we can observe, the OCSP server has confirmed the validity of the `server` certificate.

7. Now, let's check the status of the `server2` certificate that we have recently issued and revoked:

```
$ openssl ocsp \
      -url http://localhost:4480 \
      -sha256 \
      -CAfile ../root/root_cert.pem \
      -issuer ../intermediate/intermediate_cert.pem \
      -cert ../server2/server2_cert.pem
Response verify OK
```

```
../server2/server2_cert.pem: revoked
      This Update: Jul 19 20:03:56 2022 GMT
      Reason: keyCompromise
      Revocation Time: Jul 19 17:41:39 2022 GMT
```

As we can see, the OCSP responder has reported that the `server2` certificate is revoked, just as we expected. We can conclude that our OCSP setup works correctly.

We have now learned a lot about running a mini-CA. We have used many config files and commands. Those config files and commands, saved as Shell scripts, can be found on GitHub, for trying out or for future reference: `https://github.com/PacktPublishing/Demystifying-Cryptography-with-OpenSSL-3/tree/main/Chapter12`.

This brings us to the end of this chapter. Now, we'll summarize everything we have learned here.

Summary

In this chapter, we learned how to run a mini-CA. First, we learned about why a mini-CA can be useful within an organization. We also learned about the `openssl ca` subcommand and how to make configuration files for it. Then, we learned how to issue certificates using `openssl ca`. After that, we learned how to revoke certificates and issue CRLs. We finished the chapter by learning how to issue a certificate for an OCSP responder and how to provide certificate revocation status via OCSP using the `openssl ocsp` subcommand. This knowledge can help you to set up and run a mini-CA, gaining control over PKI in your organization.

This was the last chapter of the book. I hope that you have enjoyed both the chapter and the book, and have learned something new and useful. I also hope that the knowledge gained will help you to understand cryptographic and network security technologies better, develop more secure applications, and advance your career.

Index

Packt.com

Subscribe to our online digital library for full access to over 7,000 books and videos, as well as industry leading tools to help you plan your personal development and advance your career. For more information, please visit our website.

Why subscribe?

- Spend less time learning and more time coding with practical eBooks and Videos from over 4,000 industry professionals

- Improve your learning with Skill Plans built especially for you

- Get a free eBook or video every month

- Fully searchable for easy access to vital information

- Copy and paste, print, and bookmark content

Did you know that Packt offers eBook versions of every book published, with PDF and ePub files available? You can upgrade to the eBook version at packt.com and as a print book customer, you are entitled to a discount on the eBook copy. Get in touch with us at customercare@packtpub.com for more details.

At www.packt.com, you can also read a collection of free technical articles, sign up for a range of free newsletters, and receive exclusive discounts and offers on Packt books and eBooks.

Other Books You May Enjoy

If you enjoyed this book, you may be interested in these other books by Packt:

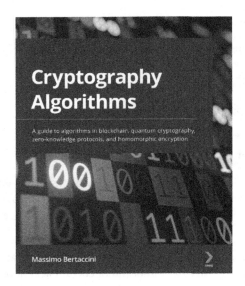

Cryptography Algorithms

Massimo Bertaccini

ISBN: 978-1-78961-713-9

- Understand key cryptography concepts, algorithms, protocols, and standards
- Break some of the most popular cryptographic algorithms
- Build and implement algorithms efficiently
- Gain insights into new methods of attack on RSA and asymmetric encryption
- Explore new schemes and protocols for blockchain and cryptocurrency
- Discover pioneering quantum cryptography algorithms
- Perform attacks on zero-knowledge protocol and elliptic curves
- Explore new algorithms invented by the author in the field of asymmetric, zero-knowledge, and cryptocurrency

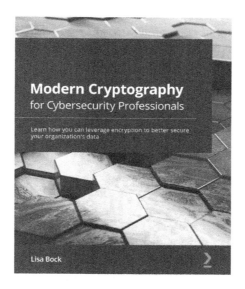

Modern Cryptography for Cybersecurity Professionals

Lisa Bock

ISBN: 978-1-83864-435-2

- Understand how network attacks can compromise data
- Review practical uses of cryptography over time
- Compare how symmetric and asymmetric encryption work
- Explore how a hash can ensure data integrity and authentication
- Understand the laws that govern the need to secure data
- Discover the practical applications of cryptographic techniques
- Find out how the PKI enables trust
- Get to grips with how data can be secured using a VPN

Packt is searching for authors like you

If you're interested in becoming an author for Packt, please visit z and apply today. We have worked with thousands of developers and tech professionals, just like you, to help them share their insight with the global tech community. You can make a general application, apply for a specific hot topic that we are recruiting an author for, or submit your own idea.

Hi!

I am Alexei Khlebnikov, author of *Demystifying Cryptography with OpenSSL 3.0*. I really hope you enjoyed reading this book and found it useful for increasing your productivity and efficiency in securing your applications or networks with OpenSSL.

It would really help me (and other potential readers!) if you could leave a review on Amazon sharing your thoughts on *Demystifying Cryptography with OpenSSL 3.0*.

Go to the link below or scan the QR code to leave your review:

https://packt.link/r/1800560346

Your review will help me to understand what's worked well in this book, and what could be improved upon for future editions, so it really is appreciated.

Best Wishes,

Alexei Khlebnikov

Made in the USA
Coppell, TX
10 April 2025